Praise f
HIGHWAY tc

"*Highway to the Sky* is a motivational primer for anyone growing up and looking ahead to what might be there for them. Her vivid and colorful descriptions of her early flight training and the Canadian landscape are very picturesque. . . She inspires the reader to understand the sky is the limit and to stay true to your own dreams and ideals—good advice for any endeavor."
—BECKY CONDON, US Navy/Delta Air Lines 757/767ER Captain Ret'd

"In this compelling memoir, Lola Reid Allin takes us into the sky, the clouds, the exhilarating joys—and a few terrors—of flying. Coming of age in the early 1970s, her path is a quagmire of misogyny in every form. Her personal life throws more missiles at her, from parental disapproval to domestic violence made worse by police indifference. This story is a page turner . . . She keeps us engaged all the way to the last page."
—ELLEN BARKER, author of *Still Needs Work*

"Granted access into the mind of a bright young girl, we see the world through Lola's eyes, feel the frustration of her own restrictions, and her awareness of the unnatural constraints on her mother and grandmother's life. An engaging memoir of boldness, determination, and an honest rendering of how painful it can be to be among the first in a field. Lola writes bravely. She doesn't sugar coat, minimize, or make excuses for the various behaviors she encounters from men in flying. And she triumphs."
—PATTY BEAR, USAF, airline pilot, and author, *From Plain to Plane*

"Lola Reid Allin has woven together a brilliant memoir that profiles her life as a young aviator during a time when being a female pilot was not a common career choice. It is a great read for someone looking for inspiration and a lesson in the importance of believing in yourself and not letting life's arrows or downturns influence your drive."

—CHERYL STINSON RODO, author of *Blind Trust: Winner, Sinner*

"*Highway to the Sky* narrates Lola Reid Allin's successful quest to follow her passion while facing challenges and naysayers. Lola skillfully tells her story of transforming her life from ho-hum job to successful pilot at a time when women were expected to stay at home. I loved the view from the cockpit and cheered Lola on, applauding her tenacity and spirit while empathizing with her frustration with a culture that devalues women. She's a wonderful role model for any woman who wants to make positive change in her life."

—KAREN GERSHOWITZ, author of *Travel Mania* and *Wanderlust*

"*Highway to the Sky* is the compelling story of a smart, strong, and independent young woman who dared defy the expectations of family, friends, and society to pursue her dreams and live her life as she chose. Lola's story will resonate with anyone who has joyfully slid into a relationship full of love and promise and then faced the challenge of extricating oneself from that relationship upon discovering it to be toxic and even dangerous."

—NANCY LESNIEWSKI, Director of Membership Development, United Aqua Group (retired)

"That several exceptional women have been able to shirk off this sexism and, not only enter but thrive within these male-dominated areas, is a testament to their ability, integrity, and tenacity. Lola is one of those women."

—ELIZABETH IVES-RUYTER, former flight instructor and retired Assistant Crown Attorney

HIGHWAY
to the SKY

AN AVIATOR'S JOURNEY

LOLA REID ALLIN

SHE WRITES PRESS

Published 2024
Printed in the United States of America

Print ISBN: 978-1-64742-800-6
E-ISBN: 978-1-64742-801-3
Library of Congress Control Number: 2024909000

For information, address:
She Writes Press
1569 Solano Ave #546
Berkeley, CA 94707

Interior design and typeset by Katherine Lloyd, The DESK

She Writes Press is a division of SparkPoint Studio, LLC.

This narrative represents my observation and interpretation of events. Some names have been changed to ensure the privacy of the individuals and their families. Certain events have been compressed or eliminated for narrative reasons. Though many readers helped me on this literary journey, I bear the responsibility for any errors or omissions.

"When everything seems to be going against you, remember that the airplane takes off against the wind, not with it."

—*Henry Ford*

CONTENTS

ODE TO JOY

"Help me, Lola!" The volume and pitch of Joy's usually velvet voice increases with each word and feels like an ice pick puncturing my eardrum. "*Please!* Take control!"

We're nearing the end of Joy's first flight lesson with me and now we're thirty feet above the runway, on final approach, seconds from touchdown. I adjust my prescription Ray-Bans, massage my temples, and say, "Re-laaax. The approach looks perfect. Besides"—I force a laugh—"I don't plan to crash and burn today."

My student's left hand chokes the Cessna 152's control column on her side of the plane. Fifteen feet above the runway, I place my hands on my knees, inching them closer to the U-shaped steering control on my side of the plane. Joy reduces engine power to slightly more than idle.

Sometimes, although a student has set up the landing approach perfectly, a gust of wind might toss the plane up, down, or sideways. If this happens, a too-hard touchdown might occur. Or the slightest wrong movement might cause the plane to land on the delicate nosewheel instead of the two main wheels. If this happens, the nosewheel might break, causing the propeller to thump against the tarmac, curling the propeller tips and possibly twisting the engine crankshaft.

With any student, anything could happen, but Joy's previous

instructors have told me about her bad landings, so I'm especially vigilant. I hover the curled fingers of my right hand around the aircraft's control column, not touching it but close enough to take control if she lets go—or if we're about to crash. I haven't had an accident with or without a student during my entire flying career, and I plan to maintain that record.

The plane smacks onto the runway. My back buckles with the impact. Though aircraft manufacturers design sturdy main wheel struts to splay and minimize damage by student pilots like Joy, the plane bounces ten feet into the air. My stomach stays behind.

After the bounce that shoots us back into the air, the aircraft begins an extended-wavelength, roller-coaster flight path, oscillating closer and closer to the runway as the airspeed decreases in preparation for landing. Similar to an S-shaped sine wave, this movement will continue unless one of us increases the engine rpm and airspeed. But if one of us doesn't act in the next ten seconds, the touchdown will be a smackdown.

"Help me!" Joy's screech pierces my ear.

I say, "Add three hundred rpm."

Her trembling hand pushes the throttle plunger toward the instrument panel and engine power increases from 1,200 to 1,500 rpm, just enough to smooth out the dipsy-doodle flight path. She manages to establish a semi-stable rate of descent but not soon enough. We thwack against the pavement and, imitating a renegade rubber ball, bounce several more times. Thankfully, our 6,000-foot runway allows for errors—like Joy's multiple touchdowns.

I lose count after three bounces, each tossing us back into the air but with decreasing height. Joy reduces power to 1,200 rpm and her final touchdown is smooth. With the two main wheels rolling along the runway, she reduces power to idle. The Cessna slows gradually and the fragile nosewheel free-falls gently onto the pavement.

We travel in a straight line until she brakes, harder with her right foot than her left foot, creating a lazy-S track along the runway. After multiple "S" patterns, she establishes directional control.

I say, "That was more collision than landing."

Her jaw tightens. "Maybe I should quit."

"Let's try a couple more takeoffs and landings," I say.

Her blue eyes flash with astonishment.

"Accelerate. Now!" I command.

Her hand quivers on the throttle, but she accelerates and demonstrates a textbook-perfect takeoff. In the air again, my muscles relax but my brain is confused.

In the practice area at four thousand feet, when asked to descend and set up for landing at an imaginary runway floating above Earth, Joy establishes the appropriate rate of descent as if we were at an airport. But she can't seem to relate simulated landings at an imaginary, high-altitude airport to an actual landing on a real runway.

Though her takeoffs are excellent, the repeated sequence of landings and takeoffs, called "touch-and-goes," are more like "smash-and-goes." Now I understand why three previous instructors at our school gave up on her. Despite my increasing doubts, I'm not ready to give up on Joy. I can't shake the gut feeling we've all missed something. *But what?*

After another excellent takeoff, Joy climbs to one thousand feet and establishes the plane in the circuit, a giant rectangular flight pattern required at airports. When she makes a final turn toward the runway for another touch-and-go landing and starts her descent, I mentally prepare for semi-disaster, hyperattentive and determined to avoid a wingtip-to-wingtip cartwheel along the pavement that might be the final landing of our lives.

This time, instead of screaming, she says, "I really need your help." Fear seeps from her words. Sweat drips down her cheek and releases a flood of Chanel No. 5 into our cramped quarters, tickling my nose.

Achoo! I smile confidently. "If you scare me—*achoo!* I'll take control, but—*achoo!* You can do this."

My pulse beats faster, throbbing like a kick drum inside my head.

We cross the runway threshold, and as the plane descends and passes the runway numbers, Joy surprises me by reducing power to idle too soon. This would be a perfect landing if the wheels were only four or five inches above ground, but they aren't. We're still fifteen feet above the runway, and, from this height, the plane drops like a dead bird shot from the sky. All three wheels smack onto the tarmac.

I say, "*Contact!*" but to be as encouraging as possible, I continue, "However, any landing you can walk away from is a good landing. And *you* did it all by yourself."

"You helped."

"Not this time! Let's do one more circuit."

She says, "You're a glutton for punishment," but obediently accelerates for another takeoff. Again, she demonstrates perfect technique until twenty feet or so above the runway, just before landing. I'm baffled. She's intelligent and educated and, perhaps more importantly, dedicated and willing to learn. *Why does she fall apart when it's time to land the plane?*

After her final thump onto the runway, I say, "I'm sure I can figure out what the problem is tomorrow during your second review lesson when you show me the remaining exercises."

But I'm not sure.

Maybe my male colleagues are right. Maybe Joy isn't pilot material. As she taxies to the ramp, snippets of conversations with her previous instructors drift through my mind. Her first instructor, Mark, taught her for fifteen hours before deciding a more experienced instructor might discover why she can't land.

Warren, a thirty-eight-year-old career instructor, gave up after three flights, saying, "She's sweet and motivated but she's never gonna be a pilot," then passed her to our chief instructor, Martin.

Three days earlier, Martin had shut the door to our shared office, then confided, "I've had two flights with Joy. She has twenty-plus hours but still can't land the plane."

I twisted a strand of my shoulder-length hair and sighed heavily. "That's a problem."

"When I suggested she take lessons with you, she agreed."

I blew air through my lips. *Pffffttt.* "Mark told me she had no interest in flying with me." Her rebuff had stung. I'm the most experienced pilot at this school, and in my six years of training students and flying as a commercial pilot, she was the first person, male or female, pilot or passenger, who had refused to fly with me.

Martin said, "She told me that, too. Maybe desperation changed her mind." He clasped his hands together on his desk and twirled his thumbs in a circle. "Why does she want to fly, anyway?"

I bristled. "Why *shouldn't* she learn to fly?"

"She's fifty-six. Makes as much sense as my mother learning to fly."

"Why shouldn't either of them learn to fly?"

He twisted his lips. "She has a life most women dream about. A loving husband. Four great kids. A beautiful home. Why would she want to be a pilot?"

"Do you question why a fifty-six-year-old man wants to be a pilot?"

Martin looked out the sliding glass window separating our office from the bustle of pilots at the front dispatch desk, then said defiantly, as if to justify his comments, "She flies with her husband all the time."

I shoved away from the desk, stood, and glared at him. "Maybe because she wants to prove to herself that she can fly." I stood and tossed my navy blazer onto my shoulder. "I'll be happy to fly with her."

I can't imagine my flight-phobic mother taking flight lessons any more than Martin can visualize his mother at the controls, but I have a good idea about the restrictions and prejudices endured by previous generations of women.

Joy and my mother were born in the decade following World War I: Joy in 1929, the year of Black Tuesday and the stock market crash; my mother in 1922, the year of Jimmy Doolittle's record-breaking flight coast-to-coast across America in twenty-three hours.

Young women in the 1940s were expected and encouraged to pursue traditional goals of marriage and motherhood. There had been no talk of chasing their dreams, going after the unexpected. Everything was all about the family, nurturing others, and prioritizing the needs of husband and children. Like generations of women before them, they weren't to concern themselves with personal ambitions.

My mother had given up, but Joy had only deferred hers.

Despite some social breakthroughs during the second wave of feminism in the 1960s, specifically the introduction of the pill in 1961 and the Abortion Act of 1967, when it came to the subjects of career, risk, adventure, and reaching one's potential, all my life I'd heard, "You can't . . . girls shouldn't . . . and women don't." My rage burbles to the surface when I think about the women denied higher education and equal pay for equal jobs, but now I have the chance to help one of them.

And I am damn well going to do it.

Two days after my conversation with Martin, I met with Joy for the first time. Before she had started lessons, she rarely came to the flight school, though her husband's a regular. Rather than dash to the airplane for her lesson, I wanted to befriend this rarity and languish in the feminine energy of another woman interested in aviation. I suggested we get acquainted over tea in the café. She agreed, casually reserved a table for us by placing her logbook on the tabletop, and asked the café's proprietor to add the cost of our tea and scones to her bill.

I cradled my cup of Earl Grey with both hands, drew in the spicy scent of bergamot, and sipped. Joy adjusted the position of the paper napkin holder on our melamine table, then rearranged the salt and pepper, once, then again. I sensed her reluctance to start a conversation, so I asked, "Why do you want to take flying lessons?"

She squared her shoulders, stating in a clear voice, "After four children and thirty-seven wonderful years of marriage, Will is encouraging me to pursue things I want to do."

I don't know Will very well, but I do know he's a living legend at our airport for his military service and for surviving World War II as a Lancaster tail gunner. Most Saturday mornings, he's at the airport, fiddling with his home-built airplane before enjoying brunch at the flying school's Compass Rose Café. When Will finishes his coffee, stands (shoulders slightly stooped with age), and says, "Time to take Bessie for a spin," my heart pangs for my Grampa, my first hero, another war veteran who said those same words.

Though Grampa and I never went flying, we'd be setting off on some adventure in his sedan, perhaps to the beach, zoo, a ride on a steam train, or, more often, grocery shopping for Gramma. But even grocery shopping with Grampa was fun. He'd treat me to a comic book and to snacks on the way home, Mackintosh's Toffee in the red-and-green tartan wrapper.

Joy's matching slacks-and-sweater outfit and white permed hair reminded me of my mother, but unlike my mother who personified the Empire State Building (massive, cold, and imper-meable), five-foot-tall Joy bubbled with happiness.

I said, "Martin told me you're studying at university."

"I've always wanted to be a writer, so, two years ago, I enrolled in a full-time creative writing program."

"Impressive. But why flying?"

"Both our sons are pilots, and when I fly with Will, I want to be more than a passenger, in case of emergency."

"You *are* an inspiration. I'll be honored to fly with you, but I heard you weren't interested in flying with me."

A gentle blush crept from Joy's neck to her cheeks. "You're young."

I twiddled the garnet ring my parents had given me for my twelfth birthday. "I'm thirty."

"I thought you were incompetent, hired like the previous two female instructors so the school would be *politically correct*."

I ran a finger along my gold necklace. "Did you fly with either of them?"

She shook her head.

My insides prickled. "If you didn't fly with them, you couldn't know whether they're incompetent or not."

She blinked, then adjusted her fashionably outsized, pink-acrylic glasses.

"One was my commercial flight test examiner and the other flies with Air Canada."

She twisted the strand of pearls resting on her collarbone. "I . . . I'm sorry. I know better than to repeat hearsay."

"What changed your mind about me?"

"When I learned you were a bush pilot in northern Ontario and have the same licenses as one of my sons, I realized you were more than a pretty face with perfect teeth and green eyes."

I reviewed the entries in her pilot logbook. "I've spoken with your previous instructors."

Her head bobbed with anticipation like an eager baby bird.

"Because you're having trouble landing, I'd like to review the basic air exercises, the building blocks for all flight maneuvers."

She nodded.

I continued. "We'll spend a couple hours in the practice area, then return to the airport doing touch-and-goes. I'm sorry but more time in the air will cost more money."

"When Mark suggested I fly with you," she said and swallowed, "I should've listened."

I stood, slipped into my blazer, and grinned. "Let's do this!"

As Joy's fourth instructor, I needed to have an open mind, ignore the assumptions and conclusions of the previous instructors, and judge her capability on merit. I hoped I wouldn't let her down.

After Joy prepared the C152 for our first flight together, she spoke confidently on the radio with air traffic control and performed an excellent takeoff. She flew to the practice area, where she demonstrated above-average skill performing climbs, descents, turns, and power-to-idle stalls. Based on the opinions of the male instructors, I'd expected her performance to be subpar. Instead, I was delighted to truthfully say, "I don't see anything wrong with your flying. In fact, you've flown well. Take us back to the airport for a few touch-and-goes."

She flashed me a shy grin of thanks and turned the aircraft toward home base. As we approached the airport, she entered the downwind leg of the traffic pattern circuit as directed by the controller. She hummed happily as she turned and descended to five hundred feet, as per standard circuit procedures.

I slumped into my bucket chair, still paying attention but convinced by her performance in the practice area and her current confidence that whatever caused her problem had been rectified by our flight today.

But soon after she turned onto the final leg of the circuit, her composure and expertise evaporated. I'd been astonished. Despite three consecutive touchdown fiascos that placed us seconds from disaster, when we returned to the school, I urged her to continue. "I'm not sure why you're having trouble landing but, if you're willing, I'll fly with you."

To my delight, she scheduled a second lesson with me.

A good instructor is a leader or mentor who communicates effectively, so when Joy arrives for her second lesson with me the following morning, I explain, "Today's lesson will mostly be in the practice area. I'll assess your skill with stalls and spins, ensuring you're comfortable with them and able to recognize and avoid them close to the ground."

She giggles with a twinge of embarrassment. "Like landings and takeoffs."

"Precisely. We'll finish with three or four touch-and-goes."

Joy burbles with enthusiasm. "I appreciate the confidence you have in me."

In the practice area, she again demonstrates above-average capabilities, so to encourage her, I say, "Joy, you've done well. Let's head back to the airport for a few touch-and-goes."

As we return to the airport, her voice trembles when she speaks with the controller. Tension floods into my shoulders, but I'm relieved when she demonstrates a textbook entry into the airport's rectangular traffic pattern. At the appropriate distance from the runway threshold, she turns toward the runway and aligns the aircraft with the runway centerline for final approach.

She's configured the Cessna for a perfect landing, so I shake the tension from my shoulders.

Then, just inches above the runway, for some undetermined reason, I see her confidence crumble. Her hands tremble like aspen leaves in the breeze and her voice squeaks like a frightened mouse when she says, "Help me!" as all three wheels thwack onto the pavement.

I have no idea why she demonstrates above-average skill in the practice area yet alternates between freezing and panic just before touchdown. Two hours of review haven't provided any clues about her inability to land the plane. I want her to succeed but plan to give honest feedback about her performance, not fill her with false hope. I mentally rehearse the kindest way to deliver the "maybe-you-should-consider-another-hobby" chat, a conversation dreaded by most instructors.

Despite the abuse she inflicts on the landing gear, Joy maintains control on the runway, then demonstrates another excellent takeoff. On climb-out, I swivel ninety degrees to take a good look at Joy, to see if her body language or face reveals anger or frustration. As I do with all students, I've monitored her hand and foot positions on the controls, confirmed that the engine and flight instruments are operating correctly, and checked for conflicting aircraft traffic. But this is the first time I've ever turned to really look at a student.

What I see astonishes me.

The crown of her snow-white head is level with my chin. I slump so that my head is level with hers, then look forward. I smile to myself, then ask, "On short final, when the nose flares up for touchdown, can you see the runway?"

"Of course not!" Joy's harsh tone suggests I'm an idiot. She pauses, then utters a cognizant gasp. "Oh! My goodness, are you supposed to?"

I chuckle. "It's like you've been driving a car without seeing the road."

Two days later, Joy arrives for her third lesson, clutching two cushions. She giggles. "Pinched these from Will's fishing boat."

We head to the practice area so she can adjust to the altered visual frame of reference created by sitting four inches higher on the bucket seat. During the next week, we fly three more hours, dedicating the first lesson to upper air work in the practice area and the next two hours to landings.

Now, when the aircraft nose flares up slightly to allow the two main wheels to touch down before the flimsy nosewheel, she can see above the dashboard. Now, her landings are better than average—and her confidence is restored.

Prior to her seventh flight with me, I say, "We'll be in the circuit doing touch-and-goes." I intend to send her solo but keep this secret.

Before sending any student solo, I fly with them for a few circuits to observe current performance before making a final decision. Students might have a bad day, a random rainstorm or haze might reduce visibility, or the wind might get stronger than the slight breeze desired for first solo. Explaining a change of plans, however legitimate, may affect a student's confidence. Also, pondering the probability of flying alone may make a student anxious and adversely affect performance.

To my relief, the weather cooperates, and her landings are excellent. After forty-five minutes in the circuit, I look at my watch and say, "Let's make this a full-stop landing."

She nods and tells our intention to the controllers.

After touchdown, she exits the runway and requests taxi clearance to the flight school. I let her continue until we're in front of the control tower, then I say, "Please stop here."

She shoots me a wide-eyed, you-must-be-an-idiot expression. Has she guessed I'm about to send her solo? Or is she wondering why we're not continuing to the flight school?

I turn to her with a big smile. "I'll be hopping out. You're going solo."

She's excited but calm. "I won't let you down."

"I know."

Then, I advise the controller that a novice pilot will be alone in the air for the first time. The controller will make allowances and expect less than perfection. I give Joy a big hug and hop out.

Part of getting out and walking to the flight school is selfish. I'm pretty sure that all twelve-minute first solo flights are as traumatic for a student as for me, their instructor. I need to burn off the tension I always feel by trying to enjoy the fresh air and ignoring the worst possible scenarios clogging my mind. *What if she makes a mistake? What if that mistake causes her to crash?* The possibility of a broken aircraft always looms, but . . . *What if she dies in the accident?* An unlikely but real possibility. If that happened, how would I explain or rationalize that to Will? Or to anyone, including myself? How could I live with myself?

Some instructors remain outside to monitor their students while others get permission from the controllers to view from the control tower. I prefer to walk to the school and wait inside, where I can't see the runway. The horrific thoughts swirling through my brain are bad enough, but watching helplessly while a student crashed would devastate me.

From my perspective, the prospect of sending Joy solo is especially traumatic. If she crashes but lives, her three previous male instructors who thought she shouldn't be a pilot will probably challenge my decision. I can deal with them but the evaluation by Transport Canada Flight Training Standards regarding my decision and my ability to perform my job might end my instructing career.

I stride back and forth inside the flight school, waiting for her to return, alive and taxiing an intact aircraft. I'm certain my decision to send Joy solo is the right decision, but in an aircraft, things can go wrong quickly and badly.

And I'm not there to help.

My stomach rumbles and growls. I'm close to vomiting, and my bladder is bursting, but I want to be here when she returns.

Finally, in what seems an eternity later, she taxis to the ramp in front of the flight school, aligns the aircraft with others parked in a row, and shuts down the engine. Seconds later, she rushes into the school and throws her books and pillows onto the dispatch counter.

I can't speak, but she says, "I did it!" I'm not sure who is more elated. She hugs me. "Your confidence in me gave me the confidence I needed."

I don't typically cry in public, but my eyes fill with tears and I'm pretty close.

Then she says, "I owe you and those two other female pilots an apology."

Tears gush down my cheeks for her success and for my wishing I'd had a female friend with complete confidence in me, someone who understood why I wanted to fly, someone to urge me on, someone with whom I could share my dreams—and doubts—without fear of judgment.

During the four weeks following her solo flight, Joy completes her training and I recommend her for the private pilot flight test—with Martin, not only our chief instructor but also our school's on-site flight-test examiner . . . and one of the male instructors convinced Joy shouldn't become a pilot. Throughout most of the two hours allotted for this test, I'm airborne with another student, but my thoughts are with Joy, wishing I could be hovering near her ear, coaching like a maternal Tinker Bell.

When my student and I land and return to the flight school, Martin and Joy are still up in the air. Inside the clubhouse, I join Will standing at the picture window.

My innards twist. Maybe she's made a mistake. Maybe Martin is judging her based on his opinion of her when she was his student.

Will casually says, "They've been a long time."

He jingles the coins in his pants pocket, a tinkling noise that annoys me at the best of times—and reminds me of my father. My anxiety spirals and I'm resisting the urge to throw up but say, "Maybe they're bucking a headwind," though I can't recall the winds aloft being strong. This makes me wonder if the wind strength has increased, causing her to misjudge gliding distance during the simulated engine-failure, forced-approach demonstration.

What if she did more than misjudge?

What if they're lying in a farm field crashed, crumpled, and flattened?

At last, Joy and Martin taxi onto the flight school ramp. Both doors of the Cessna open, but nobody gets out. After five, maybe ten, minutes of agony, Will stomps his foot and says, "What *are* they *doing?*"

Finally, Martin emerges and strolls toward the fight school, seeming to dally deliberately, pretending to enjoy the fresh air and sunshine. *Why isn't Joy with him?* I check the time, and with each passing second, get more anxious.

Martin enters the flight school, but I block him, hands gripping my hips.

He says, "She's—"

Will says, "Here she comes, wearing a big smile!"

"—an excellent pilot!"

The strain of worry vanishes so quickly, my legs turn to jelly, and I nearly collapse.

Seconds later, Will rushes to hold the door open for Joy, her hands wrapped around books and booster cushions.

He bows and sweeps his arm in a wide arc, ushering her inside like one of the Three Musketeers. "Madame Pilot, please come in!"

I say, "Congratulations! I *knew* you could do it."

With tears glistening on her flushed cheeks, Joy embraces us.

To me, she says, "Thank you, Lola. I couldn't have done it without you."

Normally, I wouldn't agree but, in this case, at this school, she's right. From personal experience, I knew that learning to fly was not beyond the reach of any motivated individual. I knew Joy could learn to soar into the sky—I just needed to discover her personal barrier, that one thing preventing success.

CLOUDS

Lola, age 3, in Mexican sombrero, with her grandfather who wears his customary WWI pith helmet and marching boots. As an adult, Lola owns many pith helmets and several pairs of hiking boots (ca 1958).

My best friend is Grampa, Mommy's daddy, the only person who doesn't tell me to act like a girl. He doesn't give me heck when I do something different from what girls are "supposed" to do. Instead of dolls and dishes, Grampa buys me *Classics Illustrated* comics, a blue-is-for-boys bicycle, and gives me keen snakeskins, arrowheads, and animal skulls he finds in the flower garden of their waterfront home on the Bay of Quinte. Mommy must know I'd rather be with Grampa than with her and Daddy because she lets me stay for days.

One sweltering summer day in June 1960, Grampa climbs the wooden ladder to the loft of his garage and pushes a folded square of sandy-colored cloth the size of my plastic swimming pool onto the floor. It lands with a thump, and I blink as dust flies into my eyes. He hauls the huge bundle onto his shoulder, and I follow him toward the water's edge. He plops it onto the flattest part of their grassy lawn, between five weeping willows, then takes off his WWI pith helmet and backhands the sweat from his forehead.

Next, he unfolds the bundle, saying, "This here tent weighs forty pounds. You could sure help by handing me the wooden pegs. I'll hammer 'em into the ground, and you can leash a tent rope to each peg."

When we're finished, he drags two canvas-and-wood cots into the tent. I flop onto one, surprised by the comfort. A summer breeze swirls through the tied-back doors, ripples the walls, and cools my skin. Grampa hangs his helmet on a makeshift hook suspended from the central wooden beam, then unbuttons his shirt and hangs it on another hook. He unties his polished black leather marching boots and stuffs his socks inside so no bugs can creep in. Together, we relax, he in his white undershirt and improvised shorts and me in my bathing suit.

He laces his stubby fingers together and puts them behind his head, making a pillow. "This here collapsible caravanserai is our private space. Gramma hates this tent 'cuz it doesn't have a floor."

"I love the way grass tickles my feet."

He says, "You shouldn't run around barefoot."

I say, "Graaaampaaa," then point to shadows on the canvas roof. "The willow trees are dancing."

He laughs. "I bought this tent in 1922—"

"The year Mommy was born!"

He chuckles. "You're a smart girl. Soon as I saw this tent, I bought it 'cuz it reminded me of the military-issue tents we boys had overseas. Neighbors would stop by just to see the zipper!"

I stick my right leg in the air and pick at the crusty scab on my knee. "Why?"

"Nobody'd heard of zippers. Trousers didn't even have 'em 'til after your daddy's war."

"How'd you do up your pants?"

"Buttons. When the Great War began in 1914, I was seventeen, three months short of being old enough to fight, but I wanted to travel and serve my country, so I fibbed."

"Graaaampaaaa, you're not supposed to fib."

"What a time we had, on leave, carousing Belgium. Couldn'a believe their capital city, Brussels—"

"Like brussels sprouts? Yuck."

"Brussels is where those nasty vegetables were first grown. And they have a statue called *Manneken Pis.*"

"Piss? Like pee-pee?"

He guffaws. "Exactly. Three-hundred-year-old bronze sculpture of a naked boy pissing into the fountain!"

My eyes widen, and I hope he'll tell me more about naked statues, but he doesn't. Instead, he says, "Didn't have potato peelers or Band-Aids."

I wrinkle my nose and pucker my mouth. "*Eee-yuck*, Band-Aids are disgusting!"

He grins as he pulls out a book from under his pillow. "How 'bout I read a Robert Service poem?"

Before I can answer, he's reading our favorite, "The Ballad of Blasphemous Bill." I listen spellbound until the last line—the best line. "'I often think of poor old Bill—and how hard he was to saw.'"

We giggle together, and as I try to imagine sawing through a frozen dead man, he says, "Would'a liked to see the Yukon, but I chose your Gramma instead."

"Grampa, please tell me about barnstorming! Or the very first airplane flight in 1903, one year before Gramma was born."

"Let's have a quiz," he says. I groan, pretending to be upset, and he asks, "What's the name of the first aircraft to fly in Canada?"

I say, "*The Silver Dart!*"

"When and where did it fly?"

"Nova Scotia, 1909."

"You mind, never tell your Gramma, but once I went for an airplane ride, a Laird Swallow. Grew up with the pilot, Art Leavens, and his brothers, Clare and Walt, right here in Belleville. Art learned to fly in America but came home to start Pottin Field."

On both hands, he extends his pinkies and thumbs outward, squishes the other three together, then moves his hands through the air like miniature airplanes. "Each second we were airborne, swoopin' and loopin', I was whoopin'."

His twinkling eyes tell me this flight was a highlight of his life, maybe better than crossing the Atlantic on a ship or touring Europe. I gaze at my hero, desperately trying to imagine his experience, and decide flying might be like jumping off my dresser or getting airborne from a diving board.

"They crashed all the time. Bits of cloth, wood, and wire. Thought I was gonna die."

Even though I get the message from almost everybody I know, including my girlfriends, that a girl's life is about finding a husband, having kids, doing boring housework, and maybe getting a boring job, I want more than diapers and dishes. I'm only five, but I already know it's not fair that boys get to have all the fun. They're allowed to try anything, go anywhere, have wonderful adventures, and only get a bit of heck for dirty hands, ripped pants, or scraped knees. When I grow up, I won't stay in one place like Mommy and Gramma. I'll have a life of travel and adventure, a life like Grampa's. Maybe something's different about me—but I don't care.

— — —

Mostly, I play with the boys in my neighborhood, but I have two girlfriends, Janice and Jo-Anne. One summer day, the three of us skip along the dusty sidewalk of Belleville, a city on the north shore of the Bay of Quinte, arm in arm, each clutching her Barbie.

When I lollygag behind, Janice, the older, bossy one, asks, "Why are you *aaall*-ways looking at the clouds?"

She's not really interested in the answer, so I ignore her. I'm more interested in the big sky that reminds me of a blue umbrella dotted with Mommy's makeup-remover cotton balls. Soon, the space between us widens. I don't understand why I like clouds better than conversation, but I do.

My Barbie points her skinny arm toward the clouds, and together we watch the mysteries in the air change from scooting, white speedboats into marching battleships. They're moving so quickly, Barbie and I decide the world must be spinning faster than usual. I twirl so we can see the whole sky but spin so fast I stumble, dizzy with wonder.

Why are some clouds thin wisps billowing like horsetails?

Why are others fat, blue splats in the sky, the color of Mommy's Delft Blue dishes?

A few clouds transform into giant, gray ships that charge through murky, blue water. Suddenly, cool raindrops splatter against my face. I close my eyes and extend my tongue, like a lizard snatching water, and decide that, one day, I'll command these battleships, ride these wild stallions, and make my own decisions.

Two weeks later, on a sunny Sunday afternoon, I'm in our shady backyard looking at the children's illustrated version of Defoe's *Robinson Crusoe* when thunder pounds my ears. I leap from the chaise lounge on our lawn, tumbling my book onto the grass. I search the sky for thunderclouds, when eight golden planes burst from behind their cloud camouflage. They scream overhead and shimmer in the sunlight. I jump up and down, waving hello with my arms, but they disappear as quickly as they appeared.

Mommy says, "Those are the Golden Hawks, Canada's aerobatic team."

Daddy corrects her. "Canada's *first* aerobatic team, and those are brand-new F-86 Sabres."

Still jumping with excitement, I announce, "I want to be a pilot."

I'm confused when Mommy's and Daddy's mouths smile, but their eyes don't. Mommy pulls me to her and combs my tangled hair with her fingers. She says, "We'll see a lot more of them because they've started flying out of CFB Trenton, just ten miles west, where your daddy was a mechanic."

Daddy corrects her again, but this time his voice is harsh. "An aircraft maintenance engineer." Then he adds, "The airbase is only ten miles west, and obviously we're below the approach path to the runway."

The following weekend at our annual August fair, the Golden Hawks perform some twists and turns in the air. I hold my breath whenever they look like they might crash into each other, but I want to be up there, twirling through the sky with them. Afterward, I beg Daddy to take me on the swirling Roll-O-Plane so I can pretend to be a Golden Hawk looping the loop inside my own mini-plane.

Mommy says, "Maybe next year when you're six."

I pout. "Mommy, I finished kindergarten. I'm a big girl now."

Daddy says, "You should be happy the Air Force formed the team last year to celebrate your fourth birthday."

I don't believe him but guess he's trying to cheer me up.

One Saturday afternoon when Daddy's at work, Mommy's in our U-shaped kitchen whipping batter with her turquoise Mixmaster. I tug the frill of her red-and-white apron. She looks at me with a smile but otherwise ignores me, so I swing the French doors of her Frigidaire oven—open . . . shut . . . open . . . shut.

"Stop playing with those doors!" she says, sounding like a TV drill sergeant. "The oven will never get warm!"

I drag our step stool toward her, and Mommy shoots me a disapproving glance as the rubber feet screech along the tile floor. I scramble up the stairs to stand on the seat and poke my finger close to the batter.

She swats my hand away. "Don't touch!"

I ask, "Why are clouds layered like your yummy cakes?" When I need answers to my questions, I always ask Mommy.

"Clouds come in many shapes and colors, just like cakes. Some make lightning. Others make rain."

"Why?" Sometimes Mommy says she's too busy or too tired, but when I catch her in a good mood, she's like my new encyclopedia—without the colored pictures.

With the back of her left hand, she brushes a permed wave from her glistening forehead, then stirs cocoa powder into the batter. "I'll forget an ingredient if you don't give me a moment's peace."

"Why do cloud layers move in different directions?"

She sighs with exasperation. "*Why* are you always asking *why?*"

"Can I help you, Mommy?"

With her finger, she dabs a blob of chocolate batter on the tip of my nose. I wipe it off, then lick my goopy finger.

She says, "Yes. Go away. Find the answers in your encyclopedia."

Chocolate is my favorite flavor, and batter is better than cake. I hesitate, hoping for another sample. After a minute or so of silence except for the whirring Mixmaster, she says, a bit angrily, "You should be grateful. Not every child has an encyclopedia. Do you remember why your grandparents bought it for you?"

I giggle. "You and Grampa *always* remind me. One night, when I was two and Grampa and Gramma were eating supper with us and talking about genealogy, I sang out, 'Gee-knee-*OL*-oh-gee. Gee-knee-*OL*-oh-gee.'"

"It was your first real word, after 'Mama' and 'Dada.' We were astonished and proud."

"It sounds like a song to me!"

The memory must've made Mommy happy because now she says, "If you leave me alone, you can lick the beaters."

I scurry into our new rec room, eager to find the answers to my questions, knowing that, even if I don't, other facts will lure me into an unexpected tunnel of discovery. Despite the difficulty of understanding many of the words and ideas, I want to discover the world. How did the Egyptians construct pyramids? Why couldn't Marie Curie cure herself? How are clouds made?

After some research that tells me the top of the sky is farther away than I can imagine, I tell Mommy, "I'm going to ride my trike."

She says, "Don't you dare go near that construction site."

With hands on my hips, I say, "I'm a *big* girl. I'm starting grade one in September."

She bobbles the wooden spoon close to my nose. "Don't. You. Dare."

"You're a worrywart." I use a weirdly wonderful word she uses to describe her mother.

She scowls. "I am not."

I dream of rocketing through the air and zooming into the blue, beyond the boundaries of my sandbox—or beyond any boundary, especially Mommy's. I hate her rules about how far I can walk alone to a friend's house, when I must go to bed, and how close to home I must ride my tricycle. But the site is only two blocks away. I'll be across our busy street and back before she realizes I'm gone. I scream downhill, tricycle wheels spinning. My blonde curls fly wildly around my face, and I giggle with delight as the wind blurs her words: *Don't go near the construction site. Don't cross the street.*

At the site, my legs judder with delight as giant earthmovers thunder across the dirt, drilling, pounding, and dumping blocks of limestone. The trucks and the stones could flatten my trike and me, but this only makes me more excited.

Suddenly, Mommy looms in front of me, towering above, seeming larger than the monster trucks. I try to escape, but she walks faster than I can pedal uphill, toward home. She canes my bare calves with a freshly cut willow stick. Each lash feels like the sting of a dozen hornets. I pedal faster, howling with pain, tears darkening my sleeveless pop-top.

She says, "You are the most disobedient six-year-old!"

For weeks, memories of her anger and the sting of the willow whip keep me within her boundaries.

One evening in late June, Grampa lays out an atlas and some maps on his kitchen table. He opens the top map. "This 'ere map is Ontario, the province we live in. Your Gramma and I are going on a road trip, and you're coming, too!"

"What's a road trip?"

He laughs. "We're going to drive our trailer through three Canadian provinces and six American states." He opens the atlas. "Come stand beside me, and I'll show you our route."

As I admire the pretty colors on the map, shades of pink and green for land, and shades of blue for water, Grampa moves his finger from our home near Toronto across most of Canada and then the northern United States.

"We'll be gone one whole month!"

I crinkle my brow. "But, Grampa, this map is so tiny. How come we'll be gone so long?"

His eyes twinkle behind horn-rimmed glasses. "You'll find out soon enough!"

Gramma serves us milk and rhubarb pie, then returns to the kitchen to wash dinner dishes. Grampa marks our planned route on the map using a black oil pencil and a wooden ruler, pointing out places we'll stop along the way. When he's done, he says, "Now, young lady, you need to spend a few days with your parents before we head out onto the trail."

I pout a little, but I haven't seen Mommy or Daddy for a week or so. I don't miss them, but I guess I should leave Gramma and Grampa's, the place that feels like home.

Three days later, my dreams of travel and adventure become reality. I sit in the back seat of Grampa's Pontiac. Grampa drives and Gramma navigates, and to pass the time we count foreign license plates. Most exciting are the cars from faraway states like Florida and California.

Another highlight is camping at Sleeping Giant Provincial Park near Thunder Bay, Ontario, named for a humongous rock that looks like a giant man sleeping on his back, arms crossed over his chest.

Grampa says, "Legend has it this man was the Ojibwa Spirit of the Deep-Sea Water. The gods turned him to stone after he betrayed his people and revealed the location of their silver mine to white men."

Late one afternoon, somewhere along Manitoba's Highway 1, Grampa says, "That darn sun is near blinding me," then pulls off the road into a gas station with a beautiful white rose on their sign.

Gramma says, "Loral, we don't need gas."

"Mildred, I have a plan."

When the man comes to fill our car and scrape the blood, bugs, and grasshoppers off the windshield, Grampa says, "Lola, let's you and me hop out 'n' stretch our legs." To the man, he asks, "Is there a campground near here?"

The man stops putting gas in the car and wipes a hand on his greasy coveralls. "Not fer a hunderd miles! Mebbe more."

Grampa gestures to an open space near the building. "Could we pay you to park there?"

The man rubs the stubble on his chin. "Gimme a couple bucks, and I'll even clean the bathroom for ya!"

I love being alone, during that silent night, with no campers nearby.

In Saskatchewan—another word that sounds like a song—we count bison grazing on the prairies. The baby bison are about the same size as the baby elephant I saw last year at the circus, chained to a tree, far from his family chained to other trees. He was crying. That made me sad, and I cried, too. I'm glad bison run free.

In Bemidji, Minnesota, we visit the massive statues of lumberjack Paul Bunyan and Babe, his blue ox. I can just barely touch Babe's tummy with my outstretched arm, and I feel so tiny standing beside these huge statues.

This whole world is much bigger than I imagined but, thanks to Grampa, I now understand this is a big world with big roads, big lakes, and big statues. Every day seems like the best day, until the next day, when I see and learn something new, and this new day becomes even better than the day before. I want to keep going and see more, but instead I have to go home.

When we return four weeks later, Mommy greets us at the door, but as soon as we're inside, she rushes to the bathroom. I follow her, then turn to Gramma. "Something's wrong. Mommy's throwing up."

Gramma spirits me into my bedroom. "Let's get you unpacked."

Mommy comes out in a few minutes and frowns. "I'm pregnant."

Gramma asks, "Have you told Al yet?"

"I'm afraid."

Gramma hugs Mommy. "Let us know if we can help."

After they leave, Mommy wipes away tears I can't see, then sniffles. "You hurt my feelings when you left with your grandparents without saying goodbye."

"You were busy doing dishes."

"You could have told me you were going."

"You're always saying, 'Get out of my hair.'" *Why's she blaming me?* She seemed more interested in tidying the house than spending the last few minutes with me. I say, "I was sitting in the car with Grampa, waiting for you to come say goodbye."

"Maybe this baby will be more affectionate than you."

I feel like a bad girl for not saying goodbye. I can't help loving Grampa best, then Gramma, then her, and Daddy just a bit, because he's either cross or distant. He kisses Mommy a lot but only sometimes kisses me good night. "How come you and Daddy didn't say goodbye to me?"

All she says is, "I can't speak for your father."

Eight months later, in April 1962, my sister's arrival tears into our lives like a tornado.

For the first seven years of my life, Mommy and Daddy often spent private time in their bedroom. I was glad they left me alone, allowing me to travel to other worlds without punishment or interruption for dodging my chores of dusting and cleaning the bathroom. I loved the fictional reality of books or my two favorite TV shows, *Sea Hunt* and *Sky King*. When I imagined myself as Mike Nelson, a frogman plunging underwater, or Schuyler "Sky" King soaring through the sky in his twin-engine airplane, outmaneuvering villains to save the world, I felt good about myself.

My first clue things have changed is that my parents avoid touching or kissing each other and me.

The second clue comes when my parents redecorate their study. This is Mommy's favorite room, so I don't understand why they move two of the three comfortable armchairs to the base-ment rec room. I'm even more surprised when Mommy's beloved books follow like Canada geese. When they fill the empty spaces with a wooden crib and change table filled with baby clothes and cloth diapers, I understand this will be my sister's room.

Dinner remains official family time but, sometime after Lynn's arrival, Daddy starts going back to his office after sup-per four or five days each week, instead of one or two, like he did before Lynn. During supper, my parents sit opposite and dis-tant, the moon and the sun. Daddy occupies the west end of the table, like death and sunset, and Mommy the east end, like birth and sunrise. I get this idea from the ancient Aztec ideas in my encyclopedia.

Lynn and I sit beside each other, keeping our parents further separated. My tummy gets upset when I wonder if dinner will be fun or awful or if my parents will even speak to each other. Sometimes Daddy reminds me of an angry storm cloud. I'm glad when he leaves. Sometimes his absence makes Mommy even more annoyed with me, even when I'm a good girl, so I escape to my bedroom, shut the door, and solve mysteries encountered by fearless teen detectives Joe and Frank Hardy and Nancy Drew, whose exciting lives I envy.

One night after supper, Mommy brandishes scissors and ges-tures toward the step stool. "You need a trim."

I hop onto the stool but when I see foot-long clumps litter-ing the tile, I can't stop the tears dribbling down my cheeks. "Mommy, please! Stop!"

She says, "I work all day and I'm too busy with two children to comb and curl your hair."

Between sobs, I say, "I want long hair."

"And I want your father's help. But we don't always get what we want."

I run fingers through the remains of my hair and cry harder.

She swats me on the shoulder. "Stop blubbering. When *I* was your age, *I* respected my parents. *I* did as I was told—the first time!"

I feel like a failure, unable to meet her expectations, unable to be the perfect daughter.

Then she shoves a mirror in front of my face. She's chopped off my golden curls and I don't even recognize the boy staring at me.

She says, "Your father doesn't care I'm home alone with you two."

Mommy hates me, but I don't know why.

One Saturday in August 1962, Mommy says, "Please watch Lynn while I finish the laundry."

Obediently, I watch Lynn in her Baby Butler, a card table on wheels that I myself survived, but after a few minutes I'm bored. Watching my sister is as much fun as watching my Betsy Wetsy doll sit on the shelf. I rush to my room, planning to return right away with *Nancy Drew and the Mystery of the Brass Bound Trunk* but instead, I perch on the edge of my bed, fascinated by Nancy's South America steamship adventure. The title made me pull the book from our town's library shelf but the picture on the cover of a steamer trunk like Grampa's sealed the deal.

Just as Nancy and I are about to solve the mystery, Mommy screams, "Lola! Come here now!"

Her words shoot me back to reality. I lose my balance and fall—*kuh-thunk*—onto the hardwood floor. *What could have happened in the few minutes Lynn was alone?* Her pudgy frog's legs are too short to reach the floor, and she's strapped in so she couldn't have slipped out. *Or could she?*

I peek into the kitchen. Lynn's seated, as I had left her. Almost.

"*Eeeekkkk!*" I screech and Mommy whirls to face me, a cigarette gripped between her teeth. She exhales through her nose, becomes Smaug, the fire-breathing dragon, then hisses, "Stop howling like a banshee. *You* have nothing to complain about."

Lynn has stretched her chubby arms to reach Mommy's shiny brass ashtray and tipped the treasure onto her tabletop, mixing ashes with juice from her sippy cup. Gooey, gray ash covers her face, and her short black hair is a crown of spikes.

Mommy hooks her finger into Lynn's chipmunk cheeks and pulls out a hidden treasure of butts that spatter onto the table.

I gag. "*Blaurggh.*"

She says, "Your sister could *die!*"

This seems silly, even to seven-year-old me, so I say brightly, "Mommy, she's imitating you!"

Mommy glowers, and I brace myself for a swat of her hand. Instead, she says, "I'll discuss this with the Man of the House."

Then, to my surprise, she sinks against the back of the chair, buries her face with both hands, and sobs. I've never seen Mommy cry, so I rub her shoulder. It's my fault she's crying so I want to make her feel better, but she ignores me and keeps sobbing, so I stop. I feel invisible.

Tonight, I'm glad Daddy works late, and bedtime comes before he's home. I snuggle into the pillows trying to help Nancy reveal the mystery but can't stop wondering what Mommy will say to Daddy about my latest "failure to meet expectations." Maybe he'll only spank me and not stop me from watching our new black-and-white TV with rabbit ears.

The following morning, I dawdle in bed, more interested in helping Nancy capture bad guys than facing parents—and punishment. Past eight o'clock, Daddy raps on my door then flings it open. "Time to rise and shine. Breakfast is ready."

He says this every day, but today his voice is full of anger, maybe even hate. I'm scared, but he'll be less angry if I get up right away. Still in my baby doll jammies, I trudge behind, head hung low.

In the kitchen, Mommy serves scrambled eggs dotted with chunks of cheddar. This is my favorite Sunday breakfast, but today the meal thuds in my stomach like raw potato. Instead of scolding me, they torture me by chatting about stupid things, such as whether Mrs. McCarthy will keep trying for a child after her fifth missed carriage, whatever that means. I can't stop wriggling in my chair, even though each fidget on the sticky vinyl seat seems to peel flesh from my bare legs. My every move makes a rude sound. *Phraaaap.*

Daddy glares at me as if I farted.

Mommy says, "Do you have ants in your pants? Sit still!"

In what seems like four hours later, Daddy turns his stony face toward me. I melt against the chair, then freeze as he speaks in his deep voice, saying each word as if it were a complete sentence. "Your mother and I have discussed your negligence."

He pops a sliver of French toast into his mouth, chewing it slowly as he watches me squirm. I remember the last time his hand slapped my bare bottom. Finally, he swallows. "We've planned—"

I can't breathe. Waiting is torture.

Mommy says, "The episode with your sister was inexcusable." She purses her lips, then sighs. "But we've decided not to punish you—"

Daddy says, "Because you're obviously too young to be responsible."

Neither their words nor their frowns make me feel good about myself.

Daddy sips his black coffee, then says, "We've planned—a—most—exciting—"

I hold my breath.

"Adventure. Instead of driving or taking the train to my folks' annual family reunion in Regina, we're going to fly."

I squeal with delight and clap my hands. I'm going to fly like Grampa.

Mommy flips her cigarette package end to end. "Passenger planes are like new kids on the block."

"Jean, the flights will be as smooth as driving on the new Superhighway 401."

Mommy wrinkles her brow. "A recent article in *National Geographic* said summer air masses are unstable. Our flights might not be as smooth as you'd have me believe."

3

FIRST FLIGHT

Lola, age 3, looks through binoculars
toward a far horizon (1958)

The next week, as I finish my slice of Mommy's cherry pie, she says, "Al, don't you think flying is a bit newfangled?"

Daddy puts down his newspaper. "Ron flies all the time."

Mommy says, "Only because his boss at Imperial Oil insists."

Daddy buries his face behind *The Telegram*. "I've already paid for our tickets."

She leans close to him and whispers. I think I hear, "We're going to crash and burn."

Daddy thumps the table with his fist. "If the Canadian government approves airplanes for civilians, airplanes are safe." Then, he folds his newspaper and leaves the kitchen.

Daddy's confidence and his war experience with airplanes convince me he's right about flying. As for Mommy, perhaps she thinks coping with my annoying sister for a few hours in the sky will be easier than three or four days in a car and overnight in hotels. Maybe she thinks showing off their second child and arriving in style by air might stop the nasty things she and Daddy say to each other every night. That is, every night when Daddy's home.

Fourteen sleeps later, we're crowded inside Toronto's Malton Airport departure lounge, wedged amidst other passengers. The room is crowded and hot. Adults pace and smoke and I can barely breathe. A loudspeaker blurts, "Pass—*crackle, hiss*—for—*gurgle*—Win—*hiss*—nipeg—*crackle*—board—*mumble*—gate—*hiss*."

Some take their belongings and hurry toward doors leading to the aircraft. We follow, clumped into a solid mass three or four people wide, exit the terminal, and wind across the tarmac toward a stairway attached to the airplane.

Daddy says in a voice loud enough for others to overhear, "There's our plane!"

Mom says, "Obviously," and grabs my hand so I don't run ahead.

I can hear the familiar sarcasm in her voice but Daddy says, "It's a turbocharged Vickers Vanguard," then he grabs the handle of my sleeping sister's lounger and guides Mommy by touching her elbow.

She stops abruptly. "I feel like we're a herd of cattle heading to the slaughterhouse."

He points at the plane. "There are four enormous engines, each with four massive propeller blades. Extra engines mean extra safety."

She sighs. "Or more that can go wrong."

Proudly, as if he built the plane, he says, "Top speed, four hundred twenty miles per hour."

Mommy asks, "Who are you trying to impress?"

At the base of the metal stairs, I gaze way, way up before I take my first step onto the silver stairway to heaven. After we enter the magical metal tube, some scramble to find their seats while others stand in the aisle of the metal cavern, looking right then left, puzzled, and waiting for assistance. Some stop halfway down the aisle, eyes darting side to side, searching for their seats, waiting for help. Nobody knows where to put their carry-on bags.

I admire the stewardesses, airborne fashion models like the beautiful actresses on our new television. The prettiest one, with a blonde bun, walks toward us.

My voice squeaks with excitement as I ask, "Will we be wearing space suits like John Glenn's?"

She kneels and takes my hands in hers. "No, we'll be flying near Earth, not outer space." She tickles my sister's chin, then stands to face Daddy. "Your baby and her lounger are blocking the aisle."

I pull at her coat sleeve. "I saw him on TV! I had the measles!"

"I'm sorry you were sick but if your folks have a TV, you're a lucky girl."

Daddy says, "She was quite sick. Missed two weeks of school in February."

She smiles and says, "I hear scientists are working on a vaccination," then gestures toward a cradle attached to the edge of a U-shaped luggage rack above our heads. "Please, use this Skycot, then take your seats."

I stare at the open shelving that runs along both sides of the cabin. A lip prevents stuff from falling onto our heads, and vertical walls prevent shifting. I clutch Lynn's hand and tug on Daddy's suit coat. He ignores me and puts Lynn into the Skycot.

Daddy points to Mommy and me and to the seats. "You two sit down."

I dive in first and glue my nose to the oval window to feel

closer to the planes sliding past us. Mommy plunks onto the seat beside me, followed by Daddy in the aisle seat. Mommy twists her hands together, and I follow her gaze upward to my sister, alone in her Skycot.

Mommy says, "Don't worry. The stewardess said babies will be safe inside the bassinet," then lights a Craven A. "Except during especially dangerous phases of flight."

Especially dangerous? Her left hand grips my right hand so hard my tiny fingers squish into each other. *What does she know about airplanes that she hasn't told me?*

After a few minutes and announcements blotted by static, I see men waving sticks in the air like music conductors. The plane lurches into motion. Mommy squashes the butt into the ashtray on the armrest she shares with Daddy. The overhead rack shakes as the plane rumbles along the pavement to the rhythm of a toe-tapping tune my parents play on their stereo—"Shake, Rattle and Roll." I bounce to the beat as buildings and other airplanes whip past, faster and faster, faster than Daddy on Highway 401. A roar like thunder blasts into my ears, then suddenly, the nose of the aircraft pitches up and the earth slips away, slowly at first but we pick up speed, and I pretend I'm a shooting star.

Soon, we leave the blue sky behind and fly into cauliflower clouds that cover the window with a veil of white and block my view. This is boring. I turn to ask Mommy for one of my books from the overhead rack. She's rubbing her forehead, holding a small white bag near her mouth and moaning. "I feel sick."

My sister wails.

Mommy vomits into the bag.

Daddy says, "Don't worry."

In a few minutes, we fly out of the white blanket toward blueberry-blue clouds with tops like the blacksmith's anvil at Upper Canada Village, towering giants with fingers stretching toward space.

Mommy grabs Daddy's hand and points. "Look! The wings are flapping!"

His gaze follows her hand. "They're designed to flap. If they didn't, they *would* rip off."

Mommy swipes her palms on her pleated skirt, then leans forward, resting her elbows on her knees. She hides her face behind her hands. "We're going to die!"

"Jean, be calm! You'll scare Lola."

"Oh, Daddy, I'm not scared. This is as much fun as riding the Rocket or the Zipper at the fair."

Mommy's voice cracks as she says, "Stop talking about those scary rides!"

Daddy smiles but his voice doesn't. "At least *one* of you *girls* isn't frightened."

Our captain makes an announcement. "Ah, folks, we're gonna circle south to deviate around a big thundercloud. Might get a bit rough, so please stay seated."

Maybe twenty minutes later, the plane enters another white cauliflower cloud, but soon the cloud becomes dark blue like the bruises on my knees. The inside of the plane gets dark, like nighttime, but it's early afternoon. The plane jerks through the sky like a bumper car hit from different directions. Our plane swoops up and down. Drinks spill. Bar service is suspended, and the stewardesses remove the china plates and silverware. We jiggle as if we're on a bumpy dirt road with washboard ridges. My teeth bounce together.

Daddy says, "Oops, we're in another thundercloud."

Something pings and thumps against the metal aircraft. This hasn't happened before and doesn't seem right, so I ask, "Mommy, is someone shooting at us?"

Mommy can't seem to talk. I get scared until Daddy calmly says, "Those are hailstones, created by the thundercloud."

A few minutes later, when he borrows a cigarette from Mommy,

I wonder if he's scared because he stopped smoking before Lynn was born. Mommy gets whiter than fresh snow, and her bugged-out eyes get bigger and bigger. She wipes sweat from her forehead, lights another cigarette, and moans. "Al, when we stop in Winnipeg, let's take the train to Regina."

Daddy's thin lips tighten. "The next flight will be better."

As our turboprop plane heaves and jolts through the thunderstorm, Mommy's face turns the color of her overcooked peas. She lights cigarette after cigarette and ignores me. I bob up and down in my seat.

"Mommy, I want to fly airplanes when I grow up!"

She grimaces and throws up again.

I hold my nose for a few moments, then, with a big smile on my face, say, "Daddy, I want to be a pilot when I grow up."

I know he'll be excited, but he scowls. "Don't be silly. Girls can't fly planes."

I pucker my brow and turn away. I hate it when he says Mommy and I are silly. She might not actually know everything, but she knows way more than he does. But maybe he's right this time. Penny on the television show *Sky King* is the only female pilot I've seen, but she isn't real and only takes control if her uncle, the real pilot, is ill or injured.

As we approach Regina, the captain says, "Folks, we're sorry about that nasty weather. But you can look forward to sunshine and eighty-degree temperatures in Regina." Suddenly, there's a big *thunk. Have we lived through the flight only to crash and die at the airport?* I open my left eye to peek outside. *Whew,* we're on the ground.

Daddy says to Mommy, "Here we are safe and sound, as I promised. Like I said, pilots know what they're doing."

The next flight is smoother, but during our visit with relatives in Regina, Mommy says to Daddy, "Let's take the train home. We shouldn't expose our girls to more bloodcurdling brushes with death."

Daddy ignores her, just as my uncles do with their wives. Whenever I don't answer her, Mommy says I'm rude, but it seems to be okay if men ignore women.

Soon it's time to return to Ontario. During the first leg from Regina to Winnipeg, Mommy is busy barfing and smoking. At Winnipeg, we race from the plane to the terminal in a swirling rainstorm. Inside the terminal, hundreds of nervous travelers cram into the stuffy lounge. An announcement advises our layover will be longer than scheduled. Events and activities during our holiday time in Regina are already vague blurs, but these flights will never leave my memory.

Mommy chats with other female passengers, who speak quietly as they fan their faces with ticket folios.

To keep me occupied, Daddy takes me to the store. Instead of getting just one of the two toys I admired during our first layover, he buys both. I'm so excited, I race back to Mommy ahead of him. In one hand, I clutch a small Sioux warrior, his painted face framed by a war bonnet of eagle feathers. He holds a spear and shield and straddles a black horse, ready to charge into battle to defend his people. I always cheer for the Indians on *The Lone Ranger*. I used to like the Lone Ranger best because his surname is Reid, like mine, until I learned he called his sidekick Tonto, the Spanish word for "fool."

I hold the warrior near my mouth and whisper, "Crazy Horse, when we get home, you can ride in my toy birch bark canoe and play with real arrowheads Grampa found in his garden. I have a beautiful Mohawk dolly named Pauline, who lives in a wigwam. She writes poetry. Maybe you can marry her and live happily ever after."

In my left hand, I clutch a metal replica of the Cannonball Express steam engine driven by railroad engineer Casey Jones, the real-life hero of my third-favorite TV show.

I scramble along the cold cement floor on my hands and knees, making the horse leap toward the steam engine. Two women seated across from our family stop talking and smack their tongues against their teeth.

"*Tch! Tch!*" One adjusts her pillbox hat. "Look at her. Playing with toys meant for boys."

The other scowls. "She's a real tomboy."

Pillbox says to Mommy, "How can you let her play on the floor?"

Mommy's cheeks turn red. She bobs Lynn on her knee and kisses her chubby cheek. "This one's an angel."

I'm sorry my behavior embarrassed Mommy, but I don't understand why people I don't know care how I act. Besides, I like playing Barbie dress-up with girls as much as playing in my sandbox with neighbor boys.

Whoever made the rules for girls is stupid.

4

FACADES

My mother, smiling at unknown photographer
four years before marriage (1943)

By the time I'm in grade six, I do homework at the kitchen table while Mom reads and smokes, using the butt of one cigarette to light the next. Her habit repulses me, but our kitchen has the best lighting. Dad's at the office. Of course. Lynn's absorbed by the television, glued to the couch in Mom's Danish-Modern living room. I say "Mom" because Dad hates the sleek style. Or maybe he just hates her.

Mom sucks on her cigarette, then perches the smelly stick on her beanbag ashtray. The spaghetti string of smoke coils toward the ceiling. Their slogan, "Will not affect your throat," must be wrong because the harsh smoke tickles my mouth. I stick out my tongue and curl my index finger to scratch the roof of my mouth.

Mom says, "Stop trying to make me believe smoke bothers you. Are you ready for me to quiz you for your history test?"

I'm not, so I say, "Your friend Miss Carson is pretty. Why isn't she married?"

Mom doesn't look up from *In the Wet*. "She had a boyfriend in high school."

"Why didn't they get married?"

"The school board forced her to choose. If she married, she'd have to give up teaching. She accepted solitude as the price she had to pay."

"Another stupid rule."

"My decision to marry ended my career as a government employee at the railroad."

Time had dulled the pain of Mom's broken heart, yet she couldn't conceal the simmering rage in her subdued voice. She said "career" . . . I heard "life."

"I wish I'd never—" She stops and looks at me with sad eyes. "Another time, when you're older."

Like the few working mothers of my friends, Mom works to bring extra money into the home.

I ask, "Why are you a legal secretary and not a lawyer?"

She explains, "'Society' encourages men to be the best they can be. 'Society' gives them approval to be scientists, professors, physicians, lawyers, or pilots." Her voice rises. She speaks faster. "'Society' says women should be happy as wives and mothers, but if we must work, they let us be nurses, teachers, secretaries, or stewardesses."

She's angry but not with me. This time.

I vow to have everything she dreamed of having. A career *and* a husband who loves me.

= = =

Two years later, when I'm thirteen and in grade eight, my parents' marriage is crumbling faster than the stale bag of Dad's Chocolate Chip cookies in our pantry. When I say, "Our home is a house, not a home," in a casual tone to Phyllis, my mother's best friend, she justifies their evenings apart with, "Your father is at the office working hard to support a family. You should be grateful."

I'm hurt she doubts me, but I understand her reaction. To outsiders, we look like a family, so we must be a family like those perfect TV parents in *Leave It to Beaver* and *The Adventures of Ozzie and Harriet*, who ooze sweetness and love for their children. My parents never treat us badly, they just don't love us, and when we attend public events or socialize with friends, a veneer of cordiality masks their misery.

But within our walls, our family is a neglected engine grinding toward disintegration. Though my parents drop their happily ever-after charade at home, daily life is tranquil. They never fight or yell because they rarely talk. Twin beds, spread far apart, have replaced their double bed. Dad works Monday to Saturday, nine to five, returns to the office every night, and on Sunday spends mornings at church, then goes for a drive in the afternoon.

I don't understand why a smart, educated woman like my mother puts up with Dad's absences, but perhaps this helps us sail past many ragged shoals, until 1968, when I become a bona fide teenager. Now, he extends his work hours until ten at night, past my bedtime, and is never around to pretend to act like a father.

I don't mind because Grampa is my best friend and has always been more like my father.

Mom starts menopause, becomes absorbed with recording her erratic cycle on the kitchen calendar, and abandons any pretense of being my friend.

Most times, this is okay with me.

Her appearance embarrasses me. I avoid looking at her and hate being seen in public with her. Though she files and paints perfect oval nails, has her hair salon-coiffed, and wears attractive dresses, her bra and panties carve cutlines into her Michelin tire torso. After Lynn's birth, Mom packed on the pounds and seems keen to add more pounds with each meal, refusing to leave scraps on anyone's plate. When I don't clean my plate, she says, "You don't know when you'll eat again."

I say, "There's enough food in our pantry for ten years."

A scowl crosses her fat face. "Why can't you be grateful?"

I dread becoming my mother with her decaying and bloated body, breathing but dead.

My parents form a storm front of resistance against me when I realize—and rebel against—their definition of a good daughter as one willing to obey and walk in their footsteps. I don't understand why they're convinced rebellious plus determined equals bad. I go to chaperoned school dances and movie matinees and come home before ten. Regardless of the situation, their favorite refrains begin, "When I was your age, I . . ." and end with how perfect they were as children:

(a) "didn't talk back to my parents."

I'd challenge, "Maybe their rules were reasonable."

(b) "didn't expect to go out on dates until I finished high school."

I don't dare insult them with, "Maybe no one wanted to date you."

(c) "studied every evening and was in bed at nine."

And I never mention, "Because you didn't have electricity or TV."

They're not interested in my ambitions, opinions, or objectives, just the opinions of neighbors. I get good grades in school, but Mom throttles any pride of accomplishment with, "You said this test was easy. If it was so easy, why'd you get only ninety-five? What happened to the other five percent?"

Mom says, "You're going to give me my nineteenth nervous breakdown."

That pisses me off. The Rolling Stones are mine—not hers.

One Tuesday night, when I'm in the first semester of grade nine, Mom sits in her kitchen chair, near the wall telephone. At the other end, I tap my pencil on the table, pretending to work on a school project. "Uh, Mom, this Friday, um, I want to see the early movie. Please."

She keeps her head buried in *On the Beach*, but her back stiffens as if her spinal discs have suddenly calcified into a single bone. She drags on her cigarette, then exhales. Smoke signals spiral toward the ceiling. I hold my breath. She turns a page.

"I want to see *Bonnie and Clyde*."

"Thirteen is too young to see a gangster movie."

I say, "But, Mom, everyone is going."

"Everyone but you."

I wheedle. "I promise to be home at nine thirty."

She spits her words at me. "Why ask? If I say no, you'll go anyway."

I smack my pencil on the table and flop against the chair. "You talk like I'm always disobeying you. Am I *really* such a bad daughter?"

Without looking away from her book, she taunts me. "I'll bet you're going with a boy."

"I'm going with Patti and Michelle."

"You have a boyfriend, don't you!"

"No!"

She says, "I know what boys want. I bet you do, too."

"This isn't 1935."

"Times may've changed, young lady, but boys have not. Don't come to me for help if you get pregnant before you're married!"

"You're crazy! I've never even kissed a boy!"

She mashes her half-smoked cigarette into a full ashtray, stomps into her bedroom, and slams the door. We often fight, but she's never run away before. I pound on her bedroom door.

"Mom, why are you so angry?"

"Go away."

I hear her snuffling, but she doesn't answer. I lean my head against the closed door for a few moments, her cruel words ringing in my head, shredding any love I've ever had for her.

In contrast to the tension that permeates our home like carbon monoxide, my grandparents' home overflows with love—for each other and for Lynn and me. One June day in 1970, I bicycle to their bungalow on the bay. Grandma greets me on her doorstep, steeped in an aroma of strawberry rhubarb pie.

In the living room, I choose Grampa's chair and fold my legs sideways while Grandma sits in her usual spot on the other diamond-tufted chair. She crosses her ankles, a perfect lady, a Norman Rockwell grandmother: salon-styled waves of pearl-white hair, shell-pink cheeks, and a ruffled apron dotted with garlands of strawberries.

"I hate my mother! One day she says find a man with a good career but treats me like a baby the next day."

"We want you to go to college, like your mom. Or maybe you'll be the first in our family to get a university degree."

"But you expect me to come back here, don't you?"

"What does your dad say?"

I snort. "He can't be bothered to offer any opinion. He goes back to work every night."

Grandma blinks in astonishment. "Every night?"

Her reaction surprises me. I thought Mom might have confided in her mother.

I nod. "And Mom's almost always cross with me."

She stands and pats me on the shoulder. "How 'bout some pie?"

As we silently eat, I wonder why I *wouldn't* want a different life from my parents and grandparents. They've whetted my wanderlust with whirlwind summers of unforgettable journeys by planes, trains, and automobiles. Leaving means adventure. Leaving makes me feel alive.

One stormy winter night, with ideas about my future still as blurry as the maelstrom of snow bashing against our house, I sit at the kitchen table, opposite Mom. My feet rest on a chair, *Catcher in the Rye* propped against my bent legs. Motivated by Holden's cynicism, I ask, "Mom, why do you let others tell you how to be happy?"

Her head remains buried in *A Town Like Alice*. "Whadoyoumean?"

"You're always asking, 'What will the neighbors think?'"

She takes a long drag on her cigarette, stabs the butt into her glass ashtray, and continues reading. "Beam me up, Scotty" filters from the TV Lynn watches in the living room, all evening, every evening.

I ask, "Why are you always reading Nevil Shute?"

"He's a British pilot whose stories are based on his life experiences."

"Far out."

"He reminds me of a chap I used to . . . know."

Now I'm intrigued. "You mean, like a boyfriend?"

She lights another cigarette. I return to Holden's sneer at adult conformity for a few more pages, then say, "I don't plan to hang around here—just waiting to die!"

"What *do* you plan to do?"

"I want to paint, like Tom Thomson and the Group of Seven."

She's annoyed. "How many times must I say being an artist won't pay the bills! You're sixteen, with only one more year of high school. You'd better figure out something soon."

"I do know I'm as smart as the boys in my class. My marks are as good, often better."

She closes her book, using the index finger of her right hand as a bookmark.

I wait for her to say something but finally ask, "Why should boys get to be lawyers, doctors, or pilots just because they're boys?"

"Maybe you should hear about my first experience in the workforce."

I wince at the pain etched on her face, surprised by an emotion other than anger directed at me.

"Soon after your father and I married in October 1947, the railroad supervisor called me into his office to discuss my request to continue working. He said he was impressed with my work ethic and performance. I was ecstatic! Until . . ." She changes her voice to a stern baritone and assumes a condescending smile. "'Jean, you know married women belong at home.'"

I gasp. "Married women couldn't work in 1947?"

"For a few private companies but not the government."

I smack my book onto the table. "Who made *that* stupid rule?"

"Men. Men make the rules to benefit themselves. I told my supervisor my husband helped around the house."

"What'd he say?"

She reverts to his baritone. "'Maybe he's helping now but trust me, when babies start coming, he won't be the one caring for them.' He scratched his chin, then asked, 'You do plan to have children, don't you?'"

"And you had two!"

Her mouth twists into something between a smile and a grimace. Is she thinking about her supervisor's assumption—or her children?

"I began to answer but he cut me off. 'Of course you do. All women want babies.' Then he pointed out I'd be twenty-five the following month and 'had better get crackin'.'"

"What a creep. Couldn't you talk to someone else?"

Her eyes water. "Your grandmother, but she was as powerless as me. After I graduated high school in 1940, the second year of World War II, I was one of a handful of girls who went to college. Most townsfolk considered educated women oddballs. Many girls dropped out of school to marry before their husbands shipped off to war."

I leap to my feet. "I don't want to get married right after school. I'd rather die than become a secretary, teacher, or nurse."

She snaps back to her defensive self. "What's wrong with being a secretary? *I'm* a legal secretary."

I regret my impulsive words. "I'm sorry. Nothing is wrong with being a secretary."

Her cheeks flush. "What makes you think you're better than me?"

"I *don't* think I'm better—I think I'm *different.*"

"I don't think you're different from me."

I didn't know how I could be similar to someone I hated but had to admit she might be right this time. I say, "Your kiss-off chat does remind me of a conversation with my guidance counselor who refused my request to take shop. He said, 'Your husband will be grateful you learned how to cook and sew in home ec.'"

Mom asks, "Why didn't you tell me about this?"

"I didn't think you'd care."

Mom flinches, then asks, "Did you tell him Grandma and I taught you how to cook and sew?"

I wrinkle my nose. "He said girls don't belong in shop with boys."

"How do your girlfriends feel?"

I cross my arms. "Jane and Brian got engaged last month. When I asked if all she wants to do is have kids, she quoted Tennyson. 'Ours is not to question why, ours is but to do and die.'"

"Sometimes we have to accept that some things never change."

"Why should a girl pretend to be stupid to make boys feel better about themselves?"

"Lola, listen to me! Your life will be easier if you stop bucking the system."

I pound the table with my fist, and her coffee cup rattles. "You mean a system that creates TV shows like *Father Knows Best*. A system with forced choice careers for women."

Her hands shake as she lights a cigarette.

I've hated my mother for years, almost as long as I can remember, but suddenly I feel sad for her.

"Mom, I'm not angry with you. I'm angry because many people think biology is destiny. I'm angry because you're smarter than Dad—yet he rules this house. I'm angry because you'd have been a good *lawyer*."

5

DREAMS

My father, sometime during WWII

After high school graduation in 1972, I get my first serious boyfriend, Duncan, a hippie barely tolerated by everyone except my twelve-year-old sister, who admires him because he's a cool dude in a rock band. Following a brief stint at art school the following year, I return home, get my first job as a bank teller, and move in with Duncan.

Mom says I shouldn't date a divorced man, especially one eight years my senior. She's right, for the wrong reasons. The age difference doesn't affect our relationship but his pathetic compulsion to screw as many women as possible, including his ex-wife, does. And his refusal to cuddle after sex seems a strange response after intimacy. Instead of feeling loved, I feel rejected.

Grampa, the only person who's always given me unconditional love, bursts into tears when he sees the ramshackle Victorian brick house I share with Duncan and the five other male members of his rock band.

Between sobs, he says, "This is not the life we hoped for you."

Grampa's pain influences my perception of Duncan and, within months, we're arguing about everything. Instead of breaking up, I suggest a short separation, a gentle letdown. He stays in southern Ontario, while I quit the bank in April and move two hundred miles north for a five-month seasonal job with a backcountry outfitter at Canoe Lake, Algonquin Park. Surrounded by the wilderness woods of northern Ontario resurrects childhood memories of tenting, swimming, and hiking here every summer with my grandparents.

I ditch Duncan. He's not going anywhere.

But I am.

I get a job in Huntsville, the town closest to Algonquin Park, hoping to find a roommate to share expenses and maximize my savings for university. My determination to decide, take risks, and move on makes me giddier than my trembling, teenage self on the hot summer night at the beach when Duncan introduced me to petting—and his penis.

Despite these decisive actions, plans for my grown-up future remain as nebulous as the clouds flying overhead.

I accept the first job I find, as a waitress at Hidden Valley Resort, a modern hotel perched midway between ski slopes and Peninsula Lake. Waitressing will be a fine job for a few months, and the benefits are great. I'll get discounted ski tickets, reduced fees for the ski lessons I need to become a skier, and inexpensive accommodation at the hotel's staff house.

To celebrate, I order a frozen margarita in the lounge, where I'll soon be serving alcohol. I laze into a tub chair beside floor-to-ceiling windows and luxuriate in the late August sun, still hot enough for warmth to penetrate the gray glass. I cross my ankles, bob my right foot in sync with the Eagles' "Desperado," and drink in the scenery. Everything reminds me of the quintessential paintings created by Canada's Group of Seven: an ultramarine lake ringed by coniferous trees; a ragged shoreline punctuated by limestone hillocks and sturdy jack pine trees, all branches windblown east by the prevailing westerlies; and a flock of red canoes nested below the hotel.

Minutes later, three tanned, muscular men stride into the room, impishly shoving each other, laughing at a private joke. I bet they're rich kids doing a gap year between university and settling down. Just one look at the athlete with land-of-the-midnight-sun ivory curls wisping around his chiseled face takes my breath away. As they order drinks at the bar, he glances my way. Our eyes radar lock. A gentle pulse of electricity galvanizes my body.

He moves toward me, beckoning his friends to follow. They sit at a squat café table three feet away. Fingers of passion tickle my groin. I hope they don't notice my hand tremble as I raise the margarita glass to my suddenly parched lips.

Midnight Sun casually waves at me. "I'm Paul; this is Clive and John. Are you staying at the hotel?"

I shake my head. "I'm living in the park, but I start here in two weeks!"

Paul leans close to me, and I drink in his spicy aftershave. "Far out. I teach waterskiing and hang gliding. Do you ski?"

"Never."

He slaps his left thigh. "Perfect! Come for a free lesson."

"Are you all instructors?"

Dark-haired, silent-film-star-handsome Clive says, "I'm downhill only. But Paul's a natural athlete."

Paul laughs. "Father first took me skiing when I was three,

to give Mom a break after my brother was born. Summers were spent waterskiing at our cottage near here."

Clive tips his head toward Paul. "He's a wild man."

John smiles and two large dimples accent his baby face. "Skis downhill—backward."

Paul winks, then orders a second round of drinks, including a margarita for me. "Skiing backward lets me watch my young students."

John chuckles. "Even the littlest kids love Paul."

I say, "Children seem possessed like Linda Blair in *The Exorcist*."

Paul and I have nothing in common.

One week later, we have our first date.

We meet at the dock, and he gives me my first waterski lesson. I'm completely incompetent but pleased when he follows through on his promise of dinner at Deerhurst Inn, an exclusive luxury resort near Huntsville. We sit opposite each other in the elegant dining room, overlooking the pool. Paul orders for us, choosing surf and turf, the most expensive item on the menu, and a bottle of Mateus.

The opulence of the restaurant and our meal awe me so much that, halfway through the meal, I say, "Hey, you've finished the bottle, and I've only had one small glass."

He laughs. "Guess you'll have to drink faster!"

I point outside. "I can't take my eyes away from the couple frolicking in the pool."

He snorts. "She's Xaviera Hollander, author of the memoir *The Happy Hooker*."

"I've . . . I've . . . never seen a prostitute before."

Two weeks later, under the rotating mirror ball at Limberlost Lodge, Paul and I wrap ourselves around each other and sway to "Stairway to Heaven." Cocooned against the rippled muscles of his torso, I feel the first pangs of true love. We sneak out of the old wooden dance hall door and make out in the back seat of his friend's car, until our friends join us an hour or so later, laughing at the steamed windows.

At the staff house, we tear upstairs to his room, past my less-private, first-floor room, grapple with belts and buttons, and tumble as a tangled heap of arms and legs onto his mattress on the floor. Fireworks explode in my brain. We make love until dawn filters into the darkness, both convinced no one has ever experienced lovemaking or love like ours. Best of all, Paul doesn't push me away after sex but cradles me in his arms and makes no demands on me other than, "Babe, you need birth control."

"You're right. A child would complicate our lives. I'd like to go back to uni—or perhaps learn to fly."

"Flying! Cool! My dad and my uncle are pilots."

"Do they fly with Air Canada?"

He laughs. "No, they fly for fun. Dad's a vet, Uncle Bob's a farmer, and between them they have three airplanes."

I've never met anyone who *owns* a plane. I'm even more in awe of Paul and his family.

Paul winks. "If you stick around here, you could take flight lessons at the nearby Muskoka Airport."

I nod, but besotted with reciprocated adoration, I let Paul's charisma change my plans to return to uni next fall, which don't seem as important as being loved. I've been desperate for love, for someone to accept me for me, not who my parents, friends—and society—think a young woman should be.

When Bill, a shared friend and ski instructor, learns of my involvement with Paul, he advises, "Slow down. Take your time. Other guys think you're pretty cute, too."

Does he mean himself? I don't ask. I don't care.

My back stiffens. "Paul loves me."

Bill swirls his rum and cola, tinkling the cubes of ice. "More than booze?"

I grab another handful of salted peanuts from the dish on the table, absently toss them into my mouth, and chew ferociously. "Everybody in our group gathers for drinks après-ski."

Bill scratches the mosquito bite on his neck. "Many of us have a drink or two"—he holds his glass aloft—"then leave. Paul doesn't stop until he's blottoed."

I cover my ears. "Stop picking on him."

With my head in the clouds and my heart cartwheeling in ecstasy, I ignore the occasional flashes of insight that suggest Paul's drinking might be a problem. I'm sure he'll stop drinking if I ask.

We fill our fairy-tale romance with days and nights enjoying each other, beguiled by the moments of first true love. Bronzed, beautiful, and towering nine inches taller than my five-foot-five, Paul's allure is more than physical. He's a daring nonconformist with a child's zest for life, apparently unperturbed by the opinions of others, unlike anyone else.

Paul and I spent three days visiting my parents at the beginning of an impromptu road trip in the off-season weeks of late October and early November. Upon our return five weeks later, I'm delighted when my parents are friendly and welcoming. Paul and I hold hands and take turns excitedly interrupting each other as we talk about touring colonial Williamsburg on a bicycle built for two; sunbathing at New Smyrna Beach, Daytona's quieter alternative; and camping at Fort Wilderness, Disney World.

Mom says, "We've never seen you happier!"

Despite my teenage ferocity to avoid the socially fabricated mold of female destiny, I allow some force—greater than yet also within me—to let love sweep my dreams into the garbage pail.

In December, only three months after our first date, we select my ring, ignoring the clerk's warning, *Pearls are bad luck for an engagement ring.* Me, a nineteen-year-old who spent her teens rejecting tradition and declared to her high school friend Michelle—*I never want to get married but I want lots of lovers!*—toss myself into a flurry of planning our February wedding. My parents' enthusiasm for my engagement and wedding surprises me until I realize marriage absolves them of responsibility for me. They don't know I never want to return to the Cold War tension of their home.

Paul has to work on Boxing Day, so I drive home alone, certain I can stand a few days with them. On Christmas morning, Mom says, "I guess you finally got yourself pregnant."

I'm speechless, remembering her scornful threat when I was thirteen, her refusal to help me if I got pregnant before marriage, before I knew anything about sex, before a boy's lips had pressed on mine.

She points to my stomach. "You're not showing."

I sip my eggnog. "I'm not pregnant."

She says, "At least *he's* from a wealthy, respectable family."

On February 1, 1975, all four parents, three siblings, and many friends attend our traditional church wedding. After we sign the register, he cradles my waist and guides me through wooden portico doors into our new life.

The impromptu honor guard of ski instructors standing face-to-face along the edges of the walkway astonishes me. Twelve men, including Bill, and women wearing crimson coats and black pants angle their ski poles above our heads. Showered by snowflakes and confetti, we promenade through their archway into a churchyard of towering pine trees. Boughs droop with snow, sun-kissed and sparkling abalone pink, Tuscan blue, and wisteria mauve, a living version of *Snow*, one of my favorite paintings by Group of Seven artist Lawren Harris.

The first few months of marriage are undeniable bliss. Our plans don't extend beyond the next few days, but his parents help decide our future by giving us an acre of land near their family cottage near Huntsville. Their generosity surprises me, but I'm grateful—especially so four months later when Doctor Brown confirms I'm unexpectantly pregnant.

"How can I be *pregnant*?"

He rubs his forehead, just above the bridge of his nose. "Birth control is *almost* 100 percent effective."

My mind swirls. "This isn't what I thought would happen, now, so soon after marriage."

"Will your husband be pleased?"

"Yes, it's just that we're so busy clearing our land for a new house."

I'm excited, and a bit terrified about pregnancy and child-birth, but reassured when Paul hoots with pleasure, then waltzes me around our living room.

With help from his male friends and relatives, Paul channels his spare time to construct our spectacular, custom-built chalet of glass and cedar siding, which we fill with love for each other and for our son, Brandon, who arrives on Boxing Day.

As with most new parents, we're ecstatic, sleep-deprived, and share an intense responsibility for our adorable, blonde baby. I have almost no experience with children, but my skills as a mother seem to flow naturally. However, Paul's attitude toward life has changed. I can't recall when I first notice, but I resent his attempts to control me with suggestions about appropriate behavior and clothing. My job as a bank teller enforces a *dresses-only* dress code for women, and Paul approves of my modest, knee-length work dresses.

But one Saturday, as I prepare to visit the downtown market

in a tube top and shorts, he peers above his newspaper. His voice seethes with disgust. "Why are you dressing like a slut?"

"Since when did tube tops and mid-length shorts become slutty?"

"Since you became the mother of my child. Nobody but me should see your shape."

I gasp. "You don't have the right to tell me what to wear!"

He leaps from the couch and lobs his newspaper toward me so forcefully, the individual sheets separate, flutter into my face, and drift onto the carpet. He stomps around the room, flapping his arms wildly and pummeling the air with rock-hard fists. He darts toward me and reflexively I step backward, but he's too fast. He towers over me, puffs out his chest, and screams into my face, "Are you trying to get another man?"

Tears fill my eyes. "My life revolves around you and Brandon."

He spins away, grabs paperbacks from the coffee table, and tosses them into the air, then struts around the room, moving his head back and forth, squawking like a chicken. I can't help laughing out loud. "You look ridiculous!"

"You're calling *me* ridiculous!"

"You're stomping and flapping like a horny male bird of paradise."

"Don't tell me how to behave!" He rakes my cheek with a backhand.

I cower and turn away, the sting reminding me of Mom's willow whip against my calves.

When he stomps into the kitchen to get a beer instead of apologizing, I tuck Brandon into his stroller for a short escape. My previous experience with aggressive male behavior is limited to television and movies. I need to be away, to examine his anger and my confusion, and to listen to Brandon cooing instead of hearing my husband roar. Though Paul's power-and-control gyrations look absurd, they're frightening. His backhand makes me wonder what else he might do. I decide to talk with him about his aggressive and inappropriate behavior that I've nicknamed the "power pace," but when we return thirty minutes later, he's crying. I've never seen any man other than Grampa cry.

Paul apologizes and I accept.

Instead of dealing with his anger, his alcohol consumption increases from two or three beers each night, to three or four. Mostly, the beer makes him fall asleep, but at other times for no apparent reason, his beer-basted Mr. Hyde persona lashes me with cutting words. I'm scared and frustrated. *Why can't he understand his drinking jeopardizes his health, my love, and our young family?*

Mostly, though, when alcohol hasn't warped his mind, he's a great guy and we enjoy good times. During one of Mom's visits to see her beloved grandson, the ski school hosts Spring Shenanigans to celebrate school break.

On dress-up Saturday, Paul creates a zany outfit: blue thermal leggings; Mom's pink-and-green muumuu purchased in Hawaii after her first plane ride since 1962; and a rainbow-colored Afro wig and red sunglasses with palm trees *à la* Elton John.

His bravery to dress up and look preposterous makes me love him even more. Mom adjusts his wig, then stands back and laughs. With horror, I realize this is the first time I've heard her laugh and begin to wonder what happened to make her so unhappy.

After a few runs on downhill skis, he switches to trick water skis with the fin removed and no poles. When Paul skies past, crouching to hold hands with two junior skiers, spectators behind the barriers along the ski slope hoot with laughter. For his next promenade, he grabs my hand.

"Babe, come with me."

A minute before we hop onto the lift, he says, "Leave your skis and poles here."

I balk and back away, but he grabs my arm and drags me onto the chairlift. "Don't worry, you'll ride down on my skis."

I gasp. "You're crazy."

"You can take the chairlift to the bottom, if you prefer."

I giggle. "What if I fall off your *water* skis?"

He hugs me closer, and our goggles knock together. "Then you *will* have to walk down."

I laugh at my shocked face reflected in his ski goggles.

At the top, he holds my hand and helps me leap from the chairlift. Then, facing him, I place my right foot on his left ski and my left foot on his right ski. We hold hands, and peering over my head, he S-curves down Lazy Lady, an easy green-circle run west of the clubhouse chalet. When he presses my right hand with his left, he's about to turn left. Somehow, we stay together, with me laughing between terrified screams. As the terrain flattens and we slow near the chalet, I start to relax. Celebrities for the moment, we face the cheering crowds and wave.

When we join Mom and Brandon on the chalet veranda, she's bouncing Brandon on her knee but can't stop laughing at Paul. She looks so pretty. I hug her, to hide the happiness welling in my eyes. "I've never seen you so happy!"

She says, "He reminds me of someone I used to know in the war."

"The man you dream about when you read Nevil Shute?"

She says, "I was a different person then."

I focus on the positives of my life and try to ignore the problems Paul's drinking creates—until one blizzardy night when popcorn-sized snowflakes obscure my sight beyond our front porch. Paul usually arrives home around six, a couple hours after the ski hills close, but tonight, he's late. I hope he's with colleagues and reassure myself with delusions. *He'll be home soon. He stopped for gas. He met some friends.*

Suppertime at seven comes and goes. My delusions slide into despair.

He's drunk. He's had an accident. He's dead.

To keep calm, I pretend everything is normal. I tuck Brandon into bed at seven-thirty and read to him until he falls asleep. I tiptoe from his room, then stoke the fire, hoping Paul will soon be home to cuddle on our love seat. I sit alone on our love seat for a few seconds, then scan our bookshelf for a novel to distract me. My fingers pause at our wedding album, bound in a powder-blue silk brocade similar to my wedding dress. I pull it from the shelf, flip through the photographs, and stop at the photo of us cutting our wedding cake. Tears blur my vision. Before this second, I adored this image. His left hand covers mine as I hold the knife; his reverent gaze and protective posture tells everyone he treasures me. Now I understand he treasures me as a possession, the way I treat my delicate Murano vase, a gift from Mother's recent trip to Italy.

I pace, angry with him, and scared for all of us. Every ten minutes or so, I peer toward our driveway into an eerie, endless void speckled with snowflakes. At eight-thirty, the phone warbles.

"Hey, babe. Harry 'n' I are gonna eat here."

"Where's 'here'?"

"Hotel."

"You're drunk! Please don't drive."

"Lov'ya." Before I can respond, he hangs up and the silence extinguishes any chance of reasoning with him.

The snow intensifies and gale-force winds rattle the windows. I flick through all six TV channels, find *The Mary Tyler Moore Show*, and adjust our rabbit-ear antenna to improve the snowy image. Mary, unmarried, independent, and professional, is an inspiration to women who want more than diapers and dishes.

Instead of heeding the words of wisdom in movies, on television, and in books, I let myself become a classic fool in love and lose sight of my goals. I can still have more than diapers and dishes, but studying will be difficult with a demanding husband and a dependent infant.

After *MTM*, I drift to sleep, convinced Paul is sleeping at Harry's place at the foot of the ski hill. Sometime later, I'm thunder-bolted awake by the loud ringing of our telephone. I dash to the kitchen and pick up the receiver. An empty hollowness whooshes into my ear. I'm furious that a crank caller is playing games in the middle of the night. Just as I'm about to slam the receiver onto the hook, a faint voice, blurred by wind and static, says, "Babe . . . wake you?"

"Where *are* you?"

"Drove truck in the ditch . . ."

A silent scream wiggles in my belly and wriggles upward. Bitter bile lodges in my throat. I struggle to breathe. I curl the three-foot-long black telephone cord between my fingers. "Why aren't you at Harry's?"

Paul gurgles. ". . . using cop phone . . . charged . . . drunk driving."

I want to wrap the cord around his neck. "When will you be home?"

". . . taken my license . . . need . . . tow truck."

"Will the police drive you home?"

Dead space hangs between us until I hear a click followed by a flat-line hum. I listen to the void, unable to accept he could shut me out so easily. I trudge into the bedroom and bury myself under our blue Star of Texas quilt. *I wish the accident had killed him.* I instantly regret this dreadful thought but then wonder if he wants to die. *Maybe he should just do the deed and end his pain.*

Most days, a mere two years after our wedding, Meat Loaf's heartbreaking song about love's elusive grail runs through my mind. Tonight's accident has rammed Paul's problems so far into my face, I can't ignore them. Months ago, I wouldn't have believed my shining knight could be an alcoholic. Alcoholics are homeless boozers wearing grubby rags, engulfed by the pungent aura of unwashed skin. Alcoholics are the men who litter the decaying downtown sidewalks of my hometown, slouched against taverns to prevent toppling onto the pavement. Paul has burst my bubble of delusion, and one of us needs to face the truth. Paul is a respectable man, a homeowner with a family and a job—and an alcoholic.

Two hours later, the front door slams. Paul stumbles into our bedroom, flops onto the bed, and spastically flails his arm across my chest. Vomit cakes his ski clothes. I remind myself alcoholism is an illness but, as much as I try to be sympathetic, I'm angry. "You're always reminding *me* about *my* responsibilities. Now you've stuck a repair bill and a big fine into our budget."

He tries to stick his tongue in my mouth. I shove him away, then tiptoe into Brandon's room. He's sleeping peacefully. I try to lull myself asleep in the rocking chair beside his crib, but I can't stop thinking about why my husband drinks. Soon after our marriage, but not soon enough for me to understand Paul might resemble his father more than I could imagine, he told me, "Dad used to get drunk and abuse Mom and me."

"Di-di-did he hit you guys?"

"Once or twice, but mostly just yelled and threatened to hurt us."

"I know how *that* feels."

Lost inside himself, he glosses over my remark. "As a kid, I was terrified, but as a teen, I tried to protect Mom and my little brothers."

"He seems so normal."

"He is normal—to everybody but us. Nobody would guess he hides booze in his basement workshops at home and at the cottage."

When I asked what was bothering his father, he grimaced. "Saw his father dangling from a noose in the barn."

"That would freak anybody out."

Long before we met, Paul began muffling these ghosts of his childhood with alcohol. I thought I could help but now realize love and understanding won't be enough to kill the malignant seeds sown by his father. If Paul continues to drink and refuses counseling, my support and understanding will only enable him to drink and to deny his role in the continuation of his family's delusion.

My help will be effective only if he acknowledges he's an alcoholic and addresses the psychological triggers that lead him to booze.

6

UNTIL DEATH

My son pretending to drive a tractor.

Fourteen days after Paul's crash, we're cocooning on another frosty winter's eve, wrapped around each other on our love seat, a cheap imitation of a Hallmark Christmas card. Almost every minute of these past fourteen days and many restless nights, I've stifled my anger and forced myself to focus on the positive aspects of our life. Though the accident strained our cash flow, we have good jobs, a wonderful son, and a lovely home.

Flames snap in the hearth; sparks spiral into oblivion. He strokes my hair and croons his everlasting love for me, in a pathetic but charming imitation of his idol, Jim Morrison.

I have to laugh. "You sound more like Leonard Cohen."

He finishes his second beer of the evening, and fighting to keep my tone casual, I suggest, "I'm worried about your drinking."

He taps the beer bottle with a fingernail. "All guys have a few beers every night."

"Maybe *your* friends and *your* relatives do, but *mine* don't." I bring my knees to my chest, wrap my arms around my legs, and sigh in exasperation. "When you're drunk, I don't respect you."

In a puzzled voice, he says, "I was drunk, but I didn't hit you."

I chew my cuticles. "Bruises disappear. Words only fade."

His rough fingertips trace lacy patterns on my forearm. "I love you."

"How can you be nasty, then say you love me?"

He lights a third Rothmans.

Why did I settle for someone with the same disgusting habit as my mother? I ask, "What happened to the happy guy who threw a mattress and some blankets in the back of our VW van and said, 'Babe, let's spend a few weeks bumming around America!'"

He grumbles, "That was a long time ago."

"Two years is not a long time!" Yet, as I speak, I realize those two years seem much longer to me, too.

He tucks my long hair behind my ear. "You're beautiful."

Tears dribble down my cheeks.

He takes a long drag, then exhales. "I don't mean to hurt you."

I burrow my face between my knees. "Your apologies remind me of confession. Drink, abuse, confess, repeat."

He coughs. "Let's just enjoy being together."

"Sometimes I think you're trying to kill yourself."

He shoves me aside, jumps to his feet, and says, "You're never happy," shifting my psyche to my little-girl self with an unhappy mother berating me. He stomps into the kitchen and slams the fridge door.

For the next few minutes, I wait in the silence of our house and shift uncomfortably on the love seat.

He returns with another beer, sits beside me, and puts his arm around my shoulders.

I look into his bloodshot eyes. "You need to join AA."

He recoils like an angry cobra, then spits words that feel like venom. "I don't have a problem with alcohol—*you do!*"

"That's twisted but right. I do have a problem with alcohol. When you drink, I'm scared."

"My father is *not* an alcoholic."

"I never mentioned your father but, since you did, nobody in your family wants to accept they have problems with alcohol."

His voice shakes with rage. "Father is not an alcoholic!"

I can't face another fight. "Honey, I just don't want our lives to be like our parents'."

When Paul introduced me to his parents before marriage, I'd seen them as wealthy, well educated, and admired for their service in the community and at their church. I'd been in awe of Paul's father, Dick, a veterinarian by profession and an eccentric by choice, a crusty Hemingway doppelgänger with two passions— horticulture and aviation.

But now, I know more about them and myself.

During one of our infrequent visits, Dick recruits Paul and Brandon to work at his maple sugar shack, while I peel potatoes and chop carrots as Eleanor makes buttermilk scones and York- shire pudding and prepares the roast. An hour later, we sit down for a few minutes of relaxation in their farmhouse dining room. Just as I break apart one of Eleanor's scones, so hot the steam scalds my fingertips, Dick barges through the back door into the summer kitchen. Clumps of mud plop from his rubber boots onto the worn linoleum and mark his trail, a ten-foot distance between the entrance and the utility sink.

He turns on the taps, sticks his head under the water, and bellows, "Ellie, where's the shampoo? Get me a towel!"

She leaps to her feet and scuttles to his aid. I can't decide which makes me more disgusted: his demands or her subservience.

When she returns, I tip my head toward their stand of pines. "Paul and Brandon were playing tag and hiding behind trees but now they're tussling in the soft snow. Paul's such a great father."

"When our boys were young, Dick was a wonderful father, too."

"He bosses you around like a dictator."

"I believe in God, and the church says a woman's duty is to love, obey, and submit to her husband."

I try to conceal my shock, but I'll never make a good poker player. "I don't question your decision to believe in God, but I do question your willingness to obey and submit. You should not be a servant to your husband!"

She bites into her scone, chewing daintily.

I ask, "Aren't you upset about the muddy floor and the extra work he creates for you?"

She raises her Spode cup and saucer for a delicate sip of tea. Accentuating her upper-crust British inflection, she says, "Let me give you some motherly advice. Marriage is forever."

"*Happy* marriages should be forever."

She narrows her eyes. "You made a commitment and you—"

"Marriage is not a one-way street. With a dead end. If one partner isn't living up to the obligations of marriage and refuses to change, the marriage should end."

She sets her teacup and saucer on the walnut dining table inherited from her parents, places both palms flat on the table, then leans toward me. "You chose my son's bed and now you must lie in it."

"Tell me why any woman should stay with a man who"—I hesitate—"doesn't treat her with respect."

Her eyes narrow. "You must honor your commitments and obey your husband."

"If your employer stopped paying you, would you stay?" She nibbles her scone.

I ask, "Tell me why a woman should stay with a man who treats his wife like the hired help—or a whipping post?"

Her long, bony face droops, reminding me of a sad Virginia Woolf. "What choice do we have?"

I refill our porcelain cups with tea, kept warm in the pot by her knitted tea cozy.

Dick bellows from the kitchen, "When's supper?" then thumps down the hall to his study without waiting for her answer.

I look at her, inquiring with raised eyebrows and wide eyes.

She plucks the lacy edge of her starched linen napkin. "When I graduated high school, in 1944, women didn't have many choices."

"That was thirty-four years ago. This is 1978."

"I worked as a nurse for three years. If I didn't get married soon, I would have been an old maid."

"Times have changed."

She sniffs. "I wanted to be a career girl *and* have children but that—"

Dick pokes his head into the dining room. "I'm hungry," he says, the irritation in his voice almost overpowered by contempt.

I hope her generation will be the last cohort of females brainwashed to believe they must accept a lifetime fate of unquestioning obeisance to men.

The next morning, after a hearty oatmeal breakfast, Eleanor and Dick become enraged when Paul refuses their offer to accompany them to worship at the Gospel Hall.

Paul snaps, "Stop trying to convert me. I hate that church. We're leaving. Now!"

I collect our daypacks, then head toward the door with two-year-old Brandon straddling my hip.

Eleanor clings to my arm and pleads, "Save yourself. Save your child."

Paul restrains her until I escape, then we run to our car. The entire fiasco terrifies me. No one in my family is loud or aggressive, even when they're angry.

I snug Brandon into his car seat, then throw myself into the front passenger seat while Paul brushes slushy snow from the windshield. Before he's done, Eleanor arrives and grabs him. He pushes her away, hops into the driver's seat, and starts to close the door. She sticks her right arm into the car, holds the driver's door open with her left hand, and repeats the refrains she hurled at us during breakfast.

"You'll burn in hell."

Paul puts the car into reverse. "Please, let us go."

She asks, "Do you want your *son* to burn in hell?"

Brandon starts to whimper. I hold out an apple wedge for him, and when his little hand meets mine, he stops crying, then sucks the sweet nectar.

Paul inches the car away from the garage, but Ellie hangs on and sidesteps down the driveway, begging us to attend church.

I grab his arm. "Stop! You'll hurt her."

"Not as much as she and Dad have hurt me."

She lets go and shrinks back from our car, her body visibly withering.

Paul screeches down the driveway, making the tires hurl gravel chunks at Ellie. As he barrels onto the highway through sloppy furrows from the overnight snowfall, a passing vehicle splatters a high rooster tail of gray mush onto our car. The wipers whine and thump. CBC Radio speculates about February's Pacific Western Boeing 737 crash in BC that killed forty-two.

Paul switches stations. Anne Murray sings "You Needed Me." I turn off the radio. A heaviness presses on my chest, squeezing air from my lungs. Silence hums in my ears. I chew my cuticles. "Was your mother ever happy?"

He expels a ripple of stifled frustration through pursed lips. "Maybe. I hope so. But Father insisted she quit nursing when she got pregnant."

"When *she* got pregnant? Wasn't he there, too?"

Paul snorts. "He expected her to stay home and raise us."

"Did she have help? A cleaning lady? A nanny?"

"Father said they couldn't afford those luxuries."

"He buys stuff he wants. A cottage, a hunting cabin on five hundred acres, an airplane, scuba gear—"

"If she complained, he'd yell, 'Which of us brings home the bacon?'"

I massage my forehead, trying to release the imaginary but very real rubber bands tightening around my head.

"Maybe I should have told you that Mom spent time in the psych ward after I was born."

"Until her bizarre behavior this morning, that would've surprised me."

Paul and I had escaped unhappy homes, filled with ignored tension, but at least my home hadn't been controlled by a pugnacious dictator. With sudden clarity, I understand Paul imitates his father's carefully calculated power-and-control tactics. I shudder, realizing he expects me to submit, just as his mother yields to his father. After a few moments, I say, "While you were helping your father in the sugar shack, I had to listen to motherly advice about being a wife."

"She's trying to be a good mother-in-law."

I say, "I got the feeling she resents the opportunities women have today."

He laughs, bitterly. "The Bible says suffering produces endurance, character, and hope."

"I wish I knew your mother before life *with your father* destroyed her character and her hope."

He turns the radio on.

I giggle, trying to make my words light. "Don't even try to destroy me."

"Babe, I love you the way you are."

"Then why do you keep trying to change me?"

A few days later, Paul says, "I have to admit you're right about one thing."

"You're going to join AA?"

He hugs me and laughs. "I'm gonna accept the job with the Feds in Chatham."

"You're making the right decision bu—"

"Our lives will be perfect. I'll have a great salary plus security and a pension."

"Will you join AA?"

"If that makes you happy, why not!"

"You need to join AA for you, not me," but I omit the ultimatum, *If you don't, I'll leave you.* With my next breath, I curse my selfishness. Instead of leaving, I should welcome this as an opportunity. He's agreed to AA, and he'll be away from his ski hill friends and their hangout bar. New friends, a new job, and a new community might help him shed Dr. Jekyll's alter ego.

Maybe, just maybe, we can fix our marriage.

I focus so single-mindedly on this objective, I don't bother to consider how the first few months without any friends or nearby relatives might impact us as a couple—and individually.

Despite my still unvoiced thoughts about ending our marriage, I agree to meet in Chatham for a spring weekend of house hunting and together time in Paul's temporary apartment. On Friday after work, I drop Brandon at his paternal grandparents' home an hour north of Toronto. Eleanor apologized to Paul for her behavior when she called, offering to babysit while we house hunted.

She doesn't acknowledge that unpleasant departure or apologize to me, but says, "We're thrilled Paul will be working for the government, like his father. It's a good move for both of you."

In the car, alone, I enjoy the rare privilege of silence. West of Toronto, fatigue overcomes me. I'd done mother duties before and after a full day at the bank, then plowed through Toronto's rush-hour traffic. I've been on the road for three hours and expect to drive at least two more.

Urged by my demanding stomach, I find a mom-and-pop Italian eatery in Cambridge, near the highway. I don't recall if his car accident marks the instant when I start to compare our marriage to an airplane with both engines running on empty, but I wonder why I'm thinking about buying a new house with him, a man whose kisses have started to chill me to the core. Every twist of tangled spaghetti I wind around my fork reminds me of the convoluted mess I've made of my life.

Shortly after ten, Paul greets me at his apartment door, beer in hand, and grabs me with delight. I kiss him with as much passion as I can fake, then ease from his grip, too tired for anything resembling romance. He sulks on the couch, glued to the television, cradling a beer.

I'm thankful for another night of reprieve from his anger and unwanted intercourse. And grateful for the female doctor willing to prescribe birth control pills. If he enforces his legal right to sex on demand, my chances of conceiving are almost zero. He wants another child, but another child will be a problem—not an answer.

The next day, after an eight-hour whirlwind of whittling through a selection of houses with our real estate agent, we fall into comfortable captain's chairs at the Wheels Inn, a modern hotel and restaurant converted from an automobile manufacturing plant. We discuss our two favorite houses over Caesar salad chased by surf 'n' turf. I lean across the table and squeeze his broad hand. "The brick house on Ebenezer needs work, but it's perfect. We can decorate the way we want."

To my surprise, he says, "I agree. We can turn the fourth bedroom into a bathroom."

He lights a Rothmans, then scoops the last bite of the Black Forest cake we're sharing into his mouth. I remember when he used to scoop the last bite into my mouth. I glance at my watch. "We should go."

He beckons the waitress, but instead of asking for the bill, he orders a fourth beer. I slump against the rounded chairback, cross my arms, and without masking my anger, ask, "Have you changed *our* minds about seeing the movie?"

He laughs and dallies over his beer.

We miss the previews but slip into two back-row seats as the opening credits begin for Michael Crichton's new suspense film, *Coma*. Afterward, as we walk to his car in the gloom of a midnight without stars, I reach to hold his hand, and am surprised when he jerks away. We continue walking side by side, together yet separated by the palpable void inside the serene center of a tornado. As we pass under a harsh cone of light from a streetlamp, I glance at him. Angry furrows line his craggy face. His powder-blue eyes shoot ice-cold darts.

I shiver, wondering why he is so angry, but attempt conversation. "Did you like the movie?"

At his car, he unlocks the driver's door of his Chevy sedan and hops inside. I stand outside, waiting. Finally, he leans across to unlock the passenger door. He clutches the steering wheel but doesn't start the engine. He faces the dashboard, then assaults me with his words. "Why'd'ya make me see that damn movie? Did you forget I work with sick and dying farm animals? Did you forget I look at corpses every day?"

I shift to face him. "We picked this movie together."

His hand darts from the steering wheel and rakes a back-hand against my cheek. I shudder, press my hand to my tingling cheek, and say nothing—nothing about the movie, his anger, or our marriage—a tactic that defuses his anger.

Why do I put up with his behavior? When and why did I stop being determined and confident? This is the second time he's hit me but—it will *be the last.*

During the five months before our house sells, I live for the weekends he stays in Chatham. I'm tired of tiptoeing around a soggy drunk with a temper as explosive as a Cambodian mine-field. Weekends without him provide the freedom of not catering to his demands or preparing each sentence before speaking. I need to discuss separating, but over the telephone seems cowardly and cruel. I promise myself to approach the subject face-to-face, the next time we're together. Yet, when that weekend arrives, he ambushes my intentions with a flicker of his incendiary temper.

How can I express my concerns without hurting him—or making him choose to hurt me, with his tongue or his hand? I'm petrified to stay—and petrified to leave.

I repeat my new mantra—new city, new friends, new lives—and hope his promotion will be the impetus for him to become the man I hope he can be.

After we move into our new home and he continues to drink, I loathe the imposter I see reflected in the mirror, yet I continue to dither. I can't predict when Paul might misinterpret—or *choose* to misinterpret—my words, or when a memory or an incident, past or present, might trigger his anger and prompt him to dance the power pace. He never throws anything breakable and never anything at me, but I fear what *might* happen and mask my fear by becoming a stone-faced spectator. After three or four min-utes of ranting, Paul typically notices his outburst isn't having the desired result. He calms down and apologizes. Stupidly, I accept, still pretending his apology means he'll never do it again.

These occasional tantrums rarely occur with Brandon present, but when he is present, I hold him in my arms or we cuddle on the couch. If Brandon appears after a tantrum begins, Paul stops immediately.

With every display, I lose respect for his inability to accept, identify, and deal with his demons. On days when my loathing overcomes fear, I push his buttons with unkind taunts, to give me a semblance of control, and laugh aloud at his histrionic bird-of-paradise imitation.

He attends a few AA meetings but one morning, over coffee, says, "Meetings aren't helping."

"Give it time."

"We're supposed to talk about our problems at meetings, but I'm afraid."

"You can talk to me."

"I left home at sixteen."

"Sixteen!"

With a timid voice like a frightened child, he asks, "Can I trust you?"

Astonished by both tone and question, I cradle his hands in mine, suddenly aware the one sure thing we share is alienation from the larger world.

He says, "Dad never hit us, but sometimes, he was so angry I thought he wanted to kill Mom or me."

I realize our estrangement not only relates to the relationship with our parents, but somehow, led us to find each other. Two lost kids looking for love. He's kept his soul-shattering emotional cargo and anger a stranger to everyone, including himself, to avoid dealing with his burden. Life must be easier with his monsters submerged.

After just a couple of months, his defiant refusal to accept that alcohol is drowning all three of us forces me to face the reality that I can't salvage our marriage without his help.

I wanted our relocation to solve his substance abuse.

Of course, it does not.

As my love dissolves like limestone in a turbulent stream, I sink into Fleetwood Mac's 1977 album, *Rumours*, a lyrical memoir inspired by the band's marital turmoil. Their songs encourage discovery quests for happiness and urge people to end stifling marriages and dead-end jobs. Knowledge of the unhappy marriages of others doesn't make me happy but does make me feel less alone.

Every day, snippets of singer Stevie Nicks' raspy warnings slip into my consciousness as she warns that the chaos of waning love, infidelity, divorce, and loneliness will litter the path to happiness. Her words bolster my determination to leave Paul and create a happy life for our son and myself. Separation and divorce will be cataclysmic for all of us, but I must accept that Paul's behavior conforms to the characteristic patterns of abusers.

After only four months in our new home, I decide I must leave. If I don't, Paul's threats and temper tantrums will continue, and escalate, in frequency and intensity. Though I'm certain he won't hurt Brandon, our three-year-old is increasingly aware of his environment. So far, he's a happy and well-adjusted child who loves both of us, but exposing him to his father's anger will warp his malleable mind. Boys need a father figure as a role model, but they need a happy father figure, not one dissatisfied with his wife. I must stop the generational cycle of power-and-control manipulation so that Brandon doesn't see and adopt anger as an acceptable solution to problems.

I want Brandon with me, but separation from Brandon will aggravate Paul's deep-seated sense of inadequacy created by his castigating father. Unmerited feelings of incompetence will gnaw at Paul's ego until a frenzied Frankenstein emerges. I doubt he'll kill me, but if that happens, Brandon won't have a mother at all.

I begin planning the best strategy to discuss my decision with Paul but get derailed when I read a pamphlet at our doctor's office stating that domestic violence by men against their partner results in death for 50 percent of women. My stomach roils like the Niagara whirlpool, and I'm even more terrified to discuss divorce. Paul has only hit me twice, and though his threats don't hurt, his promises of physical pain are an effective deterrent. My dilemma reminds me a bit of the new Styron novel, *Sophie's Choice*, where there's no right answer and no good solution.

Most days, it's easier to convince myself I'm more fortunate than others. I'm unhappy but I'm also an attractive twenty-four-year-old who, with her twenty-eight-year-old husband, has a delightful three-year-old, a two-story cream-and-red Victorian home, one rental apartment, and two late-model cars. Because we sold our house for three times the amount we spent building the house ourselves, lack of money is not complicating my problems. We have no mortgage, no debt, and can summer at Paul's family cottage in Muskoka.

Whenever I summon the courage to voice my concerns, I feel my words slip into the wind and extinguish like sparks from a campfire. Instead of an honest discussion about my unhappiness, I bathe Paul in subtle waves of sadness. I mope around the house and hum Gordon Lightfoot's 1970 hit "If You Could Read My Mind" and foolishly hope he'll sense my despair. Maybe if he initiates discussion, he'll feel in control. I take an upholstery class twice a week and meet my girlfriends more often. Just like my father, I leave home after supper and stay out past ten. When I come home, if Paul's watching our bedroom television, I ignore his advances and refuse sex whenever possible, for reasons real or invented.

When friends and family praise with admiration and a dash of envy, I smile the dead smile of a robotic Stepford wife and realize my marriage is the fruit of my parents' marriage. Flawless skin, rotting at the core.

Did they suffer as I suffer, alive but languishing, praying for paradise, praying for divine intervention to save their marriage?

I don't plan to have a fling, but one Friday in September 1978, after the bank closes at four, I join coworkers at Shores Grill. On Fridays, Paul quits work at two then picks up Brandon at daycare, so while they have father-and-son time, I have about an hour before I need to go home and start cooking. Another teller and I slide onto the bench, and Blake, the bank's accountant and the only male in our group, sits beside me. Four other women choose captain's chairs across from us and begin plans for a shopping weekend. Almost immediately, I sense a mutual attraction between Blake and me, perhaps reinforced by our status as newcomers in this clannish community. At first there's nothing definite, just a feeling, but then Blake's thigh grazes mine and a few minutes later, I feel a steady push against my thigh.

I point to his wedding ring.

His cheeks redden but he says, "My wife works late every night."

"And you feel abandoned."

I should finish my first margarita and go home, but I don't. I order a second and consider sleeping with him, each erotic thought making me happier and wetter. We flirt until I swallow the last tart sip of margarita. I remember the pain I felt when Duncan slept with other women so, instead of leading him on, I say to everyone, "This has been a blast. Let's do it again."

The following Friday, we find ourselves alone, at the end of the day, in the bank's front vestibule. Our eyes meet, and I say, "Next week? Thursday?" He smiles. Two weeks later, I skip my Thursday night upholstery class to meet him at a deserted campground. After this, we meet every other Thursday, sometimes for supper, mostly for friendship, always for sex.

One evening, lazing in his arms, he says, "Life with Deb is good, but there's more to life."

"I feel guiltier every time we meet."

"I love Deb, but she doesn't even know I'm not home."

"Paul's at home, but he doesn't seem to notice or care if I'm out."

When Duncan slept with other women, mostly groupies he met on the road, I knew his behavior reflected a desire for approval, but my affair is a desperate plea to make Paul notice my unhappiness. I want him to know I've been unfaithful, to understand he can't trust me with his love. I want him to understand that spending time with him is a prison and he's the warden, always watching, always controlling.

Yet, after seven or eight evenings with Blake, Paul hasn't noticed anything different about my behavior—or at least he hasn't commented—but my self-loathing has increased. If I weren't so frightened of his temper, I would've initiated an open discussion about ending our marriage.

One night, after fabulous sex on the beach, I say, "Blake, we need to talk."

Blake chortles. "There's a standard breakup line if I ever heard one."

We've never been more than friends with benefits, so it's easy to say, "I like being with you, but we're heading in a direction that will only create more problems, not solve the ones we have."

"I've been thinking the same thing."

We end our affair but remain friends.

As women of the seventies gather courage to speak against domestic abuse, newspapers and magazines start publishing stories about women harmed by partners. I read these like an addict, desperate for confirmation I'm not alone, that other women—rich or poor, young or old—endure mental and physical cruelty from men who had pledged to love and cherish, not berate and abuse.

I mention this to my grandmother who says, "My best friend married into a good family only to realize after her first child, her husband was an alcoholic. Five children and a few beatings later, with the emotional and financial support of her in-laws, she left."

I'm astonished that, regardless of skin color, religion, ethnicity, or country of origin or residence, many husbands control their wives with violence, implied or actual. Despite this, I'm certain I don't know any abused women.

Until I reconnect with Michelle, a close friend during my teen years. After high school graduation, our paths diverged for four years until Christmas 1977. Since then, we exchange letters, occasionally telephone each other, and meet whenever we're both at home visiting our parents. Today, we sip tea at the hole-in-the-wall Sweet Basil Café and slide into comfortable conversation, condense our time apart, and giggle at our shared choice of Denby Castile dinnerware for everyday dining.

After the other patrons leave the six-table café, our gaiety dies when she says, "Joe and I've had some nasty arguments the past couple weeks."

I spread hummus on my flatbread. "My bet's on you."

She laughs. "He wants to get a loan using my family's good name at our bank."

I shrug. "So what?"

"His plan is quasi-legal and will embarrass my parents and me."

"Just say no. Let him get his own loan."

Snow pellets ping against the window.

She says, "As long as I let him make the important decisions, we get along."

"Surprise, surprise, a guy who wants power and control."

She sucks her lower lip. "I want to leave, but I'm scared. After we moved in together, a friend told me he'd assaulted his wife, and later a girlfriend, when they broke up with him."

My tea swallows like a hard biscuit, but I choke out the question. "Has Joe hit you?"

"He's swatted me a couple times."

I shiver. "Paul and I are having problems, too."

"Has he hit *you*?"

I can trust her to keep my secret. "Twice. I'm scared to stay and scared to go. Separation will affect Brandon, but I don't want him growing up with violence. And I'm embarrassed to tell the world I've made a mistake."

Michelle asks, "How is it possible that we've both encountered angry men?"

I say, "Maybe more of our friends are dealing with angry men than we realize?"

She stirs milk into her tea. "Domestic violence is under-reported. It's easier to convince yourself your partner will never hit you again than to speak out or report him and risk being blamed for his anger."

I say, "Pathetic, but true." I sigh deeply. "I envy the relationship you have with your parents. I'm sure they'll help you if you leave, but I doubt mine would." I can't quite mask the sadness of my voice.

She says, "We're in this together. You can always call me."

My relationship with my parents had never been great, and soon after I sprouted breasts at twelve, our shaky relationship disintegrated. I became lonely and, desperate for love and acceptance, charged into a relationship with a man I loved—wanted to love—but didn't know well. I remember my comment to my maid of honor, a few days before my marriage. *If it doesn't work out, I can always leave.* The collapse of my parents' marriage had taught me that nothing lasts forever, but now I knew leaving wasn't as simple as my foolish comment.

7

SOARING

Mired in the tedium of daily life spiced with Paul's rages, my fear of the unknown blocks the exit door. I muddle along, until Friday, March 16, 1979, when Paul explodes through the double doors of our home and finds me simmering chicken breasts in my grandmother's cast iron pot.

He twirls me around and shouts, "Let's learn to fly!"

I laugh. "And after that, we'll become astronauts and fly to Mars."

"Flying is something we can learn together."

"Why the sudden interest in flying?" I wonder if we ever had any common interests.

"I was inspecting cattle at a farm when a single-engine plane like Dad's buzzed a couple hundred feet above us."

"Is that legal?"

"We can start this weekend—"

"This weekend! Where?"

"There's a flight school at a small airport twenty miles west of here."

I flip the chicken. "You've flown with your father, but flying will be too difficult for me."

He takes me by the shoulders and looks into my eyes. "You've always wanted to fly!"

"A long time ago. When I was younger."

"Dad started flying at fifty."

I study my husband's eager face, someone I used to love passionately, now encouraging me to follow my dreams. Despite his surprising support, something holds me back. "What if something goes wrong when I'm flying alone?"

"I booked intro flights for us tomorrow." He waltzes me around the room. "We'll drive to the airport together but take turns with the instructor. You'll only be in the air twenty minutes. If you don't like it, you don't have to fly again."

"Your father might finally be proud of you if you get a pilot license."

Paul grins. "Maybe he'll take me with him to his hunt camp in Temagami!"

"As a pilot, he's an inspiration. As a father, he could've been a better role model."

Flight lessons might narrow the chasm between us and bring us closer to the happy couple we once were—but I doubt it.

However, today is the anniversary of my spunky great-grandmother's birth and the coincidence is auspicious. Widowed in her sixties a decade before my birth, my mother's paternal grandmother was a single woman who maintained her waterfront home three lots west of her son, my grandfather. Lean and wiry, with waist-length waves of silver hair, she refused to follow the crowd. She'd sneak into her bathroom for a quick puff of a roll-your-own and warn, "Don't tell anyone, especially your Grampa."

As Paul drives to the airport, I'm too jittery to talk. After my first flight as a passenger across Canada at age seven, I spent hours daydreaming about my exciting future life as a pilot, even though everyone I knew insisted that flying was an unrealistic ambition, especially for a female. While my friends enjoyed silly musicals or read Harlequin romances, I escaped into books about adventurers who tackled the unknown. Aviation and famous aviators especially intrigued me, and I inserted myself into their stories, envisioning myself as the enigmatic Amelia Earhart, who flew for the fun of it and had a supportive husband who didn't restrain her with a choke hold. Other times, I sat beside trailblazer Beryl Markham in *The Messenger*, as she flew across the Atlantic and into history with her chutzpah and her book, *West with the Night*. Raised by her indulgent, divorced father in Kenya, she roamed with Maasai boys and conquered her fears and became the first female to fly solo across the Atlantic.

I wanted to be like them, a girl who soared above the crowds, a girl who accomplished something worthwhile and memorable. I hadn't expected to have enough money to become a pilot, not after marriage, not at age twenty-four, the same age as Amelia Earhart when she began flying.

Gloria Gaynor belts "I Will Survive" on our car radio as the wheels of our AMC Pacer crunch across the airport's gravel parking lot. *Could I survive without a partner at my side? And what would life be without a man?* After I dumped Duncan when I realized he thought fidelity didn't apply to men, I married Paul one year later, three weeks after my twentieth birthday. I hadn't heard the four seasons rule about getting to know someone.

I turn to smile at Brandon, our three-year-old, nested in the back seat with stuffed animals and Tonka trucks. *How will his life change if I leave?*

Paul saunters toward the cottage-style terminal, which houses the flight school, and throws open the door. I follow, carrying Brandon on my hip. A solitary man with unruly copper hair is the sole occupant of the twenty-by-twenty-five-foot room. He stands behind a wooden counter, engaged in unintelligible pilot jargon on a two-way radio, and acknowledges our arrival with a gesture to sit in the waiting room, an L-shaped arrangement of two ranch-style couches. I hold Brandon on my lap so our busy toddler can't topple the rickety coffee table covered with slithering mounds of magazines, Styrofoam cups of abandoned coffee, and butt-filled ashtrays.

On the wall behind the counter, magnetic letters on a bulletin board advertise One-Hour Cessna-150 Rental $34, One Hour Lesson $47, and the hook, a loss leader to lure prospective students, 20-Minute Introductory Flight Only $10.

Airwaves conversation complete, the man beckons us with a casual flutter of his hand. "Hello, folks, I'm Murray, the chief instructor." We approach and he smiles bashfully, revealing a disarrayed pack of stained teeth. "Our other instructor, Dan, will take you on your flights. He's a graduate of Seneca College's aviation program and won't be here long. He's waiting for his final interview with Air Canada."

Doe-eyed, freckled, and faintly wrinkled, Murray doesn't convey any of the arrogance I associate with pilots. As the only woman at this small airport, I feel highly visible, but his casual friendliness makes me slightly less uncomfortable.

When Dan arrives, Paul asks me, "Can I go first?"

I nod, and he scrambles onto the left seat of the two-seater Cessna while Brandon and I stay inside the school. He giggles at the escapades of adorable animals humanized in Richard Scarry's book, *Cars and Trucks and Things That Go*, while I flip through aviation magazines. An ad featuring a slim brunette with a salon-styled bob beside an aircraft makes me pause. The caption, "If I Can Fly, You Can Fly," suggests if women can learn to fly, men will ace the challenge. Dated September 1968, the magazine is eleven years old. How much has this attitude changed in a decade, if at all?

After the short flight, Paul bounds toward us. "Babe, you'll love it!" He scoops Brandon into his arms and flies him through the air above his head. Brandon screams with delight.

Nervous energy spikes through my body. Driving an automobile represents the extent of my experience with mechanized equipment.

I obtained my driver's license five months following my sixteenth birthday. My first exhilarating experiences controlling a vehicle occurred that same summer when my parents allowed me to be the principal driver for our vacation. In the intervening eight years, I owned standard and automatic vehicles but never drove a boat or snowmobile.

My knowledge about engines and airplanes is a blank slate, a *tabula rasa*. Shop class would have been helpful.

Dan stands beside the aircraft, waving at me. My knees quiver. I'm one footstep away from beginning my lifelong dream to be a pilot, but I hesitate. I'm afraid of embarrassing myself. Afraid to try. Afraid to fail. But I have a choice. I can choose to cancel the lesson and forfeit ten dollars—or walk my gangplank into uncharted territory into the future.

I inhale through my nose, will my right foot to move, and walk across the ramp.

Two years of college have molded Dan into perfect pilot shape, an unblemished lord of the skies attired in a crisp white shirt, a tie cinched to choke, navy trousers with a razor-edge crease, and shoes black as licorice. I shake his proffered hand and nod hello, my throat as dry as my dying houseplants. Somber and focused, he checks the aircraft in preparation for our flight. I imagine he paints Paul a probable flight-training student but wager he sees me as "the wife" trailing along for the ride, wasting his time.

He motions with his arm. "Plane's ready; let's go."

Austere but courteous, Dan demonstrates how to enter the plane. He points to a metal bar running from the aircraft to the tire. "Place your left foot on the metal rectangle on this strut, grab the doorframe with your right hand, and swing inside."

He makes hurtling from ground to strut to cabin look easy. He offers his hand, but I shake my head, clamber inside awkwardly, and half-fall into the bucket seat. Though we're average-size individuals, the confined cabin forces us to invade each other's space. To shut my door, I must lean against Dan. With the door closed, my left shoulder rubs the doorframe and my right shoulder touches Dan's left. No room for stale sweat, halitosis, or animosity. *How do two men cope canned inside this tin cylinder?*

He demonstrates how to move the seat forward toward the dashboard (aka instrument panel), then points to two identical pedals on the floor, similar to a car accelerator pedal. He says, "These are rudders. Your side has identical pedals."

Then he puts his hands on a U-shaped steering wheel, and as he turns it right then left, says, "This is a control column similar to a car's steering wheel." He starts the engine, taxis to the runway, and says, "Watch closely. When I move my control column or step on my rudder pedals, yours move, too."

The voice of fear natters in my head and suffocates Dan's words. I squeeze the voice out of my head and force myself to listen, hoping I haven't missed much. As he turns onto the runway I hear, "—takeoff, keep your feet on the rudder pedals." *Has he suggested I should do the takeoff?* Dread pumps through my body. *Maybe he's taking me too seriously.*

The engine noise masks my heaving sigh of relief when he says, "Ready for takeoff," and the Cessna 150 sprints down the runway like a desperate gazelle pursued by a ravenous cheetah. One minute, we're on the ground, the next, airborne. Dan's takeoff is so smooth, I don't sense the moment of transition from earth to air. In spite of my tenderfoot status, I recognize a textbook perfect takeoff.

Instruction begins seconds later. Enunciating each syllable like a foreign language teacher, he shouts louder than the revved-up engine. He whips through his explanation of climbs and turns. Our tiny plane races higher, away from the telescoping earth toward an infinite cornflower-blue sky, speckled with cotton ball clouds. A warm spring sun filters through the windscreen and a slight odor of gasoline tickles my nostrils. Wind whistles through the fresh-air vents and pierces my ears but cools my face, flushed with excitement.

Dan summits the three-wheeled bantam at three thousand feet, then reduces power from the takeoff power setting of 2,500 rpm to twenty-two. He points to instruments on the dashboard, first the altimeter—"We're level"—then the heading indicator—"We are straight." With the reduced power setting, I hear most of his words. The contrast in volume is akin to sticking my head inside the speaker cone at a rock concert versus standing two hundred feet from the speakers.

He turns the control column to the left. "Now we're rolling into a left-banked attitude." As the aircraft rolls past the sun, the spinning propeller sabers the sunlight spearing through the windscreen. He demonstrates a few climbs and descents and turns to me. "Any questions?"

"Seems straightforward." This is a lie. I'm boggled by the dizzying panel of instruments and the new and unusual terms. If flying requires an understanding of these gauges and controls, my assumption that all pilots possess extraordinary intelligence and aptitude must be correct. Attitudes. Movements. Straight-and-level (cruise flight). Straight-but-not-level (climbing or descending). Level-but-not-straight (turning).

I look down at the ancient lakebed filled with crops, exquisite ribbons of emerald and gold, marred by an occasional coffee-brown strip of fallow field.

Dan offers a bombshell. "Why don't you take control and try a few turns."

Is he crazy? I swivel to evaluate him. He reminds me of the larger-than-life Air Force pilots who captured my imagination in childhood. Elegant metaphors for superhuman accomplishment, heroic men who speared magnificent silver bullets into the celestial sphere.

"I don't feel ready."

An almost imperceptible smirk tickles the corner of his tight lips. I've let him down and affirmed his expectations. *Does he interpret my refusal as disinterest? Does he guess I question my ability?* The whoosh of wind through the cracks, the thrumming engine, and pilot chatter on the airwaves mask the awkward silence I've created. I shout, "But I *will* take control after an official lesson lasting more than two minutes."

He nods, stone-faced.

We return to the airport where he bookends the flight with a perfect landing to rival his perfect takeoff. The tires contact the pavement with a barely audible squeak. On the ramp, after the propeller shudders the plane to silence, I say, "Your takeoff was so perfect I didn't realize we'd 'slipped the surly bonds of earth' until I saw the ground falling away."

Dan turns to me with twinkling eyes. "How do you know the pilot's poem, 'High Flight'?"

"My grandfather loved poetry and aviation."

We gather inside the flight school and Murray meekly asks, "Want to sign up for lessons?"

Paul brushes him off with a twenty-dollar bill for today's flights. "We'll call," he says brusquely, then rushes us toward the door. Embarrassed by Paul's behavior, I smile at Murray. "I had a great time!"

At the car, I ask, "Don't you want to go flying again?"

He grins. "Don't be *stupid*! I just didn't want to seem *too* interested."

To avoid a fight, I ignore his insult. "You mean in front of Lindbergh?"

He laughs. "I knew Murray reminded me of someone."

8

FLIGHT TRAINING

One week after our introductory flights, on a sun-soaked Saturday afternoon in March 1979, we return to the flight school with Brandon in tow. We've agreed to alternate our play-time with his. One will fly while the other reads storybooks or excavates earthworks in the sandbox outside the flight school.

CFI Murray presents each of us with a folio filled with training materials.

Paul peeks inside his folio, then tosses it aside. "We can look at this stuff later. Let's go flying," he says while I run my fingertips along the embossed gold letters on the cerulean-blue cloth cover of my *Pilot's Logbook*. Each kit includes the *Flight Training Manual*, a passport-sized pamphlet designed to slip into a man's shirt pocket for reference during flight. I'm shocked that the government has made only two revisions to this minimalist manual since original publication during WWII for the British Commonwealth Air Training Program pilots, whose planes my father serviced. I thumb the scant twenty pages, then deadpan a pilot talking to passengers, "Excuse me while I review Exercise 18, Landing."

Murray chuckles and his shoulders shake dots of dandruff from his rumpled white shirt onto his Baker's chocolate brown pants. "When this booklet was written, pilots received only five or six hours of total flight instruction. A revision is expected next year, but in the meantime, you should buy *From the Ground Up* by Sandy MacDonald, also written in WWII, but updated."

While Paul leads Brandon to the sandbox, Murray and I park ourselves in the reception area because Dan and another student occupy the only private room. Immersed in the bedlam of other students chatting and asking questions of licensed pilots, concentration is difficult.

Murray uses a toy airplane with a twelve-inch wingspan to demonstrate the basic flight movements. "This lesson is fundamental to the success of flight training. There are three simple-but-essential movements: pitch, roll, and yaw."

He holds the plane's wingtips with his fingertips and moves the nose up and down. "What's this movement?"

I refer to the *Flight Training Manual* and say, "Pitch." Ten minutes later, Murray deems my basic grasp of this building-block exercise is sufficient, and despite the session's brevity, his review reinforces Dan's in-flight demonstration of these alien concepts.

We approach our aircraft, identified as GGUT, a unique registration issued by Transport Canada, and Murray says, "The pilot in command is responsible for the safety of each flight." He begins the walk-around, the preflight inspection required before all flights. He crumples his five-foot-ten frame under the right wing and opens his door. I bend my knees, duck under the left wing, and open my door—the pilot-in-command's door—and gaze, dumbfounded, at the complex instrument panel and the chaotic jumble of dials, gauges, and levers.

Murray flips on the electrical switch, and needles on gauges spring to action. He asks, "Is there enough fuel?"

Who knows? But miraculously I locate both fuel gauges, one for a tank in each wing. Feeling slightly less intimidated, I mimic the confident pilots on television. "Sufficient fuel. Check."

He says, "Get the orange rag in the pocket behind your seat and check the oil. Mind you don't hit your head on the wing."

I stick my hand into the pocket then recoil, my fingers covered with greasy globs of oil. I search for another rag, notice Murray's perplexed face, blend the sticky ooze into my hands like moisturizer, and grab the filthy rag. I back away from the cockpit and bang my head on the wing.

Murray shows me how to open the engine cover, named the nacelle, and check the oil. The oil cap and dipstick resemble those in cars. Finally, something familiar in this foreign land.

I ask, "Nacelle is French, but what does it mean?"

Murray shrugs. "Beats me. Watch me do the walk-around as I check the body for loose rivets, scrapes, or dents."

Of course, the body isn't named the body but *le fuselage*, another French word, reminding me of comedian Steve Martin's quip, "Boy, those French! They have a different word for everything."

At the propeller, he grasps each blade with his hands, does deep knee bends to jostle the nose up and down, and explains, "I'm checking the nosewheel's hydraulic pressure."

I gasp. "What if the engine starts?"

He seems unconcerned with faulty wiring, an unexpected ignition of the engine, or a whirling propeller, but my overactive imagination creates *My Own Private Horror Movie* starring Murray, who darts around the ramp, streams of blood spurting from his wrists where his hands had been.

Murray says, "Now, check your side of the aircraft," and watches me closely as I check movable flight surfaces, tires, and the fuel for contamination of water or sediment. My visual check of the tubular, cold metal body that tapers toward a knife-edged tail fin jutting toward the sky reminds me of "The Shark," E. J. Pratt's epic poem. A shudder of danger vibrates through me.

My walk-around is hesitant and bumbling, but Murray reassures me. "Not bad. Let's go!"

After his perfect takeoff, he climbs to three thousand feet, then levels off and demonstrates a turn. He talks me through the procedure of checking for traffic, then gives me control. With his encouragement, I tentatively put my hands on the control column and start turning—left, then right, then left. There's a lot to remember but, so far—flying is easy!

After a few turns, he resumes control, demonstrates climbs and descents, then says, "Let's see you combine these moves, starting with a climbing turn."

His confidence in my ability encourages me. After thirty minutes, he resumes control and returns us to the school. As he taxis to the parking ramp, I realize my first official flight lesson was fun and much easier than expected.

Inside the school, I open my new logbook. The stiff cover crackles. I write my name and address, then Murray insists I record last Saturday's twenty-minute intro flight before today's lesson. I exclaim, "I can't believe I have one hour and twenty minutes of flight time."

He says, "Most pilots need at least forty-five flight hours before becoming a licensed private pilot, but you're on your way!"

Though my adult hands had cradled the aircraft control column, in my heart I'm the same little girl who glided on widespread arms through autumn leaves in her parents' backyard, pretending to be a Golden Hawk Sabre jet. Like a bolt of lightning, I know the time has come to reclaim my youthful confidence and soar through the air on metal wings.

Flight training wasn't my idea, but neither Paul nor my instructors forced me into the airplane. I made the decision to enter the airplane and begin my journey—and no one is going to stop me.

9

THE TAXI

For my fourth flight lesson, Murray keeps me inside the flight school for what feels like hours, droning on and on about taxiing and the control of an aircraft on the ground. When I sit next to Murray or Dan as they taxi, the tiny two-seater aircraft trots obediently, turns on command, and halts exactly where the instructor desires. Most of the time, they don't seem to be looking at any of the instruments.

How hard can it be?

Finally, Murray says, "Let's go!"

Outside, I pause briefly to kneel in the sandbox beside Brandon and Paul constructing a casbah of ramps, walls, and sand pillars. Paul mixes a pail of sand and water to create another pillar, while Brandon playfully drives one of his toy trucks across my thigh.

He says, "Mommy, that's a big hill."

Murray chortles. "So glad we built this sandbox!"

I tousle Brandon's shoulder-length blond curls, then walk to the airplane. Last week, I did the preflight—but that was a week ago—and there's a lot to remember, and I seem to have forgotten what little I've learned. Murray watches me to ensure I don't miss anything; he smiles and nods as I check the movement of the flight controls, tires, and fuel and oil levels. Normally, I'm uncomfortable when people hover over my shoulder, but I'm relieved Murray watches me like a mother cat nurturing her month-old kittens.

I finish checking the exterior of the plane and say, "We're ready," but he says, "Not quite. Drain a half-ounce of fuel from each wing tank to check for foreign particulate."

I hold the clear plastic vial of pretty, pink fuel between my eyes and the sky to confirm it doesn't contain sediment or water.

He says, "Toss the fuel onto the grass and don't forget to look inside the engine cowling."

I grimace, upset with myself for forgetting so many important things.

He smiles, benevolently. "There's a lot to remember. The cowling provides shelter and safety, a perfect nursery for baby birds."

"You *did* mention that last week but I—um—thought you were joking."

He laughs, but not at me. "Actually, I've never found a nest. Let's check together."

No birds. No nest material. No wonder students rave about him.

Finally, he says, "Let's go!" I scramble into the left seat, my heart thumping with excitement.

Inside the aircraft, Murray gives more advice. "Before starting the engine, before taxiing, check for conflicting aircraft. Look for pilots and passengers walking near the planes. Listen to the radio. Then, start the aircraft, look outside again, ease forward slowly, and taxi to the run-up area."

I've committed taxiing to memory. I'm confident. I can do this.

I scan the ramp for moving aircraft and pedestrian pilots, then start the engine, setting the tachometer at 1,000 rpm, a soothing purr that hums in my ears. I confirm all instruments are operating correctly, all gauges are "in the green," then with my right foot, I push against the right rudder pedal.

Nothing happens.

My foot has intuitively mimicked the motion I use to drive a car.

Murray says, "Feet control steering, toes control braking, throttle controls power." He points to the tachometer. "Increase power to fifteen hundred rpm."

He places his left hand on top of my right hand to help me guide the throttle plunger to the desired power setting. Despite his assistance, I'm heavy-handed and the tach zooms past 1,500 to 2,000 rpm. The engine thunders and the aircraft surges toward three airplanes, parked only twenty feet away.

The image of twisted propellers and crumpled airplanes jumbles the signals from my terrified brain and I'm unable to move my hands and feet. I can't reduce power, brake, concentrate, *and* breathe simultaneously, but I must do *something*, so I reduce power, then stomp on the brakes. Miraculously, this stops the unrestrained bolt across the ramp.

Taxiing is more complicated than the text suggested and requires much coordination.

He says, "After a few times, you'll be able to brake and adjust power together."

From the corner of my eye, I peek at him, expecting a scowl. Instead, he's slouching in his seat, not even watching me. *How can he be so calm while teaching an incompetent novice to operate a fifty-thousand-dollar aircraft?*

I tentatively nudge the throttle and the aircraft shifts forward, slower than a slug. At this pace, I'll spend most of my one-hour lesson on the ground, not in the air. I tease the power setting to 1,500 rpm, and feeling the plane submit to my command, I begin to relax . . . until my uneven foot pressure on the rudders causes the plane to slither like a sidewinder across the Mojave Desert.

I reduce rpm to one thousand, a setting that slows the aircraft. Every movement is important and requires immediate *and simultaneous* attention. But when I tell my hands what to do, I forget to tell my feet what to do. Or maybe I'm telling them, but they're not listening.

Into the lesson by two minutes, we're only a few feet from where we started. I feel like a gangly puppy running downhill, tripping over feet too large for her body. I'm inexperienced, unable to anticipate possible consequences. Stimuli, not anticipation, drive my actions. *How can anyone master taxiing, the simultaneous movement of hands and feet in different directions on different control surfaces?*

I've heard pilots brag, "Good pilots can do ten things at once." Obviously, I'm not a good pilot.

Then I remember my clumsy teenage attempts to master the standard transmission of our VW camper. First gear and too much gas made the car shoot forward but, if I stopped accelerating or slipped the clutch, the VW stopped as if slammed into the Berlin Wall. Yet, driving a stick shift soon became second nature, performed without thinking about my actions.

Driving a standard transmission requires both feet, one for the clutch and one for the accelerator; driving an airplane requires both feet for steering and braking. Driving with a stick shift requires both hands, one for the wheel and one for the stick; flying requires one hand on the steering control and one on the throttle. I'm certain flying is harder than driving a car, but the similarities encourage me. I will become a good pilot just as I became a good driver.

I persevere and wrangle to find the correct foot pressure on the rudders, while silently chanting my new mantra, *Rudders to turn, toes to brake.* I pull the throttle to set the tach at thirteen hundred, a setting that keeps the plane moving, albeit slowly. The plane saunters toward the taxiway, and suddenly, a feeling of control sweeps through my body.

Murray says, "Well done."

I smirk with pride. I'm on my way, about to nail this, just as I nailed driving a standard. I shift in my seat. It's a small change in position, but in order to shift, I press my toes on the rudders. The tires squeal as the aircraft clunks to a dead stop. The aircraft nose dips downward on the fragile front tire suspension, my head jerks forward, and my chest strains against the shoulder belt.

How far will the nose dip? But before I can complete the next thought—*Will the spinning propeller chew into the pavement?*—the nose pops up to level.

I draw deep yoga relaxation breaths, then visualize my exit from the parking ramp followed by a left turn onto the taxiway. I search for a power setting to move the aircraft forward at the crawl speed of a seven-month-old baby—not a rocket-propelled grenade. Fourteen-hundred rpm seems to work. My confidence builds until I realize I need to turn onto the taxiway, an action that will destroy the equilibrium I've achieved. Instinctively, as if turning left in a car, I turn the control column to the left. Nothing happens. *Aaarrrghhhh!*

The plane charges toward the grass field sodden with spring rains. *Will the wheels dig into the soft grass? Will it flip over?*

I flash back to *The Car*, one of my favorite cult horror movies, realizing an out-of-control plane on the ground might be as murderous as that possessed old Lincoln. I can't believe driving a plane would be so damned difficult.

Ground operations looked so easy.

Do flight schools fire students?

I pinch the bridge of my nose, then attack the problem of taxiing. I tap the bottom of the left pedal, and to my astonishment, the plane turns left and glides onto the taxiway, as if I actually know what I'm doing. I clap my hands with delight.

Murray laughs. "For your first time taxiing, you did well. Not only did you do well, you didn't panic. In fact, you didn't even get flustered."

My performance isn't polished, but I appreciate his compliment, mentally noting the irony—*Paul's temper tantrums taught me to remain calm when confronted with adversity and challenges.*

Murray's voice returns me to the moment. "Let's see you do the pre-takeoff check. Point to each item and say it aloud so you don't forget anything."

I remove the folder wedged between our seats and flip to the pre-takeoff checklist. When I finish, I feel like a real pilot and ask, "Ready for takeoff?" but he pricks my confidence with, "I have control."

I flop back against the seat and let my arms drop limply into my lap.

He looks into my eyes. "Don't be discouraged. There's a lot to remember," he says, then taxis onto the numbers 2 and 3 painted on the runway. "Always position the aircraft on the centerline on the numbers. This is Runway 23, a southwesterly direction."

He talks through his takeoff, identifying each of his movements as he does them. "As we climb, I'll demonstrate a climbing right turn and then a climbing left. This has two purposes. We'll see traffic that might be hidden by the aircraft's nose-up attitude, and you'll see how these movements relate to takeoff and landing."

As he performs these maneuvers, he points to the instruments. "Notice the miniature airplane on the instruments mimics the position of the aircraft."

I say, "Cool. When the plane turns left, the little airplane inside the instrument turns left."

Murray says, "Early airplanes didn't have instruments. The pilots just looked outside, but"—he hesitates for emphasis—"instruments help pilots fly at night or in cloud. Let's see you try some climbs, descents, and turns."

Because aircraft are designed to fly, not drive on the tarmac, flying is easy compared to taxiing. I have a great time, and my successful performance of climbs, descents, and turns bolsters my confidence. When Murray says, "You fly back to the airport," I keep my cool, though my insides leap with delight. This is the first time he's letting me fly home.

Murray points to the heading indicator. "Turn east, to zero nine zero. Keep checking for planes."

On the map, he shows me our present position relative to the airport, approximately fifteen miles east. As I fly, I compare ground features to symbols on the map, a surprisingly easy task. Suddenly, I realize I'm multitasking—checking for other airplanes, monitoring the instruments, map reading, and flying. And breathing.

Following his directions, I enter the circuit, an area surrounding an airport where planes take off and land. A few hundred feet before touchdown, Murray resumes control. I'm disappointed but maybe he'll let me taxi from the runway to the ramp.

"You'll get plenty of opportunity to taxi," he says, pointing to the airplanes parked on the ramp. "Better to practice without metal in the way—or drive into the sandbox and kill your family."

I stifle the urge to say, *I don't want Paul dead, just out of my life.*

Embarrassed by my earlier impatience, I realize Murray is the rarest of humans, a person who loves his job and loves sharing his knowledge. He's a quirky bachelor, and I can't count the ways we're different, but I'm beginning to realize that such differences are life's most precious gems. I have a lot to learn—about airplanes, and people, including myself.

10

STALLED

When Paul suggested we learn to fly, I thought his idea as radical as if he'd said, "Let's hike across Baffin Island next year." Contrary to my initial doubts, seven weeks and six lessons after our introductory flights on St. Patrick's Day 1979, we both have five hours of flight time.

Paul says, "Can you believe we can actually make the aircraft climb, descend, and turn?"

I open my eyes wide. "No! But thanks for suggesting we take lessons. I'm starting to think my childhood dream of flying is possible."

I don't mention I get through each tedious day at the bank inspired by the thought, *I'm one day closer to the weekend—and my next flight lesson.* I can't imagine how flying will fit into my future or influence me, but now that Paul and I study together each night after Brandon goes to bed, Paul can't concentrate if he has more than one beer. If nothing else, his decision to drink less makes flying lessons worth the time and money.

Despite our progress, before any instructor will allow us to fly solo, we must perform stalls and spins, both classified as aerobatic maneuvers. Both must be done in the practice area, far from the airport and cities, and both are life threatening. Chatter between other students in the flight school suggests that stalls and spins function as an elimination squad, the storm troopers of aviation.

Evan, the teenage pilot who cleans and gasses planes in exchange for flight lessons, admits, after ensuring he won't be overheard, "Spins are super scary."

When I ask Murray, he says, "Some students quit after the stall-spin lessons, but once you're licensed, you never need to do spins or stalls again."

One Saturday afternoon, my father-in-law, Dick, flies to the airport where we're training. After securing his Citabria, he lumbers over to the sandbox where Paul and I are playing with Brandon.

Dick says, "Hello, Son, thought I'd fly down to see how you're doing," but ignores Brandon and me.

I'm used to his rude behavior but say, "You might say hello to your grandson."

He says, "After you've finished your lessons, I'll take you all for hundred-dollar hamburgers."

What does that mean? I'm glad to see Paul's puzzled frown.

Dick explains, "It's a pilot thing. I could drive to a local burger joint for a two-dollar burger. Instead, I spend lots of money on fuel to fly somewhere else to buy a burger." Then, he asks Paul, "Have you done spins yet?"

We shake our heads.

Dick sticks out his barrel chest, hooks his thumbs into his suspenders, throws his head back, and laughs with the bravado of a big game hunter. "Well, Son, you might get the damn pants scared off you. Spins root out the wussies."

I understand why he's more interested in his son, but he could acknowledge his grandson and me. He's treating me like the invisible woman he wants me to be.

MacDonald's *From the Ground Up* is a constant companion. Seneca's dictum, "Ignorance is the cause of fear," inspires me to study whenever possible—at work, throughout lunch, and breaks.

In bed, I read beyond when I can't absorb any more information and surrender only when my wilting eyelids blur the page.

Some things I learn seem common knowledge for the male students, learned not from previous aviation experience but from dabbling with auto repair with male friends or relatives—and from high school auto mechanics courses, the courses denied me.

Mom is right. Men do make the rules to benefit themselves.

I'm astonished to learn that the single-engine Cessna has the same engine as the VW Bug: an air-cooled, gasoline-powered engine with four horizontally opposed cylinders. I'm also astonished that a stall in an aircraft has nothing to do with fuel or the engine. When a car stalls, the problem relates to fuel, and the driver resolves this annoying and unanticipated delay with patience, a taxi, or AAA.

However, an airplane will stall *only* when the air flowing past the wings doesn't provide enough lift. Though the engine continues to operate normally, the plane falls from the sky. Or so I believe until *From the Ground Up* informs me that pilots learn and practice stalls and spins several thousand feet above ground to avoid unintentional stalls at low altitudes where insufficient time and altitude prevent recovery before crashing.

If I can defeat my fears and conquer the stall-spin storm troopers, I also must master spiral dives before my flight test. This unholy trinity of shock-and-awe aerobatic obstacles stirs my fear of failure, a fear almost as great as my fear of Paul's threats to hit me when I don't do what he wants. To my great happiness, since Paul reduced his daily beer intake to one, he's been an even-tempered and helpful study partner. Our evenings are pleasant, but despite the positive changes in his behavior and attitude, I can't rekindle the love I had for him. I come home for Brandon, not him.

I have no idea where flight lessons will lead, but the time and expense will be worth it if I can turn fear and failure into confidence and accomplishment. For the past four years, I've drifted day-to-day without an end goal, enjoying ephemeral ecstasies, cocooned in marriage. Rekindling confidence will take time, but it's time—past time—to reclaim my childhood independence of spirit. If I'm successful, leaps outside my comfort zone into unstable territory will boost my confidence. I ignore the possibility of failure and focus on the positive. I can do this.

On the day of my stall-spin-crash-burn-die lesson, Murray crams the remaining quarter of his white-bread-and-bologna sandwich into his mouth, then says, "You do the walk-around while I finish eating."

I ask, "Don't I need a ground briefing about spins?"

"Sometimes the aircraft is the best teacher."

I climb to four thousand feet before Murray takes control and reduces power to idle. He slowly pulls the control column toward us until the aircraft's nose points up and the instrument panel blocks most of the horizon. The sensation of slipping backward into the tail of the aircraft overwhelms me. I swipe my sweaty palms on my jeans, then grip the handle on the doorjamb with my left hand and the seat cushion with my right.

As the airspeed decreases, the plane wallows in the reduced airflow and staggers like an oxygen-deprived mountaineer. Staccato bursts from the stall warning horn eclipse the idling engine's gentle hum. Like a canary in a coalmine, the stall warning horn chirps, *Moron, moron, moron.*

Murray says, "Short beeps mean the plane will stall unless we take corrective action."

Gripped by fear of the unknown, I sit like a condemned prisoner, buckled in the chair. As the plane moves closer to the stall, the airflow gradually changes from smooth flow to burbling eddy. The canary's nervous squeaks become a continuous, cacophonous bleat, like an emergency vehicle's siren.

Instead of making any corrective action, Murray says, "We're about to stall."

My legs chatter. I hope I don't pee my pants. Or worse.

The disturbed airflow pummels the aircraft's thin aluminum skin, causing it to flex and straighten—*tthummp-whhummp-tthummp-whhummp*—in time with the percussive thumping of my heart. My spine trembles in synchrony with the shuddering aircraft. I scrunch my eyelids shut, shrink my head into my chest, and curve my shoulders forward to shelter my body, a turtle cowering in her shell.

A millisecond before the stall, the plane convulses, then pitches nose forward.

I shriek and shield my eyes with my hands, unwilling to witness our plummet into the ground. Despite my conviction of imminent death, my body feels buoyant, as if suspended by a magic carpet undulating across the sky. Disoriented, I peer between my fingers, expecting terra firma to dominate the windscreen. To my total surprise, instead of pointing toward the earth, the aircraft is straight and level, a position that makes air flow across the wings.

Instead of dying, we're flying.

Murray increases power to maintain level flight. We've only descended two hundred feet, a loss without consequence at three thousand feet—but critical near the ground. He says, "Most pilots don't like stalls."

Wide-eyed, I nod in agreement.

He continues, "Modern aircraft are designed to not stall easily. Ready to show me a stall?"

My sweaty hand slips along the smooth control column.

Murray says, "You can do this."

My hands tremble as I gradually pull the control column toward me and reduce power. The nose of the aircraft pitches up. Repetitive beeps from the stall warning horn jolt my body like pulsing electric shocks, and I feel like the terrified lab rats used for behavior modification experiments. I don't want to make the aircraft stall, but if I don't do it now, I doubt I'll find the courage to try again.

As the aircraft approaches the stall, individual beeps of the warning horn meld into a steady scream, piercing my ears like the practice Cold War air raid sirens of primary school.

The aircraft stalls, the nose pitches down, and suddenly we're flying. But there's a difference. When Murray demonstrated the stall, I was scared, partly because I'd never seen a stall but mostly because I wasn't in control.

I shriek, "*Woo-hoo!* That felt like a midway ride!"

Murray forces a smile. "I guess you like midway rides."

Despite my unexpected realization that the pitching and bucking of stalls resembles midway rides and the turbulence of my first flights across Canada, niggling at the back of my mind and wiggling forward is the knowledge that stalls are the prologue to the future, greater terror of spins and spiral dives. Fears expressed by other pilots (all men and, therefore, I believe, *much* braver than me) mixed with the caveat that unintentional stalls and spins must be avoided make me as jumpy as a novice tightrope artist over the Niagara Gorge.

I want to keep these fears secret from Paul. "Let's skip flight lessons this weekend and focus on Brandon."

We're at the same stage of flight training, so I expect he'll taunt me with, "Are you scared?" Instead, he says, "Great idea! Let's drive to London!"

Does he have similar fears? I don't ask—and he doesn't tell.

We cancel our next lesson. "Busy, too busy," we tell our instructors, though we continue to study the theory of spins and spirals. I'm certain I know what to expect until I try to sleep, and the festering visions of horrifying spins and spiral dives replace any clarity I've mastered.

We spend Saturday at Storybook Gardens Children's Amusement Park, have dinner at Ronald McDonald's (Brandon's choice), then go to the drive-in. Paul and I saw *Star Wars* at the theater two years earlier but want Brandon to see Han Solo and Chewie fly through the sky like Mom and Dad.

On the drive home, until he falls asleep from exhaustion, Brandon chants in his three-year-old voice, unable to pronounce all consonant-vowel sounds, "Star Whores, Star Whores."

Paul and I laugh until tears stream down our cheeks. It's a shared moment but one that revolves around our son, not us as a couple. Paul's trying to be a good husband. Though his threats and his excessive drinking seem to be in the past, those bad behaviors have destroyed my feelings for him. But he's the father of my child, and because I want to develop some type of shared parenting relationship with him, I make myself forgive him.

Two weeks later, we're back at the airport. I go first, ready to conquer my fears, ready to learn if the male pilots' verdict that full power stalls and spins are the spine-chilling ogres of my imagination. Murray has skipped the preparatory ground lesson again, stating the plane is the best teacher. I ask several questions, hoping to squeeze answers and a few more minutes on the ground, but soon, we're in the practice area, under a vast dome of blue. He asks, "Do you remember the acronym to ensure the area is safe for aerobatics?"

I nod. He waits. I can't speak.

He prods. "What does 'H' mean?"

Help! I giggle, and if we weren't airborne, I would jump out. But if I don't begin now, I might never begin, and I won't become a pilot. I won't achieve my dream. I inhale a deep yoga breath, then begin the security and safety check.

I say:

"H. Height. Three thousand. Check.

"A. Area. Away from cities so when we crash, we'll be the only casualties. Check.

"S. Security. Loose objects stowed. Check.

"E. Engine systems and switches. Check.

"L. Look for other aircraft. Clear."

Worms crawl around my stomach. I say, "We forgot parachutes."

Murray manages a limp smile. "Light aircraft don't carry parachutes."

The worms start writhing like cobras. I ask, "Why not?"

He points at the altimeter. "Only trained parachutists can operate a parachute below three thousand feet. Each parachute weighs about fifty pounds, which would significantly decrease the amount of fuel we can carry."

I breathe deeply, then begin the first of several power-assisted stalls, gradually increasing power with each stall. With increased power, the aircraft doesn't merely pitch down at the point of stall—it rolls left twenty to thirty degrees. At first, the stall-roll combo frightens me, but after a few demonstrations, my fear disappears.

He takes control and says, "Stalls with power are incipient spins. The left-rolling tendency is a reaction opposite to the clockwise spin of the propeller. Now, I'll demonstrate an intentional spin. Ready?"

I'm not ready, and his rigid shoulders and tremulous voice increase my fear—*or am I projecting?* But if he can fake it, so can I. I nod with confidence as he instructs, "Hover your hands around the control column, and rest your feet against your rudder pedals to feel the movement."

At the point of stall, he presses his left rudder pedal and the aircraft snaps left, rolls onto its back, and flings itself toward Earth. I scream, release my light grip on the control column as if it were a hot poker, and whip toward him. Nausea roils in my stomach. I grip his hairy forearm with both hands. He may not have noticed my rapid release of the control column, but he reacts to ten, long, French-manicured nails embedded in his flesh.

He recovers from the stall-spin combo, and I ask, "H-h-how—how many turns did we do?"

"Less than half a rotation."

"I thought if the aircraft points to the ground during a spin that means the aircraft has tightened into a full spin?"

He grins. "You've been studying! However, the aircraft wasn't pointing at the ground."

I don't want to doubt him, but I do. "Could've fooled me."

Murray guides the plane away from the designated practice area above farm fields and says, "Let's head home."

He allows me a few minutes to salvage some composure, then insists I take control, treating me as if I were a cowpoke bucked from a wild stallion. I take control, but the whirling image of the ground below replays in my memory. My concept of a spin as a complex, tumbling, twisting movement of the aircraft seems to be accurate, yet I have a new understanding of Pope's "a little learning is a dangerous thing." I ask, "If I keep the aircraft level and with sufficient airspeed, can you assure me the aircraft will *never* stall?"

"Correct."

I sag with relief until, seconds later, Murray shifts in his seat, fidgets with the altimeter setting, then says, "*Um-ahem-um*, generally true."

My saucer eyes stare a question mark at him.

He says, "An aircraft may stall at any airspeed or attitude."

A torrent of confused thoughts ricochets around my brain. "Explain."

The flight deck is a mediocre classroom, unintended for lengthy discourse, yet Murray yells louder than the engine, the wind that whishes along the fuselage and sneaks into tiny nooks and crannies, and the airwave chatter punctuated with static crackles. "Let's pretend we're on approach to landing."

He reduces engine power and starts a descent to simulate a landing. "Let's pretend another plane is on the runway. To avoid crashing, I'll start to climb and use full power. However, due to inertia, the plane will continue descending for a few seconds. If I try to climb faster by pitching the nose up more, the angle between the wings and the descent path might be excessive—and the wings will stall."

This disturbing information confounds me. "Don't *all* pilots understand inertia?"

He nods. "When people panic, logic leaves."

I mull this. "And if the wings aren't level, the aircraft will spin."

He chuckles. "Six minutes inside a spinning aircraft is more effective than sixty minutes buried in a textbook."

"I will *never* forget how to avoid stall, spin, crash, burn—*die!*"

11

RED LINING

The portable Sanyo radio on the flight dispatch desk crackles. "Folks, willya look at that! Polesitter Rick Mears has taken the lead in today's nineteeeeeen-seventy-nine Indy Five Hundred!"

CFI Murray sits, right leg crossed over left, moves the gracefully arched fingers of his hand over each entry in my logbook, then looks up and smiles at me. "You've done almost all the exercises required for—first solo."

My bowels gurgle, my stomach flip-flops. Though aware that first solo is a necessary facet of pilot training, I can't stop vacillating between wanting to achieve my dream of flying and plotting ways to avoid the impending event. This flight—one takeoff, a rectangular flight pattern above the airport, and one landing—is guaranteed to be the shortest (yet potentially the most traumatic) planned flight of any pilot.

"We'll review what you're learned, then I'll introduce you to a steep turn."

My knees judder. "Are they as scary as spins?"

Murray shrugs. "No, but more dangerous. If the pilot allows a steep turn to become an unintentional spiral dive—"

I say, "—the airspeed rapidly increases."

He smiles in approval. "And a sustained spiral dive may exceed engine capabilities."

"And the wings might rip off." My shoulders shudder as I recall my mother's hysterical comment during our first flight to Regina.

"Training aircraft can withstand brutal punishment."

In the air, Murray says, "I'll start with a steep turn to the right. If I were to start with a left turn, because you're seated in the left seat, gravity will make you *think* you're going to slip out the door."

He rolls the plane to the right, stops when the plane is angled forty-five degrees to the horizon, then points to the instruments. "For a steep turn, the important thing is to maintain a constant angle of bank and a constant altitude."

After a full circle, he rolls out on a heading of north, then commands, "Please take control and do a thirty-degree steep turn to the right."

I take control, buoyed by his perfect demonstration, which suggests steep turns are easy, then hesitate briefly, remembering how his skill made taxiing look easy. I recite the safety check, then roll the aircraft to the right, into a thirty-degree angle of bank.

This steep angle increases the pull of gravity, and each arm feels as if I'm wearing ten-pound weights on my wrists. I pull the control column toward me to maintain altitude, but despite my efforts, within seconds I've put us into a spiral dive.

Murray points to the airspeed indicator. "Approaching red line!"

The wind whistles, fresh air blasts into my face through the air vents, and the airspeed needle barrels toward the red-line zone—the never-exceed speed, the wings-come-off speed. But instead of fear, my inner speed demon rejoices. After six or so semi-successful attempts to perform a steep turn, I do an almost perfect steep turn and hold it for a full circle. I ask, "Can I reward myself with a spiral dive?"

He raises his eyebrows but nods.

I roll the aircraft to the left, release a smidgen of pressure on the control column, and we immediately dive toward Earth. The spicy scent of aviation gas fumes seeps into the cockpit and I inhale, energized by the scent as if it were Opium, my favorite perfume. All four cylinders howl and pound as the airspeed indicator needle spurts toward the red line of disintegration. Suddenly, I understand the thrill experienced by Formula One racers like Niki Lauda. I shriek with delight, infused with the pleasure of accomplishment—and the joy of flying.

As I fly home toward the airport, Murray says, "Next up, first solo!"

He might be ready for my first solo, but I'm not. Though no sane instructor would send an unprepared student to certain death, I want more spin practice.

For the next few days, during meals, showering, or at work, a spontaneous newsflash replays the nose-down whirling plunge of Murray's spin demonstration. With vivid clarity, I remember our plane spinning closer and closer and closer to the ground, and certain death. Multicolored farm fields, toy tractors, and miniature cows whir past the windscreen. One night, I have a similar dream but now the aircraft is only three or four hundred feet above ground. Life-sized thousand-pound animals and massive vehicles dominate the windscreen.

Why isn't Murray recovering?

I look to my right and realize he isn't recovering because he isn't inside the plane. I'm alone. And I can't remember how to save myself. I wake up seconds before I smash into the ground and leave my son without a mother. But if I want to become a pilot, I must fly solo. If Murray believes in me, I should believe in me, but I don't. I can perform spins but I'm terrified. I need more spin practice to gain confidence, but what if I request another spin lesson and Murray refuses?

I ponder the best way to persuade Murray.

On Thursday evening, the phone rings as I'm serving dinner. Paul answers, but I get the gist of the conversation. Murray has to go out of town and only Dan will be there, able to teach one of us.

Paul hangs up. "Babe, you go. I'll bet Dan sends you solo."

He's so excited and so supportive, I don't mention my fears.

Two days later, Paul and Brandon drop me at the airport. Instead of playing in the sandbox in front of the flight school and being there to celebrate my planned first solo, Paul announces they're going to McDonald's for lunch. I'm hurt, confused, and glad.

Dan examines my logbook and rakes his fingers through his auburn hair. He grins. "We'll be in the circuit today, and if all goes well, I'll send you solo. Any questions?"

"I've had nightmares about entering an unintentional spin, then crashing and burning."

Silence.

I shift on the couch and lean across the table toward him. "Before I go solo, I want to practice full spins."

He looks at me, but his face reveals nothing. "Full spins aren't required."

I say, with confidence, "They are for me. And it's my money. What's another hour in the practice area?"

To my surprise, he grins. "Why not? I love spins."

On the ramp, Dan munches an apple as he watches me do the preflight walk-around. This morning, my obsession about going solo blotted out my logistics skills. I've forgotten to bring anything to eat. My stomach grumbles with envy.

I do a good takeoff, but as we get closer to the practice area, tension squeezes my innards. I hear Dan's calm, soothing voice saying, "Re-*laaaax*! You're only climbing. You've climbed dozens of times."

How did he sense my turmoil?

He nudges me with his elbow. "Look at you. You're hunched forward, gripping the control column with white knuckles."

I force a laugh. "Didn't realize my terror was so obvious."

He flashes a grin. "I bet your hands are sweating, like Pavlov's lab dogs that drooled when they heard bells."

I wait until he looks out his side window before wiping my palms.

He says, "By the end of this lesson, you'll love spins."

"Ha-*ha*-ha-*ha*-ha-*ha*." I make my voice trill with faux delight, disputing his prediction. His willingness to forgo touch-and-goes for spins has bolstered my courage, but that only means I'm slightly less terrified.

At five thousand feet, Dan takes control. "I'll demonstrate several power-to-idle spins, then a few with various power settings. I'll finish with a full-power spin."

I'm glad he's baby-stepping me toward the precipice of the frightening, full-power, nose-pointing-toward-Earth, we're-definitely-gonna-die spin. During the gyrations, he laughs and smiles, clearly having a great time. I observe and try to maintain an appearance of cool by sitting on my hands so they don't respond to my brain, which is screaming, *Grab control from this lunatic and get us back on the ground.* Each time the plane rolls left and the wing drops, bits of breakfast surge into my mouth. I'm glad I forgot to bring lunch.

With each subsequent spin, Dan lets the aircraft rotate a bit farther. He describes each phase of the spin, as he performs it, step-by-step. Little by little, as understanding trumps fear, my jitters fade. His calm monotone relaxes me and finally, when the stall warning horn screams, I don't. My decision to forgo first solo and get more spin training was the right decision.

He says, "Here comes a full spin with full power."

I asked for this but I'm dreading it. He whirls the aircraft into a full-power, full-rotation spin. The plane rolls left. The nose pitches down. The spin axis gets tighter, and my visual reference reduces to one twirling green field. This is everything but the horrific kamikaze dive I imagined. I'm right there with him, laughing with delight, laughing with the pleasure of being alive, laughing at my fears.

He says, "First, stop the rotation." After the plane stops rotating, we plunge downward, and he says, "Now we're diving." He points to the airspeed indicator. "Check out the super-fast speed. This is the dangerous phase of a spin. Ease out of the dive. Voilà! That's all there is to it!"

He recovers from the spin, returns the aircraft to straight-and-level flight, and says, "Lola, you have control."

Who's he kidding? Yet, if he believes in me, maybe I should, too. Like a timid toddler, I crawl my way to confidence. With each subsequent spin, I use more power and allow the aircraft to rotate longer before recovering. Buoyed by success—and a decaying doubt about my capabilities—I soon embrace the sensations of these unusual attitudes. I thrill to the entry phase of the spin when, for a millisecond, time and motion cease as the plane becomes Aladdin's carpet, suspended by a cushion of air. Euphoria reigns as I float in the transitory weightlessness at the point of stall-spin, the exhilarating rotating plunge, and the electrifying dive recovery phase. What I first perceived as a blitzkrieg of screeching air seething into the cockpit during the earthbound plunge is now merry whistling, a musical accompaniment to the roaring engine pulsing with my heart, as the plane and I, united as one, streak toward the red line, the maximum airspeed, the point of disintegration.

For Dan, a stall or spin is not an abhorrent hurdle but an innervating zenith, tackled as a challenge of life, in the spirit of Amelia Earhart's "for the fun of it." And so it becomes for me. Bewitched by endorphins, transformed into a thrill junkie, I perform spin after spin after spin. I scarcely recognize the new me facing her fears—fearfully, but with determination. Ousted by my newfound competence, my fright slinks into the shadows like a rejected suitor.

I now see the bluster of male pilots as a facade masking their inner fears. With a jolt, I realize Paul's tactics are similar. He bullies me to boost his confidence and crush mine.

Flight lessons have taught me to control an airplane, an accomplishment that instilled confidence, a skill to help me take control of my life.

12

A WONDERFUL
WORLD

If I compare my progress to that recorded in the logbooks of other flight students, I'm an average pilot, competent for my level of training. Though male students seem eager to display their prowess by flying solo, I need more time—at least psychologically. Our impending holidays provide an excellent excuse to delay making decisions. Since we began flying, Paul hasn't tried to control me, but I don't think love can glimmer through my veiled anger. I'm tired of his childish temper tantrums, his threats, and almost everything about him, but when he says, "Maybe this time together will help us find love again," I smile as if to say, *I hope so*, even though I'm almost at the end of hope.

On June 14, 1979, Paul, Brandon, and I skedaddle to his parents' cottage in northern Ontario for a two-week vacation, but the fastest route meanders past Muskoka Airport's immense runway. When Paul spots the road sign with an airplane image, he consults his multi-knobbed waterproof Bulova Chronograph, a huge hunk of steel more weapon than watch.

"We've made good time. Let's check out the flight school."

"Paul, if we stop, we won't have time to swim before sunset."

He grins. "Let's take a quick look."

My pulse quickens, and faster than ground crews can holler,

"All clear? Contact!" my subconscious telegraphs, *Admit it. You want to fly during this holiday.* The Bee Gees harmonize about everlasting love, until Paul snaps off the radio. I love flying more than I love Paul. I can't wait to hear the whirring propeller but if I never have sex with Paul again, I'll be happy.

We drive in silence, along Airport Road, guided toward the flight school by amphibious airplanes aligned like silent sentinels. I open my window, feeling the breeze whirlwind my hair. A pungent cocktail of evergreen and aviation fumes swirls into my nostrils.

At the flight school parking lot, Paul hoists Brandon onto his shoulders while I grab the plastic zip folder containing my aviation textbooks brought with the intention of studying.

Inside the school, we meet Chief Flying Instructor Sandy to discuss the possibility of flying one or two times during our holidays.

CFI Sandy reviews my logbook with puckered brow, and I wonder why until he says, his voice redolent of consolation, not encouragement, "I don' wanna turn away new students but you're ready for solo on a Cessna 150. Because we train on Piper Cherokees, we'll need to fly with you a few hours to assess your competency."

Paul challenges him. "They're both single engines with three wheels."

Sandy's lips purse together and protrude like a cartoon fish. "The Cherokee is faster and, most importantly, a low-wing— the wing attaches below the body. When you look out the side windows, you can't see the ground like you can in a high-wing Cessna."

I nod my understanding and glance at Paul, who bounces Brandon up and down. Brandon thumps his tiny palms against Paul's head. "Giddyap, Daddy!"

Sandy drums his cartridge pen on the high wooden counter.

"Adjusting to a new flight school *and* a new instructor might be difficult."

I pipe up, "I've already had two. Both have the same knowledge but inspired me in different ways. One more is an opportunity, not a barrier."

Sandy smiles, adding dimension and two endearing dimples to his moon face. "Good attitude."

Paul asks, "How soon could we start?"

Sandy raises his right palm. "Hold on, buddy. These differences mean you'd need to review the exercises you learned in the Cessna. Probably four extra flight hours and—"

I moan. "—more money. Paul, let's go to the cottage as planned."

"Babe, if flying here makes you happy, I'll stay at the lake with Brandon."

"That would be fantastic!" Thankful for his support, I graze his cheek with my lips. *Does he really think aviation will steer our marriage toward recovery road?* We've been spending more time together but that's a function of studying each night and driving back and forth to flight lessons in one car—not because I've resurrected my love. Though I can't fault any aspect of his loving relationship with Brandon, I loathe my husband. I'm just waiting for the right moment to break my chains.

Sandy introduces us to my fourth instructor. "Meet Rob. He started his private pilot training here 'bout two years ago and became an instructor a few weeks ago. You're one of his first students."

Rob's a scrawny forty-something with a scraggly goatee, greasy hair, and teeth the color of burnished brass, the polar opposite of all previous instructors. Rob's sunken cheeks and haunted eyes remind me of a malnourished dopehead from the 1960s. We shake hands, mine firm, his clammy, and I silently hum "Puff the Magic Dragon." If Sandy, the CFI, had not introduced us, I would've crossed the street to avoid him.

— — —

That night, in bed, after I say, "Not tonight, I have a headache," Paul rolls away from me, even though he knows sex is usually the best cure for my headaches. I stare at the pine ceiling, excited about tomorrow's flight lesson—and worried. Flight training, as with many technical skills, has a steep learning curve. For unexplained reasons unrelated to ability or intelligence, my progress has been more rapid than Paul's. When he cheers my success with extravagant praise to anyone who'll listen, I'm flattered, but when he interrupts me—to brag about me—I'm furious.

He has no right to claim responsibility, yet he boasts as if he's responsible for my success or as if he's a parent, proud of his creation.

When I fly the aircraft, I'm accountable. Not him.

I want to answer questions about my flying. I want to speak for myself.

I turn my back to his and try to stop fussing about his problems. I need to change my life, not his. My brain cycles through the problems I created in our marriage. My lack of interest in sex coupled with evening absences screamed infidelity, but Paul didn't question my lies. I sensed he didn't believe me but wasn't ready to accept our marriage was over.

The brave and honest part of me wants to tell him the truth, to help him understand the affair was my pathetic way of showing him I don't want to be his possession. I want him to realize that living with him is my personal prison and he's the warden, always watching, always controlling. I want him to realize our marriage is over.

But the cowardly part of me trembles, afraid to unleash his anger, afraid his threats of violence will transform into actual violence. I roll over and force my brain to fret about the logistics of completing my pilot license during my two-week-holiday. The weather forecast promises warm, sunny weather, but localized storms could kibosh my plans.

The next morning, Rob greets me, "How-dee!" and, as we walk to the aircraft, pats me on the back. "Checked out your training records. Chatham's head honcho faxed 'em to us last night. Lemme see your logbook." He flips through my flight log, then nudges me in the ribs. "Your other instructors forgot to show you the sideslip," he says, then rubs his palms together, imitating a Machiavellian necromancer. His voice cackles with delight. "At the end of today's lesson, I'll show you a sideslip you'll *never* forget."

"Shouldn't I read about it first?"

"Nah. In a nutshell, it's a great way to lose height over a short distance without increasing airspeed. Used before aircraft had barn doors draggin' in the wind."

"Barn doors?"

"Flaps, to slow down for landing."

Ten minutes later, we're airborne. I climb to altitude and for the next forty-five minutes, he reviews my flight skills. Near the end of my hour-long lesson, he says, "You're doing great," then squeals with raucous laughter, "Here goes, like I promised!"

In concert, he rams his right foot against the right rudder and turns the control column to the maximum left position. Bulldozing left into a precipitous sixty-degree angle, the left side of the aircraft (rather than the nose) dives toward Earth like a razor-sharp machete through flesh. I'm a broken seat belt and one door-latch malfunction from skydiving without a parachute.

I brace my arms against the doorframe and tilt away from annihilation. Inside the confined space of a side-by-side, two-seater, training aircraft, this translates as touching Rob. With lightning speed, he takes advantage of our increased proximity and loops his left arm around my waist. I recoil and squirm from his sweaty grasp and growl, "*Aauurggh!* Let go of me."

He removes his arm and returns the aircraft to level flight.

I say, "Take me back to the airport."

He laughs. "Just foolin' around. Would'na want ya to fall out."

I cross my arms, steaming at his audacity.

He jabs my ribs and says brightly, "You have control. Fly us back to the airport. Tomorrow we'll be in the circuit practicing landings and takeoffs."

I take control and wonder if I will have a tomorrow with this guy.

On final approach in this low-wing Cherokee, my visual reference of the runway is very different from the high-wing Cessna. Thanks to Rob's helpful coaching, I make a good landing and decide not to discuss his inappropriate behavior with Sandy. I'm certain Rob's lapse of judgment is a random event.

On the morning of my second lesson, Rob introduces me to his perky wife, Candy, when she flounces into the flight school carrying his lunch.

She bubbles in a singsong voice about nothing important, yet tells me more than I need to know. I point to the airplane and shuffle toward the ramp door, trying to excuse myself, but she fluffs her short auburn curls with both hands, then twitters, "Ta-ta, gotta run, too. I'm a waitress at the burger joint in town." She points to the row of WWII strawberry-box-sized cottages west of the runway. "I live in the one with the shutters. Been there two years. Drop in sometime!"

At the aircraft, Rob sits in the instructor seat while I do the preflight. I twist-hop into the aircraft and plop onto grasping fingers cradling my derriere. I leap out and whirl to face him. "What! Are! You! Doing?"

"*Hehehehe!*" He cackles and leers like Batman's Joker. "Thought you might want some fun," he says, then curls the fingers of his left hand to beckon me. "I won't tell if you don't."

I back farther from him. "That's more disgusting than the smell of your breath."

"Okay. *Okay*. Kidding. You can't blame a guy for trying, can you?"

"Yes, I can! You're my instructor and we're married—to other people!"

"Lighten up," he says, his voice laden with reproach, as if I've offended him.

"Why would you think I'm interested in you?"

He ogles me, then drawls like a movie mobster. "Sweetheart, you're pretty friendly."

"Do you think every woman who smiles at you wants to fool around?"

"Let's go flying."

"Keep your hands to yourself."

Rob is a high-jinx culprit whose actions are neither suave nor subtle. But I *am* curious. Rob's follies pique my interest in what I sense has been an unequivocally unusual past. A few casual though deliberate questions to other students reveal nobody knows much about Rob. Though all pilots have to take their first lesson somewhere, Rob's appearance, actions, and the many holes in the stories of his life hint to a seedy past.

A couple of days later, after burgers on the barbeque, Paul, Brandon, and I skip down the hill toward the lake. Paul and I settle into about eight inches of water and sip beer from freezer-cooled bottles dripping sweat in the crepuscular sun. Brandon putzes around between us, supported by water wings, trying to swim but mostly splashing water into his face. I mention the personal touch Rob is adding to my lessons.

Paul laughs. "I'll take that as a compliment."

"Aren't you pissed off?"

"Kinda, but you're pretty hot."

"There's something odd about Rob and his wife. You met her a couple days ago."

Paul guzzles his beer. "Tiny brunette. Cute."

"She said something weird today. Said she lived in an airport cottage."

"He works at the airport. Sounds convenient."

"She said *she*, not *we*. Where's *he* been living?"

I dribble a bucket of lake water over Brandon, who blinks and giggles.

Paul crinkles his forehead. "Maybe he's a convict."

I spin to face him. "Are you *insane?*"

He laughs. "The next time you're flying, check out the big complex surrounded by barbed wire south of the airport."

"You're *serious!*"

"It's a minimum-security slammer. Locals call it summer camp because most inmates have day jobs in the community. Those I've met are reformed, ready for full release."

I arrive thirty minutes early for my third lesson, hoping for a casual encounter with Sandy while Rob is still flying. The school is empty except for Sandy doing paperwork at the front desk. We banter about weather, friends, and family for a few minutes, then I steer the conversation toward my flight training. He clarifies my questions, then I say, "Rob's a good instructor."

Sandy stops writing. "Glad ta hear it. You're one of his first students."

"I'm wondering, though . . . he loves to talk but steers conversations away from previous jobs."

Sandy knits his eyebrows together, forming a fuzzy orange caterpillar zigzagging along his brow. He studies my face and fidgets with his pen. *Click-CLICK-click.*

"His wife, Candy, said *she's* been living in one of those cottages . . ."

Sandy drums his pen on the counter. "Let's say he lives a bit south a' here."

I nod, trying to keep calm. I'm not sure what to say, how to say it, or if I should say anything. Sandy might believe me, but he'd be evaluating my word against Rob, his friend, former student, and employee. Rob might fess up, but he might also minimize or refute my allegations. As with many women who report harassment, I'll likely be accused of misinterpreting his actions, labeled a whining troublemaker—and blamed for encouraging his sexual advances.

I decide to give him one more chance. Sure, he's a former dodgy dude, a resident of the nearby minimum-security slammer for at least two years, but when this Mephistophelian felon became a flight instructor, he transformed himself from slimy worm to chrysalis, then to butterfly, and joined society as a wage-earning citizen. He's a good instructor who has paid his dues and orchestrated several monumental memories during flight training that relate to life.

But I need to remember that some men choose to interpret my smile as an invitation then blame me for their unwelcome and inappropriate actions.

13

GOING SOLO

In the next two days, I log 4.2 more hours of flight time on the school's trainer, a Piper Cherokee training aircraft. Instead of being obnoxious or jealous, Paul seems thrilled to spend father-and-son time at the cottage.

Does he miss me as much as I miss him? Which is—not at all.

During the late afternoons, after a long day at the airport, I enjoy spending time with Brandon while Paul prepares supper. He's being wonderful, but he's killed that loving feeling. Instead of returning his "I love you, babe" with a similar endearment, I can only manage, "You're being great to let me fly while you look after Brandon."

He says, "He's mine, too."

Every night when he cracks open a beer, I equate the snap of the cap to the death-rattling last gasp of our marriage. "I wish you'd go back to AA."

"Babe, I don't need those guys."

The next morning, Paul needs the car, and when we arrive at the airport, Paul notices a for sale sign stuck on a red-and-white Cessna. He shouts, "Let's buy it!"

His fervor stuns me. I don't want to accumulate things in a marriage I've started to classify as a lost cause.

He says, "Let's ask Sandy," but I'm not worried, as Sandy will surely shoot him down.

He doesn't. "Paul's plan is sensible. In Chatham, you were ready to solo on a Cessna 150. You could finish training here on your own Cessna."

I ask, "B-b-but . . . how will we get it home?"

Sandy points at me. "You *fly* it!"

"Chatham is a long way away!"

Sandy clicks his pen. "More than two hundred miles."

I back away from the counter. "I haven't even gone solo!"

"You will soon, on our Cherokee or your own Cessna." He winks. "If you're willing to fly every day, you could do your flight test before you head home!"

I fight to find another excuse. "Don't I need to pass a written exam before the flight test?"

Sandy shakes his head and grins. "The plane's in great shape."

Paul wraps his arm around my shoulders. "C'mon, babe, let's get it!"

Sandy reviews the aircraft's airworthiness documents with us and confirms that the maintenance complies with manufacturer's specifications. I'm not convinced until Rob and I take the little Cessna for a test flight. The ease of signing papers and writing a cheque radiates good karma deep into my bones. Faster than an aircraft can stall-spin-crash-explode, Cessna 150, call sign C-FDMZ (Foxtrot, Delta, Mike, Zulu), becomes ours.

The following day, Rob confirms my proficiency in the Cessna 150. "Time to solo!" This time, I'm excited until he says, "But as a Class IV instructor, I can't send anyone solo. Sandy has ta do your pre-solo check ride."

We return to the flight school where I wait with increasing frustration for Sandy. Finally, we're airborne, and after two touch-n-goes, Sandy points to the first taxiway. "Pull off there."

We're a long way from the school. I ask, "Here?"

"I'm leaving you!" Sandy beams a dimpled smile. "In fact, if you feel good after the standard one-circuit takeoff and landing, then you should go ta the practice area."

I'm more than ready. I've flown three different models of aircraft designed by two different manufacturers, with two different engines, with four instructors, at two schools, and in two different geographic regions. This diversity means I'm far from being a typical student who's flown at one school, on one type of aircraft, with one or two instructors.

This also means I could write *Your Guide to Extremely Expensive Flight Training.*

I turn toward the runway and mentally prepare to launch myself into the air. A gentle breath flutters the windsock, a silky cone of orange and white stripes. The sock ruffles and trembles, then falls flaccid, clinging like a dancer to the rigid metal pole. Cirrus clouds stretch like palomino manes across the azure sky. A pale gold sun, high in the late-morning sky, spears the earth with summer heat.

My heart thumps. A flash of heat creeps across my skin. Sweat tickles my burning cheeks. Glittering droplets of perspiration twinkle from the coal-black control column. I scour the sky, section by section, searching for aircraft without radios and therefore unable to report their arrival. Before moving onto the runway, I make a radio broadcast to warn radio-equipped pilots this is my first solo, and hope my voice radiates confidence.

I nudge the plane forward, moving in continuous motion from the narrow taxiway onto the two-hundred-foot-wide, mile-long asphalt runway, a black gash of civilization sliced through a conifer forest. I scan the runway, a gleaming oasis in the heat, and the area beside the runway for wandering moose munching grass.

I listen for the voices of other pilots but hear nothing.

I look at my hand on the throttle, unable to believe this is me checking the instruments, searching for conflicting aircraft, broadcasting over the radio, and taxiing onto the runway. This is the new me, transformed into someone different, someone about to prove her life has meaning.

Part of me wants to turn back and cancel this flight, but I slide the throttle plunger toward the dashboard. The engine revs and my brain hums with excitement—and fear. Though flying has taught me that fear is normal and that reasonable people should be fearful when faced with a reason to fear, I have also learned that panic is abnormal and counterproductive. If an emergency occurs, I must not panic; I must rely on my minimal aviation experience.

Inspired by the confidence of my instructors, I accelerate to full power, but without two hundred pounds of male instructor weighing me down, the takeoff roll is much shorter than I expect. Seconds after acceleration, my fourteen-hundred-pound aircraft leaps into the air, screaming for the ultramarine beyond. I jump with surprise. The plane feels as light as a barnstormer's silk scarf. My airspeed is only 80 mph, but it feels like I'm rocketing into space. Well, at least the lowest four thousand feet of it.

The sky becomes my playground. My body vibrates like a tuning fork. Memories of childhood flood my conscience. I feel as exhilarated as four-year-old me zooming down the hillside sidewalk on my tricycle, a sparkling blue, three-wheeled miracle. Tinsel strips stream from my handle grips, flash in the sunlight, and create an illusion of great speed. Unshackled from fettered footfall, nothing had electrified me more than gliding downhill, feet off the pedals, legs outstretched, in control. That is, until now, until flying, in control of an aircraft.

A shiver of unbridled joy ripples through my body.

I'm relieved to be the only aircraft in the area, allowed to focus on flying without the added responsibility of talking to other aircraft—or avoiding a midair collision. As I approach for touchdown, I shift in my seat, nervous with expectation about this first landing by myself. If things start going sideways, I must anticipate all possible consequences and make the right decisions within seconds, without anyone to coach me.

But the wind is calm, so I don't need to worry about wind gusts or winds blowing at an angle to the runway. The plane descends on course for the runway. When the two main wheels chirp "hello" to the tarmac, I start to breathe, knowing all my worry and procrastination about my first solo has been a waste of time.

Seconds later, the nosewheel touches down, and instead of coming to a full stop, I accelerate, sprint down the runway, and then fly toward the open territory of the practice area. My heart thrums in harmony with the purring engine as I climb to four thousand feet, then take time to enjoy the lakes and rivers below me, sparkling in the sunshine. After five minutes, I review turns, stalls, and power-to-idle spins, unable to believe I'm alone in my own aircraft.

Unescorted. Unassisted. Un*man*ned.

Satisfied with my practice and relaxed by the constant, Brownian noises of the roaring engine and the rushing wind, I turn the aircraft left, then right, leisurely, climbing, then descending, almost without purpose, admiring the checkerboard pattern of fields, untamed forests, and twisting rivers.

Ten weeks ago, not only could I not perform these actions, but I was also unaware they existed. I remember when any one of these tasks seemed insurmountable, but now I can do several simultaneously, as if they've always been familiar, as if I've always been a pilot.

Images of two childhood heroes, naval aviator Sky King and his niece Penny, blast into my consciousness. I smile as I remember soaring over Arizona, a virtual passenger seated in King's twin-engine Cessna, helping King and Penny search for villains, criminals, and lost hikers.

I admired Penny, a successful air derby racing pilot and a multi-engine pilot, but she wasn't the inspiring role model she could have been. Though the same Federal Aviation Authority that licensed all American pilots tested Penny's aviation skills, male scriptwriters created her as subordinate to her uncle, the male champion who got the glory. At the time, this casting was understandable. *Sky King* debuted on television only six years after World War II ended in 1945. While men flew combat missions overseas, women had oiled the war effort at home as ferry pilots, an achievement that prompted the producers of *Sky King* to include a female pilot who could take control and make decisions, *if* the man in charge was unavailable or indisposed.

Though the integration of women into the workforce blurred gender roles and expectations, men continued to believe women should have supporting roles. *Sky King* was art imitating the current social reality and perpetuating stereotypes. But that was twenty years ago, twenty years before I found the courage to fly solo.

My shoulders tingle with joy. Today's accomplishment is a landmark in my life, a sea change to define me and mold my idea of me . . . and what I can achieve when I find the courage to believe in me.

14

TESTING 1-2-3

My holidays morph into a whirling dervish blur of studying and flight training. After a few more days of solo flight, the pilot's bucket seat beckons like the overstuffed chairs flanking the cottage fireplace and I no longer feel like an interloper invading a private party. For the next two weeks, unless grounded by thunderstorms, DMZ and I are airborne two to four hours daily, during which I practice the air exercises and complete my first solo navigation route.

My flight test is scheduled, and though the demonstration of a multirotational spin is not required, I want to prove I can do a full spin without an instructor, *a man*, to save me. After warming up with a few power-to-idle spins, I gyrate DMZ into a full-power, full-rotation spin.

The aircraft flips onto its back, twists, then screams nose down.

Endorphins gush through my body, from brain to fingertips to tingling toes.

Until something thwacks against my forehead.

I gasp, choke for breath, and pound my chest to force air into my lungs. I can't imagine what's hit me but that isn't important right now. Recovery from the spin is. I breathe deeply, exhale forcibly, and talk myself through each facet of taming the spinning top. I speak aloud, slowly, deliberately. My voice calms me.

I ease out of the resultant dive, return to straight-and-level flight, and now start wondering what crashed into my face. Prior to the spin, I completed the required pre-aerobatic safety check to secure loose items. A quick check confirms the manual, logbook, and water bottle remain tucked into the pockets behind the seats. I've missed something—but *what?*

Something unusual. Something unique to my aircraft.

Something critical that might have made my first full spin in C-FDMZ my last.

My forehead throbs in pain, aggravated by the propeller. *Whoosh. Thump. Whoosh. Thump.* The windscreen is intact, so bird strike wasn't the cause. I scan the instruments. All are normal but blurry. I massage my forehead and rub my eyes, stunned to see blood smears on my fist. I press an oil-stained rag against the bleeding lump, then check the instruments again. All seem to be operating properly, so I bend sideways to peer under the dash to check the fuses and wiring.

A coil of black rubber leads my eyes to the culprit.

I sigh with relief.

The quasi-weightless plastic microphones in the airplanes at both schools never needed stowing, but my vintage, 1966 aircraft has a grapefruit-sized, wartime relic made of heavy black Bakelite, material that is used for telephones. When DMZ entered the spin and transitioned through semi-inverted flight, my mic became a missile with momentum that magnified its two-pound weight.

I turn toward the airport with vibrating knees and force myself to enjoy the summer sunbath streaming through the plexiglass windscreen. Today's canceled appointment with death is another crucial step toward being a pilot—and a reminder that I'm alive, with one life to live.

The time has come to live my life the way I want, not how Paul thinks I should.

===

The day before my flight test, Sandy says, "Keep prepping for your flight test, but I gotta tell ya, the weather isn't lookin' good. A massive low-pressure system rollin' in from the northwest is gonna sweep over the Great Lakes, scoop up moisture, and shit all over our plans."

My shoulders droop. "What rotten luck."

"It's scheduled ta arrive the day of your flight test."

Tears threaten to dribble onto my cheek as I listen to Sandy explain what to expect on my flight test. Then he whips out an aviation map, points to Borden, and says, "Muskoka doesn't have a flight examiner, so I've arranged for an examiner to meet you here."

"But Borden's a military airport!" My voice rises with each syllable.

"A World War I airport used *occasionally* by the military. You'll need three hours for your test. Then, instead of coming back here, you'll fly home. Should take another three hours."

"So, I'll need a high-pressure system with sunshine from sunrise to sunset over most of Ontario!"

Sandy raises his bushy eyebrows. "Yup. Another complication is the requirement for student pilots to land no later than one half hour before sunset."

I scrunch my lips together and grimace. "Sunset is around eight thirty, so I'll need to finish my flight test before four."

The day of my flight test, Sandy calls at seven. "Today's a washout. Nobody, nowhere, is goin' anywhere." We discuss my options and Sandy reschedules my test for the next day, the final morning of our holidays. He says, "Be positive. Today's an opportunity ta study more."

Steady drizzle keeps us inside all day, reading and playing games with Brandon. I study a few hours while Brandon naps.

For supper, Paul cooks burgers on the barbeque under the shelter of the back porch while I prepare vegetables for roasting. I try to convince myself this is an opportunity, rather than another day and night to fret, but two weeks of almost daily training have prepared me for my flight test, an accomplishment crowned with my triumphant flight home.

Paul says, "Don't worry. It'll work out."

Does he mean my flight test or our marriage?

In bed that night, the more I focus on sleep, the more elusive sleep becomes. Scenarios of a glorious return to my home airfield dance in my mind. As if in a stage play, I imagine the words of disbelief when I fly home to Chatham and the instructors and students recognize my voice on the radio. "Is that Lola? Whose plane is she flying?" I set the clock radio alarm, then start listing four-footed animals in alphabetical order, a memory task that redirects my thoughts and lulls me asleep.

At three, Paul's grunting snores wake me and keep me awake. I need to sleep well to perform well, but I can't stop stewing about my flight test, the flight home to Chatham, and the weather, one of many things beyond my control. I tiptoe to the windows and peek between the thick tweed curtains. Raindrops splat onto the saturated blackness of the wooden deck. I crawl back into bed, bury my head under the covers, and agonize myself to sleep.

The next time I awaken, the clock says five in the morning. Now, I envision the astonished faces as I leap from my airplane onto Chatham's ramp and their surprise when they learn we've bought an aircraft and I've passed my flight.

At six thirty, the clock radio announcer jolts me awake when he says, "Happy Dominion Day." Annoyed more than usual by his modulated chirrup, I regret not insisting Paul program the music alarm. I hurl from bed and peek through the curtains. A charcoal sketch in ten shades of gray greets me. Steam fog scrolls from the inky lake. Drizzle drapes gauze over the towering pines marching along the far shore. Gray saucers of cloud obscure the hillcrests. Joyful images of my successful flight test dissolve like honey in the tea Paul hands to me. He drapes his arm around my shoulders and kisses my neck. I cringe.

He says, "Maybe the weather's better at the airport?"

I shake my head in frustration. "The airport's only fifteen miles south."

I trudge to the telephone mounted on the log wall of the kitchen and dial the weather office. After identifying my level of experience as a fifty-hour wonder, I describe the purpose and routing of my flight and request appropriate reports. As he reads them aloud, I lean against the kitchen countertop and scribble his English words using the aviator's cryptic code, a gobbledygook shorthand created to help pilots fly and write simultaneously.

I say, "That weather sucks," and laugh aloud when he responds, "Weather's so bad, crows are walking, too."

I discuss options with Paul, then contact Sandy. "We've decided to drive home. Can we schedule my flight test for next weekend?"

Sandy says, "Checked the weather m'self. You need ta get ta Borden. Those two lower cloud levels are already startin' ta break up."

"But I can't do aerobatics in low cloud!"

"True, but you'll spend an hour or so with the examiner discussing air regs and the navigation exercise Rob gave you. When you finish around noon, the massive high should be rollin' in."

"Wouldn't the examiner rather do something else on a holiday Monday than wait for weather?"

"He lives near Borden and agreed ta be on standby."

"But if I don't start the test before noon, there won't be enough daylight to fly home."

"Plan B. You fly ta an airport near Chatham. Kitchener? London? Park at the flight school, Paul meets you in the car, and you return for the airplane on the weekend."

I give Paul a thumbs-up. "I'll aim for London, an hour from home."

Paul is strangely silent but helps organize our departure. I buzz with excitement about the challenges ahead of me, slightly unnerved by his silence. *Is he jealous I'm doing my flight test and he isn't?* I need a clear head, uncluttered with personal problems, to concentrate on my big day. *What if he initiates a fight?*

By nine, the rain has scuttled away to ruin someone else's day, but when I step outside with the first suitcase, the fecund aroma of moist earth fills my lungs with the scent of renewal and rebirth.

Paul packs the last suitcase into the car, and we head south. Mist wafts skyward from puddles on the rain-drenched highway. His continued silence spooks me, but I ignore him and review my notes. At the airport, I hug Brandon and then they leave for their long drive home.

Sandy and Rob provide last-minute instructions, and by the time I'm ready to depart at ten thirty, the latest meteorologist report indicates the high-pressure system has delivered visibility of more than fifteen miles. This dramatic improvement boosts my spirits, but I check my excitement level. *Be calm. Stay calm. Worry about Paul and your marriage later.*

Though the visibility is good, the clouds are low, only twelve hundred feet. After takeoff from Muskoka, I climb to nine hundred feet, as high as possible without touching clouds. This height limits my field of vision to an endless sea of coniferous trees with grasping tips that seem close enough to snag the landing gear and make me crash into them. Worse, the winds are thirty knots, a bonus challenge that gusts across lakes and rips into the serrated tree line, creating whirlpools of air that toss me about the sky.

At a higher altitude, I'd sail above this turbulence, and my range of vision would allow me to see major landmarks, such as Georgian Bay's ragged coast on my right. On my left, I'd see folk singer Gordon Lightfoot's hometown, Orillia, at the base of Lake Simcoe's elongated north-pointing finger. The city of Barrie would be thirty kilometers southwest, at the western tip of Lake Simcoe.

If I'm on course, these landmarks are there—I just can't see them.

I maintain my flight-planned heading and track my progress using minor landmarks, navigating like a bush pilot: a cluster of houses at a junction near an S-curve in the highway; a long lake with two antler-shaped prongs; and a pancake-round lake. Navigation would be easier two or three thousand feet higher. I'm not positive my flight path is correct but bolster my doubts with an adage I don't believe: "Pilots never get lost, just temporarily disoriented."

Ten minutes earlier than my estimated time of arrival at Borden, I spot an airfield.

What if I am lost? If this is the wrong airport, I will be late for my test.

My heart pounds like a hammer bashing my ribs as I circle overhead. The pattern of runways conforms to the miniature schematic of Borden in my *Airport Handbook*, but the decaying runways are patched and potholed, and the tarmac is as deserted as an outdoor skating rink in Florida. I'm not convinced this is Borden, but there are no other airports marked on the map within a thirty-mile radius. A new windsock, with bright orange stripes as yet unbleached by sunlight and white stripes not dulled by dirt, is the only indication this airport is operational.

I broadcast my intention to land. No one responds. My concern shifts to serious doubt. Again, I wonder, *What if I'm at the wrong airport?*

On short final, as I cross the runway threshold, I combat the gusty crosswind and touch down with a thump. The tires judder on the frost-heaved tarmac as I taxi on empty parking ramps toward a ribbon of crumbling Quonset-roofed buildings, the WWI Royal Flying Corps hangars. That is, *if* this is Borden. From one of the less dilapidated buildings, a man materializes and waves outstretched arms above his head. *Is he waving hello? Or go away! What have I got myself into?*

Sandy arranged this flight test but didn't tell me anything except the examiner's name and I stupidly didn't ask. I shut down the engine and hop out. With perfect posture, the man strides toward me. Wind tosses his straight, raven-black hair onto café au lait skin.

He says, "Heard you on my radio. Kojak D'Souza. Please, call me Kojak."

We shake hands as I wonder how his Oxford English accent had coupled with a non-Saxon name. "Pleased to meet you, Kojak. Like Telly Savalas in the TV series?"

"Cor-rect."

"Wasn't he Greek?"

"My real name's Kaushik. When I arrived here from India, some laughed at my name."

I tip my head quizzically.

"But nobody explained, until Cyril. After his second flight lesson, he said, 'Let me take 'n' tell you, what kinda gul-durned, gawd-awful name you got, boy? Who names their baby boy 'cow shit'?'"

We laugh, then he asks, "Did you close your flight plan in the air with Muskoka Flight Service? If not, I can close it via telephone."

I stop laughing, mid-laugh. "I . . . I . . ."—my voice fades— "didn't file one."

He furrows his eyebrows, one upward, the other inward.

I ask, "I know civilians must file a flight plan when using a military airport, b-b-but-but isn't Borden declassified?"

Through clenched jaws, he says, "It's true that Borden is

rarely used. Mostly for Air Cadet training in the summer, but also"—he pauses for emphasis—"rifle and weapons training! You might have been shot down."

Have I failed my flight test before it starts?

I can't move or speak until he says, "Get your documents. Come inside."

Inside the antiquated structure, we face each other across a battered wooden desk, scratched with the signatures of long-dead pilots. Forty feet above, a dozen lampshades dangle from rafters. Daylight filters through dust-clouded clerestory windows and spears ribbons of brilliance through the many broken panes.

Kojak delves into my understanding of documentation and regulations. Then I decode the afternoon's anticipated sunny weather and whiz through an explanation of my flight planning calculations, except when he holds the map upside down.

I say, "You're holding the map upside down."

Orienting the map to the direction of planned flight is crucial for neophyte me. He winces at my innocent pluck, but smiles, rotates the map, and continues quizzing me. After an hour, he stops asking questions and makes notes on the test evaluation sheet hidden behind his wooden clipboard. He finishes writing, then abruptly announces, "We're done."

My body mutates into petrified wood. *What does he mean by "done"? Done as in, "You failed," or "Let's go flying"?*

He smiles. "We're done on the ground."

I start breathing.

We emerge from the antediluvian hangar, blinded by the contrast between the shadowy interior and floodlit exterior. Sun fingers shimmer around gilt-edged clouds and stretch across the wide, blue sky. Scattered wisps of cotton-puff clouds tickle the treetops, but as predicted, the high-pressure system has bulldozed the storm away.

My heart surges with joy.

Kojak quizzes me while I do the walk-around, then beams a wide smile of perfect teeth. "Let's go flying!"

I ace the takeoff, mentally pat myself on the back, and turn northeast to my planned cross-country destination. At thirty-five hundred feet, I level off and try to confirm my position by comparing ground features to my route on the map, but nothing matches. *Something is wrong—but what?* A mere five minutes into the flight, and I've messed up. A twinge of breakfast toast twists toward my throat.

"Problems?" Kojak asks, a knowing smile in his voice.

I don't want to concede defeat, but I point to the map. "This lake should be on my right but we're above it. Am I off track? Or have I misidentified the lake?"

"Did you check your heading?"

"Yes."

"Ignore your calculations. Look at the map. What approximate heading would you select?"

I bite my lip. "North."

"Cor-rect. But you wrote zero-four, which you interpreted incorrectly as 0-4-0—northeast. Always use three digits, in this case, 0-0-4—almost due north."

This is a disaster. I'm off course because I've misinterpreted my own calculations. What had convinced me I could become a pilot? A rush of heat burns my throat, then swirls into my mouth. My cheeks flame. I adjust the cool air vent onto my face. Disgusted with myself, I start to put away the map.

"What are you doing?" he asks with surprise.

"Aren't we returning to the airport?"

"Absolutely not. Pilots get off course all the time."

I roll my eyes at him. "You're kidding, right? Pilots are perfect."

He laughs a little gasp. "*Hah!* The trick is getting back on course. From this position, revise your calculation."

I don't believe other pilots get lost, but his assurance restores my confidence. I hold the control column with my left hand, maintain altitude and my current (though woefully incorrect) heading, and reattach the map to the clipboard balanced on my knee. Turbulence bumps and jostles us against each other. The fresh air vent I need to keep my cool flutters the map, making writing difficult.

Kojak says, "Don't forget to look for other aircraft."

My legs tremble, but I glance outside, then scribble a wobbly new track line on the map. I turn the aircraft to my revised heading, a shallow intersect with my original track.

After five minutes, Kojak says, "You've accomplished much. Though you made an error, which resulted in another error, you identified the problem then quickly made an accurate in-flight recalculation."

I'm glad *he's* happy with my performance.

He says, "Equally important, you didn't panic."

"My husband's temper taught me that panic escalates a situation."

He tips his head with curiosity, but I say nothing more about my personal life.

After a few moments, he asks, "Have you learned anything else?"

I laugh. "Always use three digits for heading. This experience will keep me from making that mistake on a critical flight, in bad weather."

"*Now* put away your map."

The remaining exercises seem to go well, but as I fly toward the airport for debriefing, his furious writing on my test sheet makes me question my success. Is he rehearsing the kindest way to say, "You're a total loser"?

The afternoon sun fills the cockpit, hot as a blast furnace, scorching my face. Turbulence has also increased, buffeting the aircraft like a boat in a tempest. My innards churn as if breakfast had been strychnine-laced worms. After my short field landing, he stops writing. I try to exude calm.

Inside the hangar, I accept the Fresca offered by Kojak, hoping my somersaulting stomach won't upchuck the cool liquid. He sips orange Fanta through a straw, then says, "We'll discuss your strengths, then your weaknesses. Finally, I'll make suggestions for improvement."

These are standard words used by all my instructors, but today they sound ominous. I gaze through him, subdued by my idiotic mistake with my departure heading.

I force myself to listen to his critique and absorb his suggestions, but I can't stop thinking I've failed. When he points to a reference in the *Flight Training Manual*, I pretend to look but sneak a peek at my test sheet. The vast amount of scribbling in the margins dismays me but I notice many high marks. A shard of hope spikes every fiber of my body.

Then, *Congratulations* filters into my consciousness.

"I passed? I *passed*!" I leap up and twirl with delight.

We discuss my flight to London, then I grin. "Guess I better file a flight plan."

Homeward bound in my private metal island in the sky, I replay every second of the flight test. Though I'd rather forget my mistakes, I review them carefully and realize Kojak made my flight test a learning opportunity.

I shout to the world, "I'm a pilot! *I'm a pilot!*" and marvel at the change in weather—and the change in me, a revitalized change that vibrates through every cell of my body. My success today is neither spectacular fantasy nor wishful thinking, but a direct and undeniable result of diligent studies and determined practice. Flight training wasn't easy, but it wasn't the onerous hurdle I imagined, and now I've achieved my objective, once discarded as a foolish, unattainable goal.

For the first time in years, I like myself.

As sunlight streams toward the vast expanse of the ground below, tickling the fluffy cumulus clouds and tinting their scalloped edges a golden rose, I spread my wings and soar into the blue, into my future, away from my husband. At least for a few hours.

15

PAPER TIGERS

DMZ's wheels caress London's runway like fingertips stroking satin. I use only a fraction of the eighty-eight-hundred-foot runway, scoot onto the first taxiway, then unlatch both side windows for cross ventilation. Though the breeze tickles my face, it doesn't make much difference in the humid, 80°F heat. I fan myself with a folded map and say, "London Ground, FDMZ, requesting taxi clearance to the flight school."

The controller grants permission, and I move forward, taxiing past a humungous Air Canada L-1011 parked at the terminal. A corona of sunrays splays around the control tower, almost blinding me.

The pilot says in a slow, southern drawl, "You sound great. Air Canada should hire you."

I'll never fly for *any* major air carrier because my eyes don't meet their requirements of twenty/twenty uncorrected vision, but I appreciate his encouragement. "Thank you! I passed my private pilot flight test today!"

I park C-FDMZ in the safe custody of the flying school, and when I step outside, I feel reborn, as if I'm emerging from a metal chrysalis as a butterfly ready to spread her wings. I relax on one of the school's picnic tables and evaluate the personal growth I've experienced since my first flight lesson in March—only fifteen weeks ago—and compare this to my everyday existence, bored with the bank and unhappily married.

My new skills and today's success have revived the confidence I had before Paul began to domin—*I stop myself mid-thought*—before I *allowed* him to dominate and control me, and let his criticisms chisel away, chip by chip, everything that doesn't conform to his idea of me.

And everything that has been my essence.

When our two-tone-blue Pacer speeds into the parking lot twenty minutes later, I wave excitedly. Paul creates a cloud of dust with a sweeping U-turn and stops beside the picnic table. I hop in with a giant smile vanquished by his first words. "Traffic was terrible."

The heavy weight of anxiety crushes my chest, but I manage, "Thanks for meeting me."

He begins the fifty-mile drive.

I swallow hard, annoyed he doesn't ask about my flight test. I simmer silently.

After a few moments, he says, "I *suppose* you passed."

"Yes! The examiner was fantastic and the—"

Instead of congratulating me, he says, "I can't wait to finish *my* flight training."

His resentment seeps through our car like fog on a winter's morn, but I don't want anything to ruin this day. I try to be upbeat and say, "On our new plane! Let's get it Saturday," then hate myself for stifling my anger to avoid escalating his bad mood.

He clutches the gearshift. "I *want* to get it tomorrow."

"I work until four thirty, and it'd be seven before I'm airborne. On Saturday, I'll have eight hours of daylight."

"Let's get it tomorrow," he states firmly. Animosity seeps into the car.

"I'll call Murray tomorrow, tell him my news, and ask his opinion."

"*I said*—let's get it tomorrow."

I point my thumbs toward my chest. "A fifty-hour wonder like me shouldn't be starting a cross-country flight near sunset."

Paul doesn't respond. My thoughts return to our festering problems. On vacation, he seemed to be the man I fell in love with. But the bad behavior I thought *might* resume when we got home, back to reality, thirty minutes from now, has started already.

I want to discuss my concerns but refuse to destroy this sublime day with words sure to provoke a fight. I realize the wrong heading I selected in error for the cross-country portion of my flight test is a metaphor for my life. Just as I identified and corrected the heading in the aircraft, I need to stop deluding myself, accept the problems in my life, find a solution, and get back on track.

The next morning as I drive to work, I rehearse the most dramatic way to tell Murray my great news. Should I hint I passed my flight test? Should I mention we bought an airplane? Obligations to colleagues and bank clients force me to forget these questions until twenty minutes before lunchtime when I find a few moments for a personal call. My hands tremble with excitement as I punch the numbers for the flight school.

"Murray, this is Lola—"

"Congratulations! We're thrilled for you."

Murray's words kick like a steel-toed boot in the belly. My exuberance deflates and a canker of discontent worms into the cavity. Had Sandy, the CFI who recommended me for the test, contacted Murray regarding other aviation-related business? Worldwide, the aviation community has few members. Though I'm a newcomer, I've learned that, within it, words have wings. "Wh-what do you mean?"

"Paul called first thing this morning to tell us you passed your flight test yesterday."

I gasp, enraged. As Agatha Christie's detectives teach, I should've looked no further than the obvious suspects. "Murray, I'm calling to tell you we bought a—"

He says, "Cessna 150. Paul raved about your flight to London."

My elation crashes like Zeppelin's dirigible, the *Hindenburg*. Murray, a gentle soul who treats others with kindness and respect, cannot realize that his few words have destroyed any remaining respect I have for Paul and will change my life.

During the twenty-minute drive home, I keep asking, *Why did Paul hijack my moment of glory, a triumph only a few men—and fewer women—achieve?* But, I know why. We're products of a culture raised to believe men are entitled by birth to enforce legitimate and coercive power over women. I try to distract myself with *Today in History*, but the radio announcer's words resonate as direct messages.

When he says, "On July 2, 1885, Canada's Northwest Insurrection ends when Cree Chief Big Bear surrenders," I slap both palms against the steering wheel and realize I'm done surrendering, and then, "In 1937, woman pilot Amelia Earhart and her navigator Fred Noonan disappear somewhere in the Pacific Ocean."

Maybe Paul will disappear into the ocean.

I park behind his car and enter the wide front hall of our home, hoping my decision to adopt Amelia Earhart's advice, "The most difficult thing is the decision to act," will save my life—not end it. My throat seizes as I open the double doors separating the entryway, with its curving oak staircase, from our formal living room. Brandon cuddles against his father in the middle of our pearl-white velvet couch, giggling as Paul reads a storybook.

I cover my eyes with open fingers and whisper, "Peekaboo, where are you?"

Brandon *tee-hees* as he scrambles off the couch and toddles toward me, clutching the book. I kneel and swallow him into my arms. He snuggles against me, and I kiss his rosy cheek. "How's my little sweetheart?"

"I wove you, Mommy."

With his pudgy three-year-old fingers, he opens the book and points to a sweet-faced bear flying an open cockpit plane above bucolic English countryside. "Mommy, wook at my new book!"

Paul kisses my cheek, tousles Brandon's hair, and says, "I loved it when Mom read Rupert Bear adventure books to me."

Brandon squeals. "Wook, Wupert flies wike you and Daddy!"

Paul breaks in. "Babe, how was your first day back at work?"

There had been a time I craved my husband's affectionate greeting and the feel of his muscular hands touching my skin. But today, I smile, then crunch my lips into a sealed pucker to avoid saying something I'll regret in Brandon's presence.

Throughout dinner, my heart punches against my chest. I choke food down my throat into a stomach filled with squirming worms searching for an exit door. I need to start talking, soon, before my courage evaporates, but not before we tuck Brandon into bed. I've rehearsed what I must say to Paul, words to tell him I'm leaving, words to express my feelings without fragmenting his fragile soul, but anything I say will provoke another battle.

After eight, when our reading with Brandon is done, Paul stretches out on our living room couch, drapes his long legs over one arm of the couch, and opens his tattered copy of *The Lord of the Rings*. I light several candles and sing a few lines of "Four Strong Winds," a melancholy Canadian song about the end of love, but Paul seems oblivious. I curl sideways into a wingchair, pick up Ayn Rand's *Atlas Shrugged*. I admire Rand's heroine, Dagny Taggart, for her rational determination and her conviction that gender does not influence intellect. I want to be as brave as Dagny. I peel strips of skin from my lower lip, stopping when I taste blood. I rearrange the toss pillows.

I've passed the point of no return and am almost hyperventilating as I barrel toward terra incognita, identified on ancient maps with, "Beyond here, there be dragons." The pounding of my heart keeps time with the hum of the universe. I must start talking now before I lose my courage. "I appreciate you taking care of Brandon and letting me fly during our holidays."

"Ummmm." From experience, I know this barely audible response means he isn't listening and doesn't want to.

"Paul!"

He slaps the book onto his stomach.

"We need to talk." I scavenge for my best I'm-not-scared voice and confess, "Some part of me will always love you . . . but . . ."

He looks at me, poker-faced.

"We're not good for each other anymore."

He slams his book onto the floor. "What's bugging you now?"

Tears fill my eyes and transform the shimmering candles on the sideboard into yellow-eyed ghosts. "My day at work could've been orchestrated by Beelzebub himself, so it may as well end that way."

He picks up his book and resumes reading. "Don't blame your bad day on me."

"What do you suppose Murray said when I called him?"

Paul inhales his cigarette, then coughs. "How the fuck would I know?"

"He said, 'Congratulations! We're so proud of you.'"

Paul leaps from the couch and rushes across the room toward me. There's no escape, but instead of flinching, I plant my feet on the floor, square my shoulders, and tighten every muscle. I must be courageous, to show him he can't control me. He stops inches from my chair and towers above with a menacing swagger intended to coerce my compliance and persuade me I'm the one with faulty logic. His eyes flash with malice, but instead of bending to his opinion as I've done in the past, I clench my jaw and hold his gaze.

"Murray said you called precisely when the school opened at eight. When I was in the shower."

He stands, arms akimbo on his hips, brawny hands swelling with strain.

I tighten my fists. "You didn't give *me* a chance to tell *my* news."

He grips the armrests and shoves his face so close our noses almost touch. Smoke from his cigarette swirls into my face.

"You *knew* I wanted to tell our instructors I passed *my* flight test."

"I was just asking about hangar space for our plane."

His smirking smile reminds me of the evil Br'er Fox. I shudder with fear but realize I cannot back down. "You stole my moment of triumph!"

He spins away, returns to the couch, and resumes reading. I've had five years to master the art of predicting his reactions. Sometimes he retreats into the bottle and ignores my concerns; sometimes he belittles or threatens. Tonight's return to the couch suggests a new approach.

I won't be brushed off. "I'm tired of you"—his livid face whirls toward me—"blaming me for your anger and your bad behavior."

"Your glass is half empty."

Paul's temper frightens me, and though his threats of violence rarely materialize, I should have stood up to his bullying rage the first time he used anger to control me. But when I didn't, I enabled him to make a false image of me to love, and whenever I rejected his restrictive framework, he used temper tantrums to pound me into a submissive woman like his mother.

Living with his rages has made me stronger and strengthened my resolve to leave him and stop the cycle of generational, learned violence. I exhale, despondent but resolute. "I'm moving to an apartment near my office."

He says, "You're not taking Brandon."

"I'm entitled to have sole custody, but I want joint custody."

"You'll never make it on your own."

I sense a subtle threat beneath his taunt. Life alone will be challenging but better than living with a human incendiary bomb. In the strongest voice I've used in years, I declare, "Yes, I will," and shred my fears, my paper tigers.

16

ESCAPE:
THE HOMEWRECKER

I wake alone. When I come downstairs, Paul's cooking scrambled eggs for the three of us. He says, "I thought I should sleep on the couch."

After breakfast, we sit on the front porch and watch Brandon ride his tricycle. Paul says, "For Brandon's sake, please stay here until your apartment is ready." I smile but later arrange to stay with a friend, if necessary.

Later that day, Paul arranges an appointment with our lawyer, Phil, owner of a small-town, one-stop shop for legal matters and our go-to for all things legal. Phil agrees to see us next Monday.

When we arrive the following week, Phil's head jerks backward in obvious surprise.

Paul asks, "Did I get our appointment time wrong?"

Phil rubs the half-inch stubble on his chin with thumb and forefinger. "I never imagined you'd come together."

"Doesn't an agreement need both of us here?"

Phil steeples his fingers. "Lawyers don't usually represent both litigants. However, I'll represent both of you unless you start bickering, then I can't represent either of you."

We agree, then Phil examines our handwritten suggestions.

"Your financial proposal is excellent, but we need to discuss custody."

Paul says, "We've agreed to joint custody, but for the first while he'll stay with me during the week—"

"And with me on weekends."

Paul smiles. "Brandon's life will be less topsy-turvy if we don't change his routine too much."

I say, "He'll continue at his regular day care."

Phil makes a check mark on our handwritten agreement. "You forgot alimony."

"I don't want alimony."

Phil clasps his hands together on his desk. "In my experience, all women want alimony."

"I want independence."

I dither about packing, certain such definitive action will provoke Paul, but collect my courage and start with personal items. Instead of angry threats, he says, "You can have all the furniture and dishes your grandparents gave you but *nothing* else."

"That's not fair, but it won't stop me from leaving. In fact, I agree. If I leave most of our furniture, the house will look almost the same, and I don't want to disrupt Brandon's life any more than necessary."

For the next two weeks, Paul's almost the man I married. He's home earlier and helps with chores around the house without being asked. We eat breakfast and dinner together, tell some friends we're separating, and sleep in the same bed. A casual observer noting we rarely speak to each other and never touch would identify us as a long-married couple, focused on our son, and very familiar (or bored) with each other. His interactions with Brandon are unchanged; he remains involved and attentive, kind and loving.

I'm a little surprised he doesn't woo me with chocolates, roses, and empty promises until he says, "Since I started this job, before you moved here, I knew something was wrong."

"Oh?"

"You didn't want another baby. You didn't even want sex."

"Why didn't you complain?"

"I was afraid to lose what I had."

"So, you were relieved when I spoke up?" Tears form in his eyes. "I'm not the wife you want—and I don't want to become the wife you want."

"I don't know why I tried to control you."

I say, "Nobody likes being forced to be something they're not meant to be."

He hugs me. "I understand. My dad wanted me to be something I'm not."

Our last few days together-but-separate gives us time to adjust to our impending separation and let Brandon know we don't love each other, but our love for him hasn't changed. We enjoy some quality time together, as friends, and debate logistics about finances and childcare. Twice we lapse into a familiar pattern of arguing but stop ourselves before the argument escalates.

We're getting along so well as friends, we decide my seventeen-year-old sister should visit as planned for two weeks of school summer holidays, even though her visit will bracket my moving day. Though Paul's moods fluctuate between agitation and acceptance of our impending separation, he's on his best behavior during her visit. Lynn and Paul always enjoy each other's company, and her presence calms him.

On moving day as I pack my clothing, he lounges on our bed, his torso supported by the antique wooden headboard, swilling his second Labatt Blue. My shoulder blades clamp together. "You promised you wouldn't drink until after Brandon went to bed."

He says, "He *is* in bed."

I say, "It's noon. He's playing with Lynn, not sleeping."

He guffaws wickedly. "I've changed my mind about letting you take any furniture."

I shrug. "Furniture is stuff."

"Where will you sit?"

I glare into wild eyes that indicate our cease-fire is over. "Freedom is more important than furniture."

He taps an index finger against his beer bottle and sneers, "You're not a virgin. You're damaged goods. No guy will want you."

"Your bizarre ideas remind me of my father. What happened to the bohemian I married five years ago?"

"I grew up. You should try it." Suddenly, he whips his left leg across the bed and shovels my blouses onto the floor. I fold them again and fill a second suitcase. He crosses the room, flops into one of our matching tub chairs, and swigs his beer. "A woman needs a man."

"No woman needs a man who threatens her."

He studies me like a wildcat observing prey. "You had an affair."

I squeeze my eyes shut to block the tears. "I'm truly sorry. He was a friend when I needed one. I shouldn't have let him become anything more."

"You're dating, aren't you?"

"No, I'm not, but"—I straighten my back and hold my head high—"I'd rather be celibate forever than live another minute with you."

Gripping a suitcase in each hand, I turn toward the door, then hesitate, suddenly aware his position in the chair blocks my pathway. Our eyes meet and he cackles like the Wicked Witch of the West, then propels the beer bottle toward me. Instinctively, I duck and drop both suitcases. Behind me, the bottle explodes against the wall.

Paul dashes toward me, his face deformed by rage. He pauses a few feet from me, then swings the flat of his foot against my abdomen. I crumple to the floor and cower, arms cradling my abdomen, a howling hunchback contorted with pain.

The clash of broken glass alerts my sister. She dashes into our room, then kneels beside me. Her gaping mouth and wide eyes tell me Paul has toppled from his pedestal of perfection I helped her create by shielding her from his bullying.

He glowers. "Get out."

Lynn helps me stand and hobble into the hallway. Paul tosses my suitcases onto the hallway floor, then shuts the bedroom door with a thud.

Lynn asks, "Should we call the police?"

I shake my head. "He's just angry I'm leaving. Let's spend some time with Brandon while Paul calms down."

She doesn't look convinced but after we read with Brandon for twenty minutes or so, Paul joins us. He says, "I'm a jerk. Go get settled."

I hope his fierce dropkick will be his final comment about my departure.

Three or four weeks later, on a Friday in mid-August, I drive to my former home to pick up Brandon for a scheduled weekend at my apartment.

Feelings of impending doom niggle in my primordial brain. Paul hasn't answered my phone calls during the past week, and I worry he might be playing power-and-control games regarding my visitation with Brandon. I'm relieved to see his Chevy Caprice in the driveway of my former home. Tears gloss in my eyes as I realize this house is full of life and memories, more welcoming than my sterile beige apartment.

I knock on the hand-carved, double doors, knock again, harder, then try the handle. The door, unlocked as usual, sways open. I query, "Hello?" and stroll into an empty hallway, peek into our vacant living room, and enter the dining room. Golden fingers of a late afternoon sun lance through slatted blinds of the bay window, striping the love seat. Part of me expects Paul to be relaxing here, at the end of the work week, reading to Brandon, but nothing prepares me for the sight of Paul, sprawled, boozed-up, face down, on the floor. His navy pants and white shirt, rumpled and soiled from his day inspecting farm animals, contrast with our Persian carpet. A spent beer bottle lolls on the gleaming oak flooring, a few feet from his splayed arms. Two unopened beer bottles stand nearby, ladies-in-waiting, ready to please.

Paul drifts into semi-consciousness and grunts garbled words. My head fills with the shrill scream of sirens warning, *Danger-danger-danger.* My legs buckle. *Where's Brandon?* I race upstairs, relieved that Brandon's playing on his bedroom floor, surrounded by a carpet of Lego blocks and his work in progress, a Lego dump truck.

He drives a Tonka trunk over my toes. "Hi, Mommy."

I want to grab him and run but decide Paul is too drunk to move fast, if at all. I hope Brandon hasn't seen his father on the floor. We play smash-up derby, Brandon steering his new Lego creation to destroy my metal Tonka truck, until he asks for supper. I intended to treat him to dinner at a restaurant near my apartment but instead prepare a quick meal with food from Paul's fridge.

I carry him downstairs and put him into his booster chair at the dining table. In the kitchen, I slice carrots and leftover roast chicken into fingers, add celery, tomato wedges, and cheddar cheese, then prepare a similar cold plate for Paul. Though I don't want to encourage him or relapse into a caretaker role, he's still my husband, a good man who lost his way. He doesn't drink to torment me—he drinks to kill his pain. He'll be happier if he awakens to the sound of voices rather than the echoes of an empty house and a brief note of explanation.

For Brandon's dessert, I select a Macintosh apple, putting it on the table with a paring knife. As I serve supper, Paul moans and lifts his head, posturing like a bearskin rug. With ham-fists braced against the floor, he flops onto his back. He tries to stand but teeters and tilts like a human Tower of Pisa. Finally, he props one hand against the wall and uses the arm of our love seat as a crutch. He totters toward me, struggling for balance.

"You're pathetic," I say, my voice filled with disgust.

He mashes his face into mine. His droopy eyelids are rimmed rose pink by the flush of alcohol-fueled blood. "Ya don' live here anymore. Git out."

Fuck everything and run flashes like neon through my brain. He's drunk but bigger, stronger, and very angry.

I sidle toward Brandon, but Paul says, "Doncha think a takin' my son."

Paul staggers toward me, zigzagging left, then right, gyrations so wild that he seems like an actor playing a part.

I dart toward Brandon. Paul's strong hands grip my shoulders and twirl me to face him. He glowers with glacier-blue eyes, steps one foot back, then whips a savage backhand. His heavy gold and diamond ring whishes past my eyes. I feel searing pain as the ring's square corner rips my right cheek. The force of his swing spins him to the left. He wobbles, then slumps to his knees, a boxer going down while I careen backward. My head smacks against the wall, then I thud onto the floor. I curl into a fetal form and play dead. Rivulets of blood tickle my cheek.

Paul pries me open, forces me flat against the floor, and straddles me.

Brandon screams, "Mommy!" I turn my head, heartbroken to see his horrified face.

Paul pauses to glare through slit eyes, then his rock-hard fists take turns hammering my face. Every second or third smack, he pauses, wraps his left hand around my throat, and guzzles another gulp of beer. When I squirm, he tightens his grip. "Don't move, you bitch. You deserve this." Drool burbles from his taut lips onto my face, and the bitter taste of beer mixes with the tinny taste of my blood.

"Daddy! *Stop!* Please don't hurt Mommy!"

My face numbs from the agonizing blows. Time slides into a void, and I lose any sense of myself. I see myself floating in a Zen emptiness above the scene, disembodied, a passive bystander, a lost soul, seconds away from being transported to another dimension. My heart aches for the toddler standing on the dining room chair, a marble garden statue, immobilized by the horror. He wants to help the woman, but his little legs are too short to climb down from the chair.

After a few more wallops with each fist making its mark, this round ends, and the man flips off the woman. He rolls onto his back, then turns toward her and whispers, "I love you so much." His right arm flops across her motionless body. "If you'd been here where you belong, lookin' after me, I wouldna hurt ya."

I want to change the channel and stop watching this terrifying B-movie, but I can't. I'm paralyzed, unable to touch her, unable to help. *Why does he think violence will change her mind? Why does he blame his behavior on her?*

I hear the little boy scream. "Daddy! Stop! Please don't hurt Mommy!"

The man's hand grasps her breast and hot lips nuzzle her cheek. "If ya stay, I promise I won't hurt ya again."

The woman doesn't move. *Is she dead?*

Within seconds, the man lapses into unconsciousness.

I slip back into myself and feel Paul's warmth settle against my body, swathing me in a repulsive embrace, his arm a dead-weight across my chest. I gag on his aroma, a fermented blend of cigarettes and beer, and on his words.

Brandon's eyes rivet on us. I blow him a kiss but linger beside

Paul for several minutes, petrified to move. I shift slightly, to see if Paul reacts, then begin to writhe away, inch by inch. Pain ricochets through my body with each squirm. I move my feet first, then my buttocks, shoulders, and finally my head, and repeat this slithery rhythm three or four times, locking my eyes on Paul. In the lull between each wriggle, seconds hang and become hours.

Reassured his stupor is genuine, I free myself from the leaden burden of his arm and fold it across his torso. I tiptoe toward Brandon, pausing after each step. I hold my forefinger against my lips.

"*SSSssshhhhh.*" I scoop him into my arms. We clutch each other, with love and dread. I feel his tiny body tremble in my arms. I seize my purse from the antique oak sideboard and slink along the murky hallway toward the foyer. Blood throbs through my aching head and hammers against my temples.

The ancient metal door chirps as we step toward freedom. I exhale, exultant.

A tug on my hair jerks me backward. Spikes of pain pierce my scalp. I hear the hiss of Paul's voice. "Where the fuck duh ya think you're going?"

Paul must have dashed from the dining room, through the living room, to the hallway. I say, "You told me to leave. We're going to my apartment."

His clenched fist flies toward my face. I leap backward, then freeze. He's snatched the four-inch blade of the paring knife I'd put on the table to cut Brandon's apple.

Paul waves the blade inches from my face and laughs, a sickening chortle that prickles my flesh. "Still wanna leave? You try 'n' I'm gonna slice your beautiful face."

How could he have gone from flat-out cold to clearheaded mobile in ten seconds? When he'd straddled me on the floor and pummeled my face, I experienced an ethereal distancing. Now, faced with the sharp point of a cold steel knife, I'm in this world and his cunning terrifies me. I shuffle backward, enough to distance me, but not enough to suggest I'll bolt for the door. I grip Brandon closer to my chest and rummage my aching head for a solution. Brandon clamps his arms and legs around my torso and buries his face in my shoulder.

Paul twirls the knife. "Your boyfriend won't want ya all sliced up."

"I *don't* have a boyfriend."

He points the knife nearer to my face. "Prove it."

"Put down the knife."

He does and I feel slightly less terrified. The worst is over, for tonight, and hopefully forever.

I ask, "Shall I get Brandon ready for bed?"

He nods.

I hope my small measure of compliance will soothe him until he regains sobriety and sense. Since Brandon was a few months old, Paul's been controlling me with threats of what might happen if I left him, but he's never attacked.

Experience has taught me that when Paul's temper clouds our day like lightning in a fast-moving cold front, attempts to pacify him stoke his fury, but if we remain calm, his tempest fizzles.

As we retreat to Brandon's bedroom, I wonder how Paul could get so drunk in the hour since his workday ended. *What if he isn't as drunk as he appears?* I remember seeing only one empty bottle. *Are his actions a deliberate ploy to convince me I need to come home?*

Brandon picks a favorite book for me to read aloud, then we burrow together in his bed, snug within the safety of his coverlet, and soar North African skies with Saint-Exupery. I gaze at my son, an innocent, thrust without choice into his parents' battle. As he enters dreamland, I hope he'll imagine sand, stars, and great adventures and forget the odious dance his once-madly-in-love parents performed.

Paul needs counseling. Maybe we both do. During our four years of marriage, his two backhands against my face represent the only acts of physical violence. But those two incidents, coupled with threats of physical violence, kept me from leaving sooner. I've always known his threats had an endgame.

After a few minutes, Paul stumbles into the room, a beer bottle in one hand, and a glint of metal in the other. "I warned you not to leave me." His eyes radiate a toxic mix of lust and hatred. He says, "Sweetheart, if you promise to stay, I promise never to hit you again."

Staying with him is the last thing I plan to do, but saying that now would be suicide. I shiver. "I promise."

I drowse, my mind a whirlwind of worries, my head pounding in agony. How can I get out of this mess? Though tonight's attack was vicious, his angry outbursts have steadily increased during the past year. *What if he'd attacked me with the knife?* Would a few scarring slices have satisfied his thirst, or would his hysteria have skyrocketed? Would he have stabbed me? I never want Brandon to witness his father's violence again.

I revisit a conversation with my sister, who'd said, "You're strong but even strong women need time to heal." I fall asleep, mulling her comment, "Paul has damaged you in ways neither of us can imagine." She's only seventeen and her only experience with relationships is observing our parents' marriage and divorce, but she understands better than me that I've checked my battered baggage into a locked compartment of my brain.

Several hours of restless sleep later, I wake up, shift, and wiggle, and try not to disturb Brandon as I contemplate my best strategy.

If I stay tonight, and we impersonate a happy family enjoying Saturday morning, Paul will interpret my presence as weakness. My inertia will be his victory. Our marriage was a dreamer's mistake, but staying won't correct that mistake; staying will be another mistake. I need to leave, to be away from Paul, and most importantly, away from the spineless creature I'll become if I stay.

If I leave Brandon, he'll be a comfort to his father, who loves children. As a teen, he'd been camp counselor, babysat neighborhood children, and gone beyond setting an older brother example to his two younger brothers by defending them against their father's sarcasm and physical threats.

If I take Brandon, Paul will be wild with fury. At best, he'll interpret this as a deliberate attempt to contravene our joint custody agreement; at worst, he might convince a judge I've kidnapped Brandon and then *I'll lose all custody.*

Though my decision to leave is the best for everyone, I created my personal perdition by jumping into marriage and then by deluding myself I could help him, even though he wasn't ready to be helped. I hope Dante was right when he wrote, "The path to paradise begins in hell."

I need to take control of my life. Helen Reddy's song "I Am Woman" roars in my ears. From now on, no one's going to keep me down or stop me from living my life the way I want to live it.

I kiss Brandon and snuggle him between the three-foot-tall Raggedy Ann and Andy dolls I crocheted for him. I step over Paul sprawled on the floor, creep downstairs, grab my purse, and search for car keys as I dash toward my car. *Where* are *those keys?* I dig deeper, sifting through the contents. I can't breathe. My heart pounds. I dump everything onto the hood and fumble with each item twice, finally accepting Paul swiped my keys and sabotaged my freedom.

Not knowing where to go or what to do, but propelled by fear, I run as fast as someone not built for running runs. I sprint, surging with adrenaline, past the tidy lawns and nineteenth-century houses bracketing our street.

Past Broadway. As I pass the house of a friend, I consider knocking on her door, but then remember her cruel words last month when she said, "Go away! Please! My husband said I can't see you anymore." When I asked why, she said, "He's afraid you'll persuade me to leave him," then slammed the door in my face, shutting herself inside her own personal hell.

Past Church. Pain pierces my temples with every slap of my feet against the pavement. I must get to my apartment, in another town, thirty kilometers away, but I can't run even a fraction of that distance. Bus service is nonexistent in this town, and taxi service ends at two when the bars close. I need help but I can't knock on the doors of strangers in the middle of the night. I need my car—and my keys. Maybe I can find a phone booth and call a friend in Chatham.

Two conical shafts of light swoop around the corner, piercing the oppressive gloom. I dash behind a manicured hedge and crouch. My left calf muscle cramps but I dare not move. Cicadas shriek like air raid sirens, blotting out all other sounds. The vehicle approaches, in slow time. Not my husband but a Holstein, slang in this agricultural community for a police car.

I hurtle from the bushes, energized by the knowledge they can help. I wave my arms above my head and bring the car to a screeching stop. The shotgun window rolls down. The interior light flicks on.

Gawking with raised brows, two goggle-eyed officers scrutinize me. The younger cop in the passenger seat asks, "What the hell happened to you?"

I wince. Escape had been my goal, but now I realize my appearance is well below any standard of female beauty. The black mascara that stings my eyes and drips down my cheeks is the least of my concerns. I suppose my face is bloody and distorted. I glance at my clothing. A ripped sleeve of beige silk droops from my left shoulder. Blood splats have converted my blouse into a nascent Jackson Pollock canvas.

"I don't always look like this. I left my husband last month but returned home tonight to get our son for a custodial visit. My husband was drunk. He swiped my keys. Please, help me!"

The junior officer asks, "Ma'am, is he at home?"

"Yes, passed out on the floor."

Junior looks into my eyes and smiles a sad smile. "We'd like to help but—"

The driver, tubby from sitting in a squad car, says, "The law considers the home to be the man's property."

"I legally own half the house."

Junior says, "We're sorry but—"

"That's ridiculous! I own the house as much as my husband does but can't invite you inside unless he gives permission?"

Tubby says, "Revision to this old law is expected in a few months, early next year."

I force my mouth into a wry smile. "I can't wait until 1980."

They nod.

I think quickly. "Would you consider standing on the front veranda, near the threshold? You won't have to come inside, but I'll leave the double doors open so you'll be able to hear me. If he tries anything, I'll scream, 'Officer!' He won't try anything if he realizes you're nearby."

The cops swap glances.

Junior's smile transforms his face into a beacon of help. "Hop in."

Tubby unlocks the rear door, the prisoner door. I leap inside.

I tiptoe upstairs to Brandon's room and return to a scene frozen in time. Brandon is sleeping, breathing gently, still snuggled by Raggedy Ann and Andy. Paul snores, face-planted on the carpet, each breath rumbling like a misfiring cylinder. I mince around his prone body, hoping to see my keys on the dresser or near him on the floor. I stand above him, feet straddling his torso, and fold forward. My heart is pumping, and a wave of pain floods my forehead, but I don't care. I twist until I see the silver tips of my keys poking from his front pants pocket.

He moans, suffering in his own way, then settles. With thumb and forefinger, I pinch the keys and tug. His body jerks. I clasp the coveted keys in my fist the same moment he rolls over and hooks my wrist with an iron grip.

I shriek, "Officers!"

Paul's eyes flash disbelief until he hears the male voices. He releases me and springs upright, galvanized by their presence. His drunkenness vaporizes, again.

The veranda beacon illuminates the officers' upturned faces. They stand, shoulder touching shoulder, a sturdy wall of navy blue, dominated by Tubby the Tank. Paul greets them with pleasantries, as if we're strolling through High Park on a spring day. Paul's deceit repulses me, but I seize his attempt to present a good face as my opportunity to escape.

I step onto the top stair but he grapple-hooks my arm. I wince and try to twist from his grip. "Don't touch me."

Tubby beckons with his hand. "Ma'am, come on down."

"She wants to fly off and be a pilot."

"You may not agree with your wife, but that doesn't allow you to mistreat her."

Paul says, "She's seeing another man."

Do the officers hear the indignant whine in his voice?

Tubby says, "Sir, your wife told us you were separated officially. Is that true?"

"She deserted our son and me."

"I did not. We share joint custody."

Tubby the Tank puts his hands on his broad hips. "Let her go."

I scramble to the bottom of the stairs, scurry between the officers, who step aside, and run to my car. Fast-moving footsteps thunder on the wooden veranda, and I whirl to see the officers blocking Paul, who lunges forward, trying to get to me. I'm lucky I encountered sympathetic officers.

Paul shakes clenched fists in the air. "She's my wife. She's mine. She asked for it."

Junior says, "Nobody *asks* to be abused."

Paul tries to sidestep them but Tubby puts both palms flat against Paul's chest. "*Stop* right there. Do *not* move closer to your wife's car."

My hands quaver as I unlock the door. I jump in, lock the door, and stab the ignition with the key, two, three times before it slips into place. The engine catches and the radio explodes with Phil Collins singing about true love. I snap the radio off, but Phil's next words about safety and security play in my head.

Junior walks to my side of the car. I roll down the window and he asks, "Do you want to press charges?"

I hesitate. "Can't *you* arrest him?"

"If we witness domestic violence, we can make an arrest."

"Look at me. Obviously, he attacked me."

"We can't be sure your husband is the attacker."

"So it's *my* word against *his*? I thought you were on my side!"

Junior touches my arm. "Based on what we saw and heard, I believe you, but we can arrest him only if *you* press charges. If you don't, all we can do is keep him overnight."

"Do I need to decide now?"

"I wish you would."

But I don't.

All three watch me back out the drive away. My heartbeat pounds against my temples, and my body vibrates until I pass the town limits. During the drive, I mull my decisions. Guilt soon overwhelms logic. America might be embracing the Second Wave of Feminism but in this small-town wedge of Ontario, few doubt that a woman's status as wife and mother determines her worth. Our family is demolished, and some friends (some friends!) and relatives will blame me. For leaving my husband. For leaving our son.

I force myself to be logical. Paul is a devoted and gentle father who understands children better than me. As a husband, he's a mercurial bully who learned from his father that husbands have the right to control their wives. If I return, his belligerence will intensify and result in murder, possibly witnessed by Brandon, possibly excused by the legal system as a crime of passion.

Never again will I expose our son to the trauma he witnessed tonight. Though guilt electrifies every nerve in my body, my decision to leave is best, for all of us.

I'd rather be guilty and alive, able to mother my son, than dutiful and dead.

17

THE END

I slink into my seventh-floor apartment sometime between darkness and dawn, shattered and suffering. Two rectangles of slatted moonlight pattern my living room floor like a scene from a Raymond Chandler noir thriller. Paul had used only my head as a punching bag, but my entire body feels as if I've been mauled by wolves.

I seize the pitcher of skim milk from the fridge, gulp a full glass in one swallow, then traipse down the hall to the bathroom. I grope for the light switch, squinting when the light pricks my eyes like porcupine quills, then gasp at my reflection in the mirror. Caked blood streaks my distorted purple face. I bare my teeth. They're all there, and they're intact. I turn on the shower, brush my teeth, throw my blouse into the garbage, and drop the rest of my clothing into the wicker laundry basket.

When steam roils inside the room, I open the shower curtain a few inches and slip into my makeshift sauna. I face the showerhead, brace both arms against the wall, close my eyes, and tilt my face upward. For several minutes, I luxuriate in the enveloping cascade of soothing heat, then peek through wet lashes. Narrow streamers of my blood mix with water, then swirl like a peppermint pinwheel down the drain into oblivion.

I wish I could eliminate the memory of tonight as easily.

I slip on my turquoise silk kimono and call the hospital emergency department. "My husband assaulted me. Nothing is broken, but my face is swollen. Please, will you tell me how to minimize swelling and bruising?" Instead of censure or demanding my presence at the hospital, the nurse provides advice. Her understanding fills me with gratitude, and I feel less alone in the world.

Hours later, as pale strips of daylight wiggle between the blinds, the raucous jangle of a ringing telephone drills into my skull. I'm in bed, exhausted and sore, on my back, in the corpse position, forehead and eyes covered with an icy, moist compress, as instructed by the night nurse. Throughout the night, pain had jerked me awake every two hours.

The ringing stops. The clock says eight. I slip out of bed for more Tylenol, then ease my body back into bed. The ringing begins, again, an assault to my ears like a dagger stabbing my eyes. I consider ripping the telephone cord from the wall, try to ignore it, give up, get up, go to the dining room, pick up the receiver, and hear the distinctive sound of someone inhaling a cigarette, then coughing. But the caller doesn't speak.

I'm just about to hang up when I hear, "Sorry about last night."

I'm sore, angry, exhausted, and unwilling to accept his apology. Voices from his television natter in the background. Blood pulses against my temples, each thump like pounding fists on a locked door.

He says, "Shouldn't have hit you."

"Let me talk with Brandon."

Seconds later, my son's cheery voice fills my heart with joy. "Are you coming to the beach with Daddy and me?"

"Sweetheart, Mommy has a headache. You two have a great time. I love you."

Brandon giggles. "Daddy's tickling me. I wuv you, too."

Paul returns. "Will you forgive me?" He hacks a heavy smoker's cough. "Please."

I hate him. "I believe your apology is sincere—"

"That's a relief."

"But there's no excuse for your behavior. I'm not coming back."

I slam my poppy-red Contempra phone receiver against its cradle. I want to charge Paul with assault but am equally aware that an official charge won't likely result in conviction but will refuel his rage. I want to be friends with the father of my only child—not enemies—and I have to admit that, without his support and encouragement during my flight training, I might never have followed my dream and set my soul on fire.

With sudden clarity, I realize our five-year relationship, launched during the carefree summer of 1974 when I was nineteen, will become a real-life, long-term stay at Hotel California. I can check out of marriage anytime, but the memories will never leave.

I spend the next thirty-six hours in bed or reclining on the couch, reading and exchanging one hot compress for the next. The heat treatment recommended by the emergency room nurse works miracles. The deep purple I expected to see in the mirror for several days has transformed from thundercloud blue to a freakish jaundice yellow within forty-eight hours. My head aches constantly with a dull pain until I open my mouth, touch my face, or move, and then, the pervasive ache transforms to piercing pain.

On Tuesday night as I prepare Cobb salad, the ringing phone interrupts my thoughts. My body tenses with frustration when I hear the forced gaiety in Paul's voice. "Hope you're feeling better. When're you going back to work?"

"Yesterday."

His angry retort deafens me. "Are you *crazy*?"

I laugh. "Not anymore."

"Did your face actually look *normal*?"

"Only if you consider the colors of rotting peaches normal."

"What about the swelling?"

"I had chipmunk cheeks."

"You should *not* have gone to work." He inhales, then huffs, "Did anyone notice?"

"Probably everyone! But only one woman dared ask."

"What'd you say?"

"The truth. You beat me up."

"What if my friends—or my boss—find out? This isn't a big city."

"Maybe you'll behave better to your next wife."

Calling in sick would have been easy—the coward's escape. I want people to know the root cause of our separation is alcohol and anger, in a society that excuses inexcusable violence by men against women. If women continue to accept this behavior and hide our shame behind closed doors, we'll always be chattel. Many will attribute Paul's behavior to some unspecified failure of mine as a wife. Only two years ago, in 1977, some of my parents' friends blamed a female friend for her husband's affair. I learn the men who created *The Mary Tyler Moore Show* wrote her as an independent divorcée but scratched that because divorce is a socially unacceptable method of reconciling differences between a man and his wife.

I kept my decision to leave a secret from everyone, and because I enabled Paul to hide his alcoholism and anger management issues, I'm sure no one suspects our troubles. Soon after we separated, I read that fewer than six percent of couples divorce. I guess some women decide to plod through life. Marriage for a woman might be hell but it is better than having your lifestyle and financial health nose-dive and being ostracized by family and friends. But now that I've catapulted our lives in new directions, the time has come to tell our parents.

The month after I leave Paul, and nine years after the debut in 1970 of *The MTM Show*, the marriage climate is changing. *People* magazine's August 20 issue features Farrah Fawcett on their cover, provocatively draped in a long white shirt and apparently nothing else. The inside tagline, "Liberation Made Her Drop Her Majors," explains her career gave her financial security—and the courage to break free from her husband, Lee Majors. She wants to be more than the compliant, dependent woman who cooks Lee's meals and cleans his house. I'm not happy our marriages have ended, but Farrah's willingness to face public condemnation inspires me. Her defiant pose informs the American public that life doesn't end for divorced women.

After Paul tells his parents I've left him for another man, Dick wants nothing to do with me, and Ellie takes an opposite tack. Several nights weekly, she telephones in the middle of the night. The first few times, I explain my position without mentioning her son's problems. They'll eventually learn without my interference, and anyway, she won't believe me.

She scolds, "We knew you were a hussy, sleeping with Paul before marriage!"

"*He* slept with me."

"Go home to your husband, where you belong."

"Your opinion is a perfect example of the double standard that keeps *all* women second-class citizens."

"If you accept God into your life, He will show you the way."

"Your God believes women are property."

She slams the receiver against its cradle and never calls again.

My maternal grandmother says, "Your grandpa and I always liked Paul but figured five years of him would be all you could take."

"Our marriage lasted four-and-a-half years. How could you have known?"

"Well, my dear"—she speaks with the learned assurance of the elderly—"you remind me of your grandpa, two headstrong thoroughbreds that balk at restrictions."

18

ON MY OWN

By September 1979, Paul owns the house and I own C-FDMZ. A perfect arrangement. I decide Charles Lindbergh had the right attitude when he declared, "If I could fly for ten years before being killed in a crash, it would be a worthwhile trade for an ordinary lifetime."

Soon after I pass the private pilot written exam, I jump into five hours of instrument flight training, which licenses me to fly at night as well as during the day, then step up my training regimen to refine my skills and accumulate the two hundred hours necessary for a commercial license.

Occasionally, I fly to other airports throughout Ontario to expand my cross-country skills, familiarize myself with procedures at other airports, and meet other pilots over coffee. I'm always the only female. In early September, only two months after my flight test, I fly to Wright-Patterson AFB near Dayton, Ohio, to visit the Air Force Museum, an impulsive adventure across Lake Erie's open waters—and my first international flight.

Many won't fly single-engine aircraft over water because, in the event of an engine failure, your airplane-that-is-now-a-glider is going in one direction—down.

Aviation regulations specify (and good judgment dictates) that single-engine flight over water must be within gliding distance of shore. But stronger-than-predicted headwinds may prevent the plane gliding to the safety of land. Moreover, some pilots spook themselves, convinced any little rumble is a gremlin chomping on the engine. So far, my airplane hasn't let me down, as some people have.

When I agreed to take flight training, I thought the shared experience of learning might save our marriage. Though our marriage had deteriorated and I no longer loved Paul, social conditioning and some primordial aspect of my brain persuaded me to keep trying to make my marriage work. Another part of me understood that familiarity with a world broader than the village of my birth made staying together for life more difficult than it had been for my grandparents' generation, even without the adverse influence of alcohol and anger mismanagement.

After the first few lessons, I decided flying was fun, but not for one millisecond did I consider learning to fly would instill confidence, provide a goal, and transform my life.

Of the many cross-countries I conduct during my first months as a licensed pilot, the flight to my hometown in late September excites me the most. I'm certain my seventeen-year-old sister and my father, a former WWII aircraft mechanic, will be proud and eager to experience the thrill of flight with me, but I imagine the gentle refusals of my mother and grandmother.

"Wouldn't dare step into one of them newfangled contraptions."

The direct route for my flight home passes above Toronto's two million inhabitants and through the high-traffic airspace surrounding Toronto International Airport. I could have chosen to fly around Toronto's busy airspace, but instead, I tackle my fear of getting lost, smashing into the CN Tower—the tallest free-standing structure in the world—or causing a midair collision.

As I fly closer to the western periphery of controlled airspace encircling one of Canada's major airports, pilot and controller voices jam the airwaves. Finally, just as I'm close to entering their airspace, I make contact with air traffic control and obtain permission to transit the airspace monopolized by transatlantic jumbo jets. Bedazzled beyond expectation, I follow the controller's directives to track south of the airport, along Lake Ontario's shoreline.

Massive passenger planes whoosh left and right, toward exotic destinations I can only dream of visiting, and leave my little two-seater far behind in the atmospheric dust. High above, contrails crisscross and streak above my head, then dissolve. My neurons buzz with apprehension because, if I'm not hypervigilant, I'll cause a midair and become as significant as an eviscerated bug smeared onto a windshield.

When I exit Toronto's congested airspace toward the east, I realize my concerns were overblown and I'm glad I followed Eleanor Roosevelt's advice to "do one thing every day that scares you."

At the grass strip airport near Belleville, I land and whirl into a vacant tie-down spot between two taildragger airplanes. I gather my overnight bag and aviation paraphernalia and walk toward my father leaning against the clapboard clubhouse. He bestows his typical hunched-back hug, an uncomfortable compromise between a handshake and the embrace of two homophobic guys.

"How'd you know when I'd be landing?"

"Your mother was listening to the local FM station, waiting for your call from the clubhouse phone. Suddenly, the music stopped, and she was astonished to hear your voice talking with Trenton's military controller about flying through their zone."

I puzzle about this briefly, then say, "Makes sense. FM radio stations and aviation radios use VHF—very high frequency—electromagnetic waves."

A scowl flashes across my father's face, reminding me he resents any display of knowledge or intelligence by women. I'm relieved when his scowl dissolves and he says, "Let's stop for donuts at Tim Hortons before I drop you at your mom's."

"Thank you! I'm hungry," I say, glad for the chance to learn how he's doing as a single man after thirty years of marriage.

We load my bags into his midnight-blue Malibu, and as he drives, I ponder the oddity of his suggestion to stop for coffee. He never initiates visits. I try to recall our last one-on-one—it was eight years ago, the day I passed my driving test in his previous Malibu.

At the coffee shop, he buys an apple fritter and a black coffee for himself, orders a bran muffin and tea for me, then chooses a table for two in a corner, far from the nearest patrons. We chat about work and the weather, more like distant friends than father and daughter. I'm trying to ignore the fact he hasn't said one congratulatory word about my pilot license, when he suddenly snorts, "So he beat you up, did he? Serves you right for screwing around."

I choke on my muffin and clear my throat with a sip of tea. My father's blunt words are a dramatic shift from the conversation we've been having, though more typical. My fingernails dig half-moon darts into my palms. I grit my teeth. "Why do you think I was unfaithful?"

"Paul said you'd left him for another guy. Said he hit you a couple times."

Who is this man, the man supposed to be my father? I corral my astonishment and muffle the pain in my voice. "Father, your logic is faulty for at least two reasons. Number one, I did not leave him for another man."

His jaw tenses, as it always does when he feels challenged. "He said you did."

"I left because Paul won't deal with his personal issues."

My father looks at me, then toward passing traffic, downs a mouthful of coffee, and states, "He *said* you have a boyfriend."

My shoulders stiffen with rage. How can he believe Paul without consulting me? How can he support violence of any kind—especially to his daughter? I want him to know his words hurt but I don't want to fight, so I digest his hateful opinions and swallow the venom in my voice. "It's always easier to blame someone else."

We sit in mute opposition for a few minutes. My father sticks the tip of his left pinky finger into his ear, then vibrates the tip rapidly up and down for a few seconds. When he removes his fingertip, I notice short white hairs sprouting from his ears.

I wrinkle my nose in disgust. "You should trim those hairs if they're tickling you."

He sips his coffee.

"Paul told you I left him for another man because that delusion allows him to compare himself with another man—in this case, a fictional one."

He chomps a chunk from his apple fritter.

I force myself to speak rationally. "Secondly, you believe Paul without questioning his motives, but you couldn't be bothered to pick up the phone to ask me."

He chews slowly, head bowed. *Is he preparing an apology or a rebuttal?* He chases the last bite of his apple fritter with the dregs of coffee. "I've been busy."

I gasp. "Busy? Too busy to ask how your daughter's doing? Too busy to ask how your only grandchild's doing?" I'll never understand this alien who stares at me without emotion. "I was thrilled you suggested we come here and was enjoying myself until you attacked my personal life and insulted me."

"There's a friend I've been seeing."

This discordant statement frustrates me, but I'm thankful he's finished his skewed assessment of my personal life. "I'm glad. How'd you meet?"

"She works at the store as my jeweler's assistant. We've been"—he gazes at me—"uuhh . . . dating . . . uuhh, awhile."

"For many years, I've known you and Mom were unhappy. People change and fall out of love. Then the right person comes along and soon you're following your heart, even though you know cheating isn't right."

He says, "Actually . . . Annie and I've been together . . . ten years."

I hear myself shouting, "Ten years!" I glance around. My outburst hasn't turned heads in the crowded restaurant, but many must have heard.

I hiss between clenched teeth, "Ten years is a long time to screw around."

He flinches, then says, "I stayed with your mom 'til I had a sure thing with Annie."

"You mean Mom was your *backup* plan?"

He pokes at crumbs on his plate.

I ask, my voice shrill, "Do you have any idea how awful my teen years were? Mom constantly criticized me. I thought she hated me!"

He starts prodding his gums with a Stim-U-Dent stick.

I press, "When you left us in the evening and said you were working, were you lying?"

He drops the Stim-U-Dent onto his plate and tosses his crumpled paper napkin on top.

"Do I understand you were with *Annie*?" I spit her name at him. Angry with his treatment of Mom. Angry he's shutting me out as I've seen him do with Mom. My voice rises as I ask, "On Sundays, after church, did you leave us to be with her?"

I persist, no longer caring whether patrons overhear. He has to live in this town, but I don't. "Did Mom know about Annie? If she did, I'll hold you partly to blame for cheating Lynn and me of a happy mother."

My father's head wobbles side to side. I watch in shock and stumble through an incomprehensible *Star Trek* universe as his head mutates to a multiheaded monster, becoming two, then three, then two. Suddenly, I realize he isn't moving but I'm swaying side to side, teetering on my chair as if drunk. Father's staring at me. I grip the table to avoid toppling onto the floor. A siren screeches inside my ears and blocks all external sound. I manage to say, "So because you cheated on Mom, then left her for *your* lover—you think I've done the same?"

His lips flatline, an immobile slash across his face.

I spring to my feet. "This conversation is done."

During every second of the fifteen-minute ride, I regret not taking a taxi from the airport. My father's calm, almost inaudible, breaths punctuate our silence. I open my window to inhale a stream of fresh air. He parks in Mom's driveway. I gather my bags, slam the door, and start to walk away. I stop myself. My father hasn't behaved honorably, but he's not an axe murderer.

I open the passenger door and wait, hoping he'll say something . . . anything. He looks at me, eyes questioning my continued presence. I fight tears clumping in my lashes and ask, "Maybe we can talk later? When I'm less angry."

He looks at me with disinterest, without expression. "If you want."

"I guess you're not interested in an airplane ride tomorrow?"

He says flatly, "I'll pick you all up after lunch."

Mom runs outside to greet me. We talk late into the evening about her trip to Hawaii—"Orchids grow beside the roads," she says with awe—and my flight training, but nothing about my father's behavior. In bed, inside my childhood and unchanged bedroom, despite a long day preparing for the flight and the flight itself, I lie awake. I remember that soon after Father ditched Mom in 1977, two years before my marriage dissolved, I'd been stunned to receive a telephone call from him, one of a handful that happened only on Sunday, the only day Bell Canada offers a discount.

He'd pointed an imaginary finger at Mom. "I can't take her nagging any longer."

When I was a teenager, Mom's ceaseless sarcasm had more barbs than a porcupine's quills. I hated her and left home at seventeen, three months after high school graduation. When he was actually home, Father complained about her so often, I couldn't imagine why he stayed.

When he'd said, "I've moved into a bachelor apartment," I had sympathized and said, "What took so long!" I thought he'd rented a bachelor apartment because of his frugal upbringing and a desire for an ascetic lifestyle. His praise for *Jonathan Livingston Seagull*, Richard Bach's new novella, surprised and pleased me. I'd never seen him read anything but the newspapers delivered to our door, but his earnest sincerity made me wonder if I'd misjudged him.

He'd insisted, "I'm looking for meaning in my life. The book helped me understand I was unhappy because I married the wrong person. Your mom forced me to conform to middle-class materialism."

Now, I realize Father had posed as a single man and rented a bachelor apartment to deflect suspicion of a decade-long love triangle.

Now, I understand the significance of his words. "Annie, a lady at work, suggested Bach's book."

I assumed my introverted father and extroverted husband shared no similarities, but events of the past months have revealed common ground, the learned expertise of blaming anybody but themselves for mistakes and failures.

How much had my subliminal psyche driven me into Paul's arms?

At the airport the next day, I open the doors to DMZ so Mom, Dad, and Lynn can get a good look at my aircraft before we go flying. Since our first flights in 1962, Mom had done a cruise and decided seven days at sea was worse than seven hours in an airplane. She'd wanted to see Europe and the Pacific Islands so badly, she'd swallowed sedatives before each flight. Though the airplanes we flew in 1962 from Toronto to Regina—a forty-eight-passenger Vickers Viscount and a one hundred-and-fifteen-passenger Vickers Vanguard—are small compared to modern jumbo jets like the L-1011 or a DC-10, all are massive compared to my two-seater Cessna.

Mom and Lynn stand on either side of the plane and stick their heads inside while Dad stands ten feet away, legs spread, arms crossed on his chest. I say, "Dad, come take a look." I know he can hear me, but his failure to respond or move is puzzling.

Mom declares, "*Lynn* wants to go flying."

I nudge the soft flesh of Mom's upper arm. "Just sit inside and move the controls."

"No thanks. I'll stick with big airplanes."

I press my lips together. "I kinda hoped you'd come flying."

Lynn leaps into the passenger seat and grabs my arm. "Let's go!" she says, as Mom wraps her arm around my shoulders. "I'm one hundred percent terrified," she says, "but one hundred per-cent proud of you."

I've waited all my life for this percentage and manage to say, "Thanks, Mom," without bursting into tears.

Lynn and I are soon airborne, seeing our hometown from a new perspective, circling above the rectangular speck of our house, farm fields salt-and-peppered with grazing Holsteins, and sailboats on the bay. The rushing air and the engine drown her soft voice, but her smile tells me she's enjoying herself.

On the ground, we run toward our parents. She is excited to tell them about our flight, and I'm excited to treat my father to a flight. I want him to be proud of me. I need to hear his praise. I grab his hand and drag him toward the plane.

After takeoff, I glance at him, expecting to see the back of his head.

Instead, he's slumping in the bucket seat, chin against chest, shielding his soul with crossed arms, each hand clenching a robust bicep. Maybe the bumpiness created by the midafternoon clouds and the twenty-knot wind rolling across Lake Ontario is making him queasy, so I reach across the plane to adjust his fresh air vent, and ask, "Are you okay?"

He grunts. *Does that mean yes or no?* I turn the aircraft to the right, his side of the aircraft, to give him a better view. "Look, there's our house."

He unwraps his arms and stares at the short spiky hairs on the back of his fingers. I'm mystified by his bizarre behavior but force myself to concentrate on flying. His palpable displeasure escalates with each minute and a premonition of uncertainty leaches into my stomach. The propeller strobes through the sun's rays, freezing each silent, insufferable second.

"Please tell me what's wrong."

But he doesn't, so after thirty minutes of agonizing proximity, I return to the airstrip sooner than planned, crushed by his sullen disinterest. His quarrel with Mom must include me, but—why? I turn away and blot my collecting tears with a Kleenex. I thought he loved Lynn and me, but not Mom, just as Paul and I love Brandon but not each other.

Back at Mom's house, he stops the car against the curb, hands clenching the steering wheel. The engine idles. Mom and Lynn exit from the back seat. Dad mumbles, "Bye," then turns to face me with eyes that scream, *Get out of my car. Get out of my face.* His behavior stings like a poison dart. More than my visit with him is over, but I've no idea why he's unwilling to continue any charade of family togetherness.

During yesterday's flight to my hometown, I anticipated various scenarios, all featuring proud parents. I predicted Mom's misgivings about flying would eclipse my request for her to be my passenger, but I'm delighted she's proud of my accomplishment.

I envisioned an admiring father, thrilled by my success in a field linked with his wartime service. As a child, I spent hours with him in his woodworking shop surrounded by vintage aircraft parts, visual testimonies to his love of aviation: a wooden propeller; an altimeter; and a radio with a microphone, eerily similar to the one in my aircraft. His tools fascinated me, and though he cautioned, "These tools are too dangerous for girls," he let me observe and listen to his wartime aviation stories. Though they lacked Grampa's enthusiasm and visuals, I was glad to be with him in his shop.

I expected to cherish the memory of treating my father to a flight, with me—his eldest daughter—at the controls. Instead, I can't purge the image of his revulsion. Before my success in aviation stripped his false veneer of affection, I assumed he loved me as fathers were supposed to love their children.

Today's flight reveals he's been an outstanding impersonator for most of my life. *Why does he hate me? Why did he have children?*

After dinner, I question Mom about their marriage. When I hint about Annie, Mom folds her arms onto the dinner table, cradles her head, and weeps. "I thought he was going through a phase, a midlife crisis."

I'm heartbroken she knew about his infidelity and angry that she transferred her frustrations with him to me.

Even though I sometimes sensed her anger was misplaced, I hated her. When I couldn't avoid her, I argued with her and made it easy for my father to twist my mind. I was a pawn in his game, his ally against her. He swayed me to his side and made me believe *he* needed to escape *her* but, in reality, she was miserable because he was a lying cheat. I'm furious she believed there was no choice but to allow his deceit.

I finally understand the depth of her words, spoken nearly a decade ago. "Men make the rules to benefit themselves."

Lynn and I clean up after Mom's delicious homemade lasagna

dinner, then, while Mom returns to reading another Nevil Shute book, we rummage through boxes in the basement storage room, searching for tucked-away childhood memorabilia. Instead, we discover old photo albums. Side by side on the shag rug, we begin a black-and-white journey through Mom's life in three-by-three-inch miniatures. I shove an album into Lynn's face. "This one's full of her in her twenties, before marriage, traveling with girlfriends."

Lynn marvels, "Here's one at the beach with girlfriends—check out her cool shades and long, wavy hair." She finishes that album and moves to another. "Here she is at one of the Air Force dances. All the girls hoped to snag a pilot."

I say, "Once, when I came home to visit, she gave me an engagement ring with three diamonds. When I asked why she was giving away a gift from Dad, she said, 'It's not from him!'"

Lynn purses her rosy lips. "Who's it from?"

"Rory, a British pilot from Newfoundland who left for war in 1942. Flew Spitfires. I positively drooled for more information!"

"Did she break off the engagement when she realized Dad was Mr. Right?"

"He only became Mr. Right after Rory's pilot friends told her he'd *never* be coming back. Her eyes glistened, but she clammed up and lit a cigarette."

"Did Daddy know about that engagement?"

"Apparently Mom had been dating Dad but dumped him to date Rory."

Lynn says, "I'm confused—why didn't she marry Rory?"

"I guess he was shot down in Europe. Dad said, 'I should never have taken her back.'"

Lynn gasps. "That's so sad. I guess marriage to second-best was better than being single."

"When they married in 1947, Mom was twenty-four, an old maid by the gossip standard of the day."

≡ ≡ ≡

Two days later, on an evening when Mom and Lynn have previous plans, I visit Aunt Phyllis, Mom's best friend of thirty years and a passionate gossip who maintains, "I'm not gossiping; I'm telling you current events!"

Tonight, she doesn't waste time on small talk. She waves a bottle of Glenfiddich, pours me a generous ounce, then says, "I hear you're upset with your dad."

We sink into the overstuffed floral couch in her family room. I sit sideways, facing her, and fold my legs onto the couch. "I thought he'd be proud of me. Instead, he was hostile."

Gentle creases frame her black eyes. "Marriage is difficult at the best of times."

I chortle at her admission. "Right on!"

She sips her scotch. "Your dad wouldn't listen to your mom when she tried to talk about things, but on the day he left, he handed her a grocery list of complaints."

"Does he blame *her*?"

Contempt oozes in her words. "Haven't you heard that a woman is responsible for keeping her man happy?" She pauses for a drink. "Their divorce settlement didn't work the way he expected. She got the big house, and he got the small cottage. He told their friends the lawyers sided with your mom because she's their secretary."

My mouth makes little Os like a captured fish struggling for life. I grab my scotch, swirl some around my mouth, and swallow. "What nerve! He cheated on her. He dumped her."

"Your parents' marriage would've been okay if she didn't get pregnant."

I crinkle my eyebrows. "They didn't want children?"

Phyllis pales, looks away, downs her glass of wine, then sputters, "I . . . I . . . I thought you knew."

I focus on deep breathing. Inhale, exhale, inhale, exhale. I'm stunned, not so much by the truth but from her articulation of the truth, unmasked, without fanfare, a previously unspoken reality that long ago had crept into the core of my being.

I lean forward to kiss her sun-leathered cheek. "I've always known something was wrong. Maybe they wanted to explain, but what would they say? 'Please pass the butter, and by the way, you're an accident.'"

"Your dad thought children were rivals for his time, his money, and his wife."

I bang the back of my head against the soft couch. "Father blamed his parents for making too many children and not enough money. He's never forgiven them for making him quit high school to support their family."

She wags her finger. "Your generation is privileged to have birth control."

I slice an oval from the crusty French baguette. "I *do* feel fortunate."

"He joined the military, hoping to be a pilot." She winks. "Like every other man."

"Mom said war was his ticket from the poverty of his family's prairie farm."

"He was furious when the military slotted him as an airplane mechanic, but he needed a job. Now you've accomplished his unfulfilled dreams."

She pours another generous ounce of scotch into my glass. "She considered abor—"

I choke on a chunk of cheese. "Abortion!"

She grimaces. "I'm sorry. That slipped out."

I twirl a lock of hair around my finger. "Keep talking."

She sighs. "Doc Russell told her that, even if your father gave permission for *her* abortion, it would only be approved if pregnancy endangered her health."

We drink silently until Phyllis says, "Things were okay until she got pregnant again."

"Was he angry?"

She snickers. "All hell broke loose. The worst of it was he blamed *you* because *you* gave her chicken pox and messed up her monthly."

I say, "As if he had nothing to do with it."

Phyllis shakes her head. "He can't forgive or forget."

We finish our drinks, and nighthawk that I am not, I'm snuggled in my childhood bed by ten, before Mom and Lynn return from the theater. The scotch lulls me to sleep, but I wake up two hours later, drenched in sweat. Relieved, yet burdened by the information and events of the past few days, memories and questions spin through my mind like a gerbil going nowhere inside a wheel, pushing me further from the fringes of sleep. My aunt's revelations. My parents' fractured relationship. My fragmented interactions with my parents.

I force myself to accept that the crux of my father's dismay is his love for flight but not the pilot, the child he never wanted, the child who became the pilot he wanted to be. Jealousy has shredded the fabric of his love for me—if love ever existed—and his bitterness will prevent any stitching together of these fragments.

How different Mom's life might have been with Rory or as a single woman focused on her career. I doubt we can seal the rifts I helped create during my adolescence, but I'm going to try. Mom deserves another chance.

$=$ *19* $=$

LEAVING
THE TWILIGHT ZONE

In the morning, my body aches as if I've endured a long-haul flight crammed in the cheap seats with my knees around my neck. Night had been one long ricochet from bed to toilet to kitchen for another drink of water.

After a breakfast of yogurt and fruit, I haul my teenage ten-speed from the wooden shed Father had built years ago and cycle three miles to my maternal grandparents' home. With each pedal push to the seventy-foot-high zenith of the new bridge, I strain, deceived by the gentle slope of this modern arch that's replaced the old swing bridge.

Grandma meets me on the veranda, wraps her plump arms around my torso, and kisses my cheek. "What a delightful surprise—we weren't expecting you until suppertime." She ushers me inside. "I'll fix us tea and cookies."

In the living room, we sit on French provincial armchairs angling toward their picture window on the world. Kitchen scents of fresh apple pie and bubbling beef stew waft into the living room. We sip orange pekoe tea, hers with sugar and mine with lemon, as sailboats sashay between whitecaps. We chat about the weather, then she moves on to family news.

"My brother's legs were amputated above the knee last week."

LEAVING THE TWILIGHT ZONE

"From his diabetes?"

She shakes her head and wipes tears from her eyes. "He's been in a wheelchair for years. Didn't listen to his doctor who told him to lose weight, stop his diet of daily desserts, and walk at least thirty minutes every day."

"Good advice," I say, and silently vow to avoid sugars and exercise regularly.

"And my sister . . . I don't know why Philena lets that darn spider monkey run loose around the house."

I bite into one of her delicious oatmeal raisin cookies. "You're as different from Philena as I am from Lynn."

She chuckles. "Why can't Philena be normal and get a dog?"

"Speaking of differences, I'm having a terrible visit with Father. He *loathed* flying with me, but worse, he accepted Paul's side of the story."

Grandma nods, as if this sounds familiar and, perhaps, predictable.

"I didn't expect unconditional approval but thought he'd ask my side of the story before making a decision."

She jiggles her partial plate of two upper teeth and clicks it back into position. "Your father has been surprising us a lot lately."

"He said I deserved whatever my husband dished out!"

Grandma spins her Eastern Star ring around her finger.

"As if that weren't strange enough, last night I spent two hours chatting with Auntie Phyllis. Her tongue, liberated by alcohol"—I catch the eyes of my teetotaler grandmother—"revealed many surprising details about my parents' marriage." I finish my tea. "Phyllis said they hadn't planned children . . ." I let my voice trail off.

Grandma raises her voice. "She has *no business* telling you that!"

"I was surprised . . . a bit."

Grandma's tongue traces her upper lip. "We never expected grandchildren, but we were delighted."

I gobble another cookie, devouring it without pleasure.

Grandma's seventy-five-year-old eyes glaze as she says, "We'd wanted at least two children. But after forty-eight hours of labor with your mom, the doctor said another pregnancy would kill me. Grandpa vowed he wanted me more than another child."

"I need a man like Grampa who considers me a partner—not a possession!"

"Your folks' troubles got worse with Lynn. We looked after both of you to give your parents time alone so they could work things out."

Their glass-domed clock chimes, reminding me of my luncheon date with Michelle. I stand to go, and Grandma hugs me against her ample breast. "My fondest memories are with you and Grampa."

Grandma cries tears of joy, I hope.

I peck her cheek and hold back my tears. To say, "Without your love and guidance, I'd likely be a junkie on skid row instead of a pilot in an airplane," would tell her too much about growing up in her daughter's house and hurt her without purpose. Instead, I say, "I can't imagine growing up without you two in my life."

"You and Lynn are the daughters we didn't have."

I cycle to the bridge, tears streaming down my cheeks. Minor road repairs on the eight-year-old bridge delay traffic and provide extra time for me to evaluate the past few days. My newly found puzzle pieces provide unexpected insight into my parents' struggles, clarity to past actions, and guidance for my future.

The first thing I can do, today, is to treat my mother as a friend, not an adversary.

The second thing I will do when I return to Chatham is meet with Paul to explain the many reasons I will never return. Before marriage, Paul loved my independent spirit, but after marriage, he tried to force me to become a clone of his mother, his idea of the perfect wife and mother, obedient and forgiving. Now, I believe

LEAVING THE TWILIGHT ZONE

he expected me to follow the traditional wedding benediction, "Now, we are one," with its subtext, "Now, we are the husband."

I crave the comfort and stability of marriage, and Brandon would be happier to see his parents together, but I don't want him to see—and adopt—the bullying tactics of his grandfather and father. Our society needs to teach boys to respect girls as equals, not teach girls to be compliant and demure, a teaching that must start at home.

Despite this, I can't shake my guilt for ending our marriage, leaving my husband, and forcing our son to bounce between two homes.

When traffic moves ten minutes later, I imagine the flag-man's wand transporting me from the bizarre conversations and unexpected discoveries of my personal Twilight Zone into a world of new beginnings.

Michelle waves from a plantation-style rattan table in Paola's Patio. The noonday sun filters through spiky palm leaves and glistens on water tinkling into the lion's head fountain. Our wine spritzers, Greek salads, and the pizza arrive within minutes. She leans forward and whispers with a conspiratorial squeeze of my hand, "Did you hear our gorgeous grade nine teacher is a convicted pedophile?"

A cucumber chunk lodges in my windpipe, and I thump my fist against my chest until it dislodges. "You can't be serious?"

"It's in the news. He *admitted* to molesting boys."

I arch my brows. "Appearances can be deceiving. Remember his girlfriend?"

Michelle sticks out her tongue. "Miss Prim 'n' Proper with her beehive hair and cat-eye glasses—"

"And sweater sets with knee-length skirts."

We squeal like tweens, then I say, "Guess he dated that scrawny sourpuss to *avoid* sex!"

Michelle raises her eyebrows up and down, imitating Groucho Marx. "Speaking of sex, how's your new life?"

"No sex, but life without *Paul* is fantastic. Life without *Brandon* to cuddle every night rips me apart. When he's with his dad, sleep only comes after I force myself to stop thinking about him."

"When do you see Brandon?"

"Every Friday I pick him up at day care and return him Monday morning. Day care is a great third-party buffer that lets me avoid Paul."

Michelle sips her spritzer, then explodes with triumph. "I left Joe."

We clink our glasses together.

"When I refused to help him get a loan, he yelled"—she juts her chin toward me—"but I yelled louder."

"Weren't you frightened?"

She stretches her mouth into a wide grimace. "Not really. He ranted for a few minutes, then flopped on the couch and got lost in some stupid TV show. The next morning, he didn't mention our argument. I figured he'd accepted my decision until he came home after I'd fallen asleep and threw a bucket of ice water onto me."

I freeze, my fork of salad poised between the plate and my mouth.

"He dragged me onto the floor, twisted my arm like a wet towel, and stomped on my foot."

I imagine her terror. I can't speak.

"He kicked me with his steel-toed boots, then suddenly stopped, undressed, and hopped into bed."

I start to breathe. "Then what?"

"I lurched like Igor in *Young Frankenstein* into the spare bedroom."

"*Then* what?"

Her eyes widen. "I shoved the dresser against the door. In the morning, my foot was so swollen, I had to hop. Joe apologized and dropped me at Mom's on his way to work. She drove me to the hospital. I had a ruptured eardrum, but my foot wasn't broken."

Her calmness in the face of adversity bonds me closer to her.

"I stayed with my parents, who encouraged me to ditch him. Joe came by several times with flowers and apologies. He'd say, 'I'm sorry but—'"

"An apology including *but* isn't an apology."

She whines an impersonation of Joe. "'But you hurt my feelings.'"

"Have you heard from him lately?"

"I hear he's found a new victim."

We clasp hands and I say, "We both need to move on."

As I cycle home to Mom, I realize my inherent optimism prevented me from a critical examination of human motives and actions. My naivete—and a society legally blinkered to all but the most heinous domestic abuses—had sheltered me from the awareness that neither alcoholism nor spousal abuse heed income or education.

20

THE NEAR NORTH: TRAINING CONTINUES

The altered landscape of my personal life challenges me. Sometimes, I'm lonely, but loneliness won't kill me—my angry husband might. When Brandon is in my custody, Paul occasionally stalks us if we leave the apartment. He trails us to restaurants or movie theaters, then asks to join us. At first, this frightens me, but he seems more like a lost puppy. His presence is awkward, but because Brandon wants to be with both parents and Paul seems forlorn, not angry, I often agree.

I hope time will dampen Paul's bitterness, but in October 1979, I add distance to the equation and transfer to CIBC's Computer Conversion Team at Head Office. On weekends, I'll be home with Brandon, but during the week, the bank will post me to bank branches throughout Ontario. The team will convert all documentation from paper onto computers.

Each Monday, in predawn light, I drive my TR6 ragtop to the Toronto airport for a breakfast flight with twenty other female employees to whichever far-flung bank branch Head Office selects as the next victim, in the minds of some branch employees. No other Canadian bank has introduced computers, and many employees resist the transition from a manual accounting system to a computerized model. Every Friday afternoon, I fly back to Toronto and drive home to be with Brandon and train for my commercial license.

Monday to Thursday, after work ends at five, no matter where the bank sends me, I fly at a local flight school. The shortened daylight hours of a northern winter mean my weekday flights are night flights, conducted at airports in the Canadian Shield north of forty-six degrees north latitude—Sault Ste. Marie, Sudbury, North Bay, and Timmins, to name a few.

During winter, the wind howls and the temperature climbs to –11°C—during the day. After sunset, the wind typically dwindles. When I do my preflight check, the hardpack snow squeaks like a mouse with each step of my rubber-soled mukluks. But even though I'm cold and my nostrils stick together when I breathe, I relish every minute. Soon, the engine heat will warm me.

Airborne and away from airport lights, I transit a surreal and silent space, sandwiched between a counterpane of snow-flake-speckled obsidian skies and unblemished snow. The air is smooth, as if I'm skating on glass. Some imagine stars as pinprick holes in black canvas, miniature doors to another dimension, but flying in this universe is all the escape I need. Each moment airborne creates the illusion of drifting through a dream. The few electric lights illuminating the cities and villages don't overwhelm the stars sparkling in the black velvet sky.

On weeknights, I fly alone. After a chaotic day dealing with frustrated bank staff forced to tackle unwelcome technology, I'm desperate for the solitude and the opportunity to practice stalls or spins, maneuvers verboten with passengers. For me, flight without aerobatics is as satisfying as sex without orgasm.

Despite the inky serenity of night flights, if the engine fails, spotting a safe landing area in the dark will be difficult, perhaps impossible. Because of the increased risk, I monitor the engine instruments and plan for emergencies. If the engine quits, a road will provide my best (only?) chance of survival. If the aircraft can't glide to a road, I'll have to land on a snow-covered farm field where the wheels will dig into the snow and flip the aircraft onto its back. If I survive the forced landing, I might wait hours for a passing vehicle.

But—I have choices.

Don't go flying.

Don't challenge myself.

Or place my faith in the airplane, the maintenance crews, the compliance of the flight school with prescribed maintenance schedules, and my increasing confidence in myself. I remind myself the plane has no concept of time or place. If the engine and instruments are working properly but I hear an unexplained *burp-burble-burp*, I pull a knob on the instrument panel that redirects engine heat to the carburetor before ice accumulates and blocks fuel flow to the engine. Though these various improbabilities cycle through my mind continually during night flights, they're worth the risk.

Since every night flight has been perfect, I bring a colleague for a quick zip to North Bay for supper. During our return trip, the northern lights shiver kiwi-green and turquoise and a slivered crescent moon glistens on endless fields of white.

We've made good time and have lots of gas, so I offer to end the evening with an aerial vista of Sudbury. I scan the instrument panel to preempt disaster, just as automobile drivers scan mirrors and blind spots. Moments later, as we're looking at Sudbury by night, the black sky glows fiery orange and the radiant glow illuminates the cockpit's shadowy interior.

Gail jerks upright, grabs my arm, and screams, "What's happening?!"

Supper's greasy hamburger roils up my esophagus.

The only possibility is an engine fire, but she doesn't need to hear that until I'm sure. Instead, I say, "I don't know—yet."

To reassure her—and myself—I point to the dashboard. "The instruments and gauges are fine." Invisible hands choke my throat, tighter and tighter. I roll the plane left, then right. "I don't see flames, so it isn't an engine fire."

The orange light fades and the interior returns to murkiness. Gail asks, "Maybe the fire burned out?"

My shoulders relax a smidgen, but my brain keeps spinning. "I can't imagine what caused the bright light or why it faded so quickly." Suddenly, to my horror, the underside of the wings flares bittersweet orange again. Another scan of the panel reveals nothing amiss. My brain pounds with confusion. I decide to sideslip and see if a change in perspective reveals flames. Not wanting to scare her as Rob scared me with his sideslip demonstration, I say, "Hold on, I'm going to tip the plane sideways to get a better look at the engine and nose."

If there's a fire, I'll need to shut off the engine so we don't explode, then dive nose down to put out the fire. If the fire stops, I don't dare start the engine again but must find somewhere to land. I brace myself for a terrifying image, but instead, I burst into laughter. I turn to the right so Gail can get an unobstructed view of the ground directly below. I say, "We're above an open pit mine. They're dumping slag!"

Bonfire rivers of molten ore stream down mountains of cold, hardened slag and transform the landscape into a panorama resembling El Capitan's annual spectacular firefall in Yosemite. Enthralled by eruptions equaling volcanic extravagance, we circle for thirty minutes, before returning to the airport.

With each accumulated hour of flight time, the freedom of flying lures me from the captivity of a job inside a building, with unhappy people who have regrets, for many different reasons. I understand their reluctance because the old me stood in their shoes, afraid to end my marriage, afraid to live the life I wanted to live. I chose to face my fears and become the independent woman I wanted to be. Though the first months alone haven't been ideal, I'm on an airborne road to happiness. Best of all, my courage allowed me to understand that, faced with fear, I'm calm and decisive.

But I'm not ready to face all my fears.

I persuade myself I need to work a bit longer to pay for my commercial pilot training. This logic seems sound, but my rationale is a crutch. Without my salary, I can dip into my small savings account or sell DMZ. I tell people I'm not ready to commit to aviation, but in reality, I'm afraid to be unemployed, to jump into the void. I'm not as brave as I pretend.

I slog through the remaining two months of a five-month stint in Sudbury, then, in February 1980, go with the crew to Elliot Lake to start the manual-to-electronic conversion process at the town's only bank. Though inhabited by about sixteen thousand people, the hamlet is a speck in the wilderness perched between two cities 160 km apart. This dismal has-been uranium-mining town, 30 km north of the Trans-Canada Highway, seems a forsaken village halfway along the Highway to Hell.

Though some employees at other bank branches resented computers, this branch manager retaliates, and instead of reserving rooms at the attractive two-year-old hotel with a swimming pool, he slots us into the Algoden Hotel. Constructed on the cheap in 1957, the dive served beer-guzzling miners 2.4 million bottles of beer in the first year. This first drinking hole in the fledging town began its career on April 1 with a murder behind the hotel.

By the time we arrive, the Algoden is only twenty-three years old but can pass for a chain-smoking, hard-drinking, eighty-year-old hooker with alligator skin. The walk to my room along the top-floor hallway is an obstacle course skirting galvanized metal buckets filling with melting snow that creeps under curled shingles.

Elliot Lake doesn't have an airport, so I blitz-study for my commercial pilot written exam, holed up in my tawdry room, during the long darkness of winter evenings.

On Friday afternoon of this first week, I return as a passenger on Air Canada to Toronto, then drive home for my weekend with Brandon. I now feel safe picking him up at my old house, where they still live, but when Brandon sees how well his daddy and I get along, he asks, "Mommy, when are you coming back?"

This breaks my heart, and I wonder if I should return to picking him up at day care. But then, I won't be able to confirm Paul's keeping the fridge stocked and the cleaning lady employed. On the plus side, Brandon seems to be enjoying day care and is otherwise happy. We have a great weekend together, swimming at the local indoor pool, two flights in my airplane, two trips to McDonald's, and a movie. He chooses *The Black Stallion*, based on a book we cherish. We have a great time, but I'm always sad when I have to go to work and he has to return to his father.

On the return flight to Elliot Lake the following Monday, I investigate the local seaplane base. After work, I drive six miles farther from civilization, pull into the narrow gap between eight-foot-high snowbanks, and park my rental car beside the only vehicle, a red Ford pickup. Centered above the hangar door, light trickles beneath a coolie-hat lampshade. A silvery moon shimmers on the snow-covered lake. Only five in the early evening, but the sky's already coal black.

Inside the hangar, Carl, the owner, tinkers with some gadget on his cluttered workbench. I introduce myself, show him my pilot license, and say, "Hoping to get my ski endorsement in the next week or two."

"Happy to make a few bucks." He glances at my license, then tosses his head toward a Cessna 180 inside the hangar. "She's in for service. We'll use the Super Cruiser at the lake."

I stifle a snigger at the Cessna's unusual registration, CF-SEX. "Pretty provocative for the Canadian government."

He grabs a flashlight and pops a stick of gum into his mouth. "Go figure. If ya asked for that registration, ya prob'ly wouldn't get it."

At the shoreline, I decide he has the most unusual aircraft registrations. Our plane for tonight is C-GOAT. We hop in—I'm in the left seat. He points to a flattened, plowed section of the frozen, snow-covered lake. "There's the runway."

Though we're slender and the fuel tanks are half-full, the heavy skis top our weight at the maximum takeoff weight. He snorts as the plane lumbers across the snow. "Getting the old GOAT into the air with skis takes a while."

Finally, just when I'm considering I might have to abort and start the takeoff again, we're airborne, soaring away from an all-white ground into an ebony sky.

Carl says, "Easy-peasy. Show me a few touch-and-goes."

Landing the aircraft between snowbanks feels a bit tricky, but in the air, the plane handles like other aircraft. After fifty minutes, he says, "Don't see any problem, 'specially since your first shot at skis is at night. Jes' to be sure, come back in a couple days when it's windy. A few more circuits and that'll be it."

All flights offer freedom from the mundane and the predictable, but flying in the wilderness offers freedom from restrictions and rules—and the chaos of civilization. I haven't felt this happy with life since my first solo and my first solo cross-country.

During the second week of my three-week perdition in Elliot Lake, I get my ski plane endorsement, another accomplishment at the end of a million steps—and the first step toward my next goal.

I expect to pass my upcoming commercial pilot flight test in Waterloo and want to begin instructor training immediately. If I don't pass, I'll need remedial training. Regardless, the only way I can complete my instructor training and start flying professionally by summer is to quit work. When I give Nancy, my senior supervisor, my four-weeks' notice, she snorts derisively. "Have you ever *seen* a female pilot? In twenty-five years with the bank, I've gone as far up the ladder as the bank will allow women to go—second rung from the bottom!"

Motivational gurus preach that anyone can become whatever they desire and are responsible for the outcomes in their lives, but my life and work experience suggest this isn't completely true. In 1970, I'd been inspired by Kate Millett's *Sexual Politics* and Germaine Greer's *The Female Eunuch*, two seminal books integral to the Second Wave of Feminism. Ten years later, more women pursue professions but few hold positions of authority.

In March 1980, I finish my commercial flight test at Waterloo, evaluated by Maureen, a Class II supervising instructor and the first commercially employed female pilot I've met. She shakes my hand. "Congratulations. You've joined the ranks of fewer than two hundred women in Canada with a commercial license." Speechless and honored, I grin with delight.

She stares solemnly. "You should be proud, but don't get too excited about your prospects. Many think women can't or shouldn't fly, so our options aren't equal to those for men. Most commercially licensed females are instructors."

"Tell me more."

"Transport Canada's Flight Training Standards hired their first female instructor in 1977, only three years ago, and I can count the remaining female pilots on one hand. One flies a CL-215 for firefighting and three are first or second officers for airlines."

"That's discouraging, but—will you to teach me to be an instructor?"

She agrees, so I arrange to sublet a room in a house near the

Waterloo Regional Airport for six weeks. Since beginning work with the bank's computer division, I haven't been in the same city for more than four consecutive nights, though every weekend I travel home to be with Brandon, who still lives part-time with his father in Chatham, and fly DMZ.

However, because government regulations specify that instructor training must be done using flight school aircraft, I can't use my airplane. I'm thinking about selling DMZ but I'm hesitant to abandon the aircraft that helped me soar higher than I ever imagined, a place of solace and joy. While I dither, the farmer who owns the adjacent property takes decisive action. He objects to planes flying low—something planes need to do during takeoff and landing—and he erects a silo only three-hundred-and-fifteen feet from Chatham's runway, making departures and approaches nerve-racking.

CFI Murray says, "Unless you're low on approach, you're never going to hit it."

I inhale deeply. "It's an illusion, but it seems like the wheels are going to hit the silo."

He nods wisely. "Focus on your objective, the runway, not the silo, an obstacle that can be overcome. The silo's only seventy-five feet high, so fly over at three hundred feet."

His helpful advice makes me less uncomfortable on my next approach to landing, and I realize his wisdom can be applied to other life decisions. I arrange to sell my beloved aircraft and use the proceeds, not my savings, to pay for advanced flight training.

To celebrate Easter and my grandparents' fifty-eighth wedding anniversary on Saturday, April 5, Brandon and I drive home Thursday afternoon.

Brandon says, "Daddy has a new girlfriend."

My heart pings with foolish jealousy, but I say, "Your daddy deserves to be happy."

"On weekends, she sleeps over."

I'm even more jealous when he points to his knee. "I got this boo-boo last week when I fell off my swing, but she's a nurse like Gramma. She cleaned my knee and put red stuff on it."

We stay at my childhood home where Mom and Lynn continue to live. Within the first half hour, the four of us cluster around the kitchen table sipping Mom's delicious hot cocoa overflowing with marshmallows.

I tell them about my recent decisions, and Mom leaps up, her cheeks pink with excitement. I think she's going to hug me but then she stomps to the pantry, slams the pantry door, and says, "Last year you left your husband. This year you're quitting your perfectly good job at the bank! Your grandfather's first career was at the bank. I guess that's not good enough for you?"

She's rarely supported my decisions, so her reaction doesn't surprise me. "I guess it's okay if men change careers?"

She ignores me and lights a cigarette.

After supper, Father pops in. Mom leaves us to read a bedtime story with Brandon. I'm certain my father's response will be negative, but I still hope he'll surprise me.

His words echo Mom's. "Quitting a perfectly good job. Ridiculous."

Why is it so hard for them to be supportive?

"You're like my sister Aileen who left her perfectly good job as executive secretary with Eaton's to be a missionary."

I grit my teeth. "I admire her for following her heart."

"She's a fool. At thirty-five, she should've been getting married, not gallivanting around the world."

I'm angered that he never misses an opportunity to express contempt for his unmarried sister by ridiculing her personal achievements, but doubt anything I say will change his attitude. "I hear you're planning a vacation in New York?"

"Annie's never traveled outside of Ontario, and she's always wanted to visit the Finger Lakes."

"Should be beautiful in May and less busy now that the Winter Olympics are over."

We make small talk until he leaves. Brandon's asleep, so I call my grandparents, sure they'll be supportive.

Via their antiquated Western Electric rotary tabletop telephone, Grandma says, "We worry, but you'll be fine."

Tears fill my eyes as she passes the heavy Bakelite receiver to Grampa, my favorite person in the stratosphere and the only one who gives me unconditional love.

He says, "You shouldn't be quitting a perfectly good job."

Have they rehearsed their responses? I reassure him. "Don't worry. The barnstorming era is gone, and planes are safe now."

"Yes, but—"

"I'll be flying commercial aircraft, serviced by licensed mechanics."

"You'll be taking jobs from men who need to support their families."

His words slash as if he'd eviscerated my throbbing heart and sacrificed my soul in a ritual of male supremacy. *How can he say men deserve an aviation career more than women? More than his grandchild?* My neurons misfire and I become a zombie, with a befuddled brain and paralyzed tongue.

Then, the faintest of muffled sobs trickles into my ear, and I remember the only other time I've known him to cry—the day he looked at the scrap heap of a house where I lived with Duncan. That day, my heart broke as I watched tears creep down his cheeks, follow the gentle furrows of his face, and drip from his square jaw onto his starched shirt collar. Now, I say nothing and try to understand his perspective. Because I love him. Because he's eighty-three.

Moments later, I hear, "I'm an old man who's seen many changes. I shouldn't feel this way. Fly safe and always remember I love you."

"I love you, too, Grampa."

I hang up the phone feeling immense relief. My grandparents are still on my side. Not for the first time, I wonder what kind of a mess I'd be if they hadn't cherished me as their child.

Two weeks later, when I arrive for my first instructor lesson, the dispatch clerk, Cookie, says, "Maureen passed her Class I instructor rating and got a better job."

My shoulders sag. "I really wanted to train with Maureen."

"She reassigned you to Chris."

"You've hired another female!"

Cookie flinches. "Actually, Chris is Christopher—but you'll like him."

I'm devastated to have missed an opportunity to train with a female, but Chris is an excellent instructor whom I trust after he trusts me enough to say, "I don't blame you for being upset. Maureen didn't leave because she got a Class I rating. She left because the manager hired a guy as chief instructor even though she had more seniority and was more qualified."

"That's a slap on her face."

Chris says, "The manager and the new CFI are buddies from the military. Welcome to the old boys' club."

I train all day, every weekday, and six weeks later become a neophyte Class IV instructor. I mail resumes to five schools in southern Ontario, a selection based on the size of the school (more than two aircraft), the type of aircraft used for training (Cessna 150 and 172), a charter division with multi-engine aircraft (I plan to fly charters in the future), and the school's distance from Paul's new home in Niagara. To work for any of these schools, I'll be relocating, but my new location won't compromise our joint custody arrangement.

The first call is from my school of choice because I'll be less than an hour's driving distance when we exchange Brandon for weekends, holidays, and summer vacation. One week later, I start teaching, and for the first time in my life, I'm earning good wages in a career I love plus commission for every hour I teach. As my student roster increases, my wages increase. As I accumulate flight hours and acquire advanced ratings, my pay level will increase. Moreover, I receive the same amount as a male pilot, with the same qualifications, doing the same job.

During the first few weeks, I notice that, in contrast to my hesitation during my intro flight, my first five male students take control during their intro flight. Some do hesitate, seeming to gather courage, but all are determined to uphold the glorified ideals of masculinity.

One says, "Wouldn't want to look scared in front of a girl."

Another pales but grips the controls and starts to sweat. He says, "Mind if I open the vent? Sure is hot in here."

Their right to be in control has been ingrained since birth, but my confidence was acquired well after my introductory flight.

Sometimes, I join my fellow instructors for a drink at the local bar and quickly learn that being a pilot is a surefire pickup line . . . if you're male.

Even though the guys I'm with are pilots, a guy who is chatting me up asks, "Are you the secretary at the flight school?"

I'm interested in him so I smile. "I'm a commercial pilot, too." To my dismay, he moves his right hand to cover his balls and steps backward. He laughs but I don't. Soon, he moves on.

After another fellow asks something similar, I ask, "What makes you think I'm not a pilot?"

He says, "Women can't do anything so technical—can they?"

Despite this negativity, flying is my dream job. Every day is an exhilarating adventure. No longer am I jammed inside an office, eyes squinting, nerves jangling from flickering fluorescent lighting. Every day, I'm excited to get out of bed. I love teaching, and my colleagues—the instructors and the maintenance crew—are friendly and helpful. Instead of gazing toward the outside world, I bask in sunlight and warm breezes. I'm a pilot, a skilled professional in an exciting career, one brimming with opportunity for advancement and travel.

Life can't get better.

But it does.

One of the other instructors introduces me to his student Steve, a scholarly looking guy about my age with a moustache and wire-rimmed glasses. We chat a few times after his lesson on the ramp or in the clubhouse. He initiates conversation but it never leads anywhere. I sense a mutual attraction, so one day I gather my courage and ask, "Want to grab a burger sometime?"

I'm nervous asking a guy out, but to my relief and delight, he says, "Let's drive to Windsor for dinner and a movie. How about *Urban Cowboy*?"

"Perfect. I love John Travolta. Did you see *Grease*?"

He laughs. "Didn't everyone?"

Over dinner, I ask, "How can you afford to fly so often?"

He says, in a gentle voice, "I live with my folks, but mostly because my job testing plastics in a lab pays outrageously well."

When I mention the reaction I typically get from men regarding my career, he says, "I already have a great career, so you're not taking a pilot job from me." The suggestion that women aren't as deserving of a job in aviation as men irks me but he's a nice man, who treats me well. After several dates, I introduce him to Brandon and feel the instant karma between them.

21

UNWANTED

One afternoon in early July 1980, I cluster with the other instructors around the dispatch desk for a short weather briefing from Dwaine, the manager of the flight school. During my first few weeks as an instructor, most days begin with blue skies and light breezes but morph from perfect flying conditions to towering cumulonimbus clouds racing across the continent, tossing turbulence, heavy rain, thunder, and lightning onto our heads.

As the meeting ends, Dwaine asks, "Hey, Lola, this Saturday, if another thunder-bumper threatens and you cancel your students, I want to check out your teaching skills."

I don't want to seem ungrateful. "I've been here a few—"

"I know the CFI checked you out on our aircraft before he turned you loose on unsuspecting students." He laughs and glances at the other instructors as a cue for them to laugh at his joke. They do. Dwaine brags, "Bet you don't know I used to instruct?"

"Bet you don't know that one of your old girlfriends is a friend of mine."

"Really?" He looks dubious, I guess because he's at *least* fifteen years older than me.

"Bev Ryder."

His head jerks back in surprise. "What a coincidence. Let's make this fun. We'll puddle-jump a couple miles east, you can do touch-and-goes on my friend's grass strip, and then we'll join his pool party."

Two of the instructors exchange raised eyebrows.

I ask, "Why don't we take the 172 so all four of us can go?"

Dwaine says, "Because most teaching occurs on the 150."

I say, "Let's just do touch-and-goes here, at the airport."

Dwaine runs his fingers through his thinning hair. "Bring your swimsuit."

His cheeky persistence surprises me, but because of Bev's fond memories of him as her instructor and casual date, I'm certain he's a stand-up guy. Besides, the chance to swim, one of my favorite pastimes, and meet new friends in a new town is too good to refuse.

That evening, I discuss Dwaine's suggestion with Steve, my new steady, who says, "Sounds like a plan. I work until six. Let's get together after that."

On Saturday, the weather is an encore performance of previous days. Lessons start at eight in a crisp, cloudless sky, but by midafternoon, multihued, anvil-shaped clouds of blue-gray scrape the roof of the sky. At one thirty, Dwaine and I hop into the plane, but to my surprise he assumes control and starts the engine.

I ask, "I thought you wanted to assess my flight skills. Or are you going to act as my student to assess my teaching?"

He shrugs away my question. "Let's get there before the storm."

Our destination pops into view within five minutes. In addition to a well-maintained, grass landing strip, this private complex boasts a hangar, an in-ground pool, a sprawling ranch-style bungalow with colorful flowers—and an empty driveway.

Suspicion sneaks into my head. "Where's everyone?"

"Should be here soon. Let's wait in the pool!"

Though Bev spoke favorably of Dwaine as an instructor and

boyfriend, I'm beginning to second-guess the wisdom of joining him at a rural estate, on a gravel side road, ten kilometers south of the nearest secondary road. But, since I'm here, I may as well swim. Inside the change house, I shed my instructor's uniform—navy blazer, white blouse, and gray skirt suitable for an elite private school—shimmy into my one-piece suit, tie a floral sarong around my hips, and saunter back into the muggy cloak of summer air.

Dwaine's paunchy body bounces on the diving board. The loose flesh of his protruding abdomen and budding breasts wiggles and surges. His balls bob in unison like synchronized swimmers and test the integrity of his wafer-thin, spandex bathing suit. Revolting. At least he's not naked.

With increasing concern, I say, "Most hosts arrive *before* their guests."

He rakes me with his beady eyes, then, without warning, whips off his suit. With a cavalier flick of his wrist, he tosses the tiny black triangle onto the deck.

I reflexively back toward the exit and consider doing a 180-degree turn, putting on my uniform, and going. But . . . *where?* Our flight was a five-minute, crow-flying-in-a-straight-line hop but walking will be a ninety-minute endeavor. I'll be lucky to encounter a passing car before the main road, and if I do, being a lone female will present a different risk.

He says, "Take off your suit and hop in."

Should I call the flight school? Someone might be teaching theory or doing paperwork, but I doubt this as we have the afternoon off. I cringe with shame as I consider the possibility that colleagues suspected Dwaine's underlying intentions. Knowledge about my virtue might win respect from colleagues but they aren't responsible for hiring—or firing.

How will Dwaine react if my rejection of him becomes gossip at the flight school? I don't care if he's embarrassed but—*What if he's vindictive?*

I don't plan to teach flying forever, but I'd hoped to stay more than five weeks. I've found an apartment suitable for Brandon and me and don't want to relocate so soon.

I shift from foot to foot near the edge of the pool, at the shallow end. Dwaine treads water, twenty feet away. At this point, I'm *almost* sure he lured me here on false pretenses, but if others do arrive, I don't want to be naked, in a pool, with my boss. I've skinny-dipped with a mixed group my own age and with my husband at our cottage, but this is different—and creepy. However, he hasn't been a boor like my instructor Rob who grabbed my ass and suggested we go to his house while his wife was at work. Dwaine just wants to skinny-dip. I hope.

My skin tingles as the cool pool water seeps under my suit. I swim about twenty lengths of the crawl until an impatient tug on my foot halts me.

Dwaine asks, "Why don't you let me toss you into the air? My son loves it."

Instead of the alarm bells that should be clanging in my head, I hear Grampa's voice. When I was little, he'd link the fingers of his hands to create a platform. I'd place one foot on this temporary podium, he'd push up, and I'd spurt into the air before plunging into the water.

He tosses me a few times, then says, "Glad you're not upset with me." I expect he'll pester me about removing my bathing suit but instead he asks, "Why don't you float on your back, across my arms, and I'll toss you in the air?"

I relax against his outstretched arms.

He says, "Close your eyes," then slips underwater, leaving me on the surface. I steady myself for his thrusting push, waiting for the thrill of surging into the air. Instead, soft wet lips plaster my mouth and a rigid tongue strains to pry open my lips, puckered to keep out pool water. I kick and scratch, wriggle away from his arms, and flop underwater.

I surface, spit out the pool water, then step six feet backward. "I trusted you."

He pinches the bridge of his nose.

"You're my *boss*! My *married* boss!" My voice gets louder with each syllable.

I wait for him to respond, to apologize, to say something—*anything*—but he just stands there, open-mouthed, as if *he's* shocked by *my* behavior.

I say, "You *lied* to me!"

"I thought all divorcées missed having regular sex."

Dumbfounded and disgusted, I climb onto the deck, swaddle myself under the false protection of my oversize beach towel, then slip into my uniform inside the change house. Back at the plane, I lock both doors and consider flying to the airport. Dwaine deserves punishment, but deserting him will force him to contact someone and more people will learn about my stupidity.

Some might accept he's the predator, but he might spin-doctor his actions to discredit me. My mother, a legal secretary, tells me that when women report sexual harassment without clear physical evidence of rape, the police, the courts, and public opinion often transform her from victim into villain.

Ten minutes later, Dwaine arrives. I unlock his door. He doesn't apologize, just starts the engine, and flies us home without a word.

I hope my next boss uses power and authority appropriately.

For the next few weeks, interactions between us are frostier than the Yukon in January, until the day Steve sallies into the flight school, Brandon on his shoulders. He's doubling as chauffeur because my TR6 needs maintenance, an uneven trade for the fun of having a British sports car.

Dwaine inserts himself into our conversation as if we're great friends. He tousles Brandon's hair and gives him a toy airplane, saying, "I keep these on hand for all the kids!" His avuncular behavior with Brandon pleases me, but his ability to disguise himself as quickly as a chameleon frightens me.

After the pool debacle, I discussed Dwaine's advances with Steve, who responded with disgust, "Didn't think Dwaine was such a slime bucket."

Today, Steve's every response to Dwaine is sarcastic and surly, but Dwaine doesn't respond. Or maybe he just doesn't care.

For the next few days, Dwaine casually asks about Steve or Brandon. Unable to convince myself that his interest and congenial manner are genuine, I deflect conversation away from my personal life. The less he knows about me, the better.

When late August rolls around, I drive to Paul's house to pick up Brandon—and discuss a new custody arrangement. Paul hasn't arrived from work but Jeanne, his partner of eight months, invites me into the backyard with a nervous smile. Brandon stops playing on his swing set with friends and rushes to greet me but, after a few minutes of cuddling, returns to his friends.

Jeanne looks at her watch, shifts in her lawn chair. "Paul should be here soon. I'll make iced coffees for us and call his office." About five minutes later, she returns, hands me my coffee, and glances at her watch. "The office said Paul's just finishing with a trucker at the Peace Bridge."

I ask, "What's Brandon been doing the past two weeks?"

"We went shopping for school clothes in Buffalo. Clothes are much cheaper there."

"He loves clothes."

"And we went camping at Darien Lake, the waterpark south of Buffalo." Talking seems to distract her, but after her description of the park waterslides, she checks the time again. "I don't know why Paul's so late."

I wouldn't want the unexpected role of entertaining an ex-wife, so I say, "I don't care if I ever see him again."

"I thought . . . you might want him back."

He must have said *he* ended our marriage. "I'm only here because of Brandon."

She relaxes in her chair. "Paul's the best thing that's happened to me."

"I'm glad he's found someone as wonderful as you."

She beams with pleasure.

Paul arrives, only thirty minutes late, explains a problem with a customs shipment, and says, "Now that Brandon is older, he needs to stay with one parent for the school year instead of changing homes each school year."

"If he continues living with me, he'll be at the same school but, if you prefer—"

Paul says, "That's okay as long as he lives with us for the entire summer vacation, Christmas, and long weekends."

Jeanne says, "This will minimize the upheaval in Brandon's life."

Paul takes Jeanne's hand and says, "I'm looking forward to having him spend time with me—and my fiancée!"

Jeanne blushes, head lowered, demurely.

"I'm happy—for both of you!"

Problems soon surface.

Though my salary is good for a single person, as a single mother, I have unexpected school and medical expenses. We've agreed the custodial parent is responsible for Brandon's expenses, but I hadn't fully appreciated how much I relied, emotionally and financially, on Paul's support of Brandon throughout the year. Paul earns more and now has a dual income situation from Jeanne's nursing job. He'd help, if I ask, but I hesitate to reveal problems in my new life—or do anything to make Paul reconsider our joint custody arrangement.

I feel fortunate to have Madeline, a great seventeen-year-old sitter, who meets Brandon after school, includes him in a family dinner with her parents, and then plays with him in our apartment until I get home. He hasn't displayed any acting-out behaviors at home or school to suggest maladjustment, but I worry he's spending too much time with sitters instead of parents.

To complicate these concerns, Steve starts inserting his own kind of pressure. One morning as we cuddle under my fluffy comforter, he pulls me closer. "We could spend *all* our time together if I moved in with you."

"*Um-hmm.*"

"I work twelve-hour shifts, three days a week. You work twelve-hour split shifts, six days a week."

"I won't be home any more often."

"We'd be together every night . . . and I'd be able to spend more time with Brandon."

I say, "He loves being with you. In fact, when he's with you, he likes going to the grocery store as much as the playground."

"Plus, I could do the grocery shopping and laundry and cleaning, so you'd be able to spend *quality* time with Brandon on your day off."

"The only man I know who does housework is my grandfather and he only vacuums because my grandmother has a bad back." I laugh. "At least, that's what *she* claims!"

"I'm here almost every night anyway. Let's make it official. Please!"

His rationale is sound, but my intuition tells me not to rush. "I want to discuss this with Paul and his partner, Jeanne."

"Does he still control your life?" he asks, with a peevish note of jealousy.

I kiss him on the cheek. "He's the father of my son. I won't break up with you if he disapproves, but life will be easier if he's comfortable with my living arrangements."

"Why her?"

"She's part of Brandon's life so she's part of mine. She's the perfect *Leave It to Beaver* wife Paul's always wanted."

During my next visit at their home to pick up Brandon after a long weekend, we discuss my plan to live with Steve. Paul and I've agreed to do what's best for Brandon, not what's best for us, but I don't know if jealousy might taint his reaction.

Brandon bounces on his father's knee and says, "Last weekend Steve took Mommy and me to a waterslide park and then we had ice cream and then we went to McDonald's."

I'm relieved when Paul says, "Sounds like a nice guy." To Brandon he says, "Lil buddy, let's get you packed."

Jeanne touches me on the arm. "Let's you and me have coffee in the kitchen." As soon as she pours coffee, she moves closer and whispers, "I *have* to ask you something. Brandon insists he saw Paul attack you—"

My throat constricts.

"But I told him he must be wrong. His daddy would never hit anyone."

I wince. "I hoped Brandon wouldn't remember."

"You mean Paul *really did* attack you?"

"Only once, after . . . we separated. One Friday when I came to pick up Brandon."

She says, "He hates being alone."

"He was drunk." I deliberately catch her eye. "Is he still drinking?"

She doesn't look away. "Only a couple of beers on weekends."

"You seem to be good for Paul—and Brandon adores you."

"He's a wonderful child."

I steer the conversation back to Paul's anger. "One attack was one too many. Before we separated, Paul threatened me when I didn't comply with his wishes, which was often."

She sympathizes. "He can be cranky."

"*Cranky!* Has he ever threatened *you?*"

Her plucked eyebrows rise above her plastic Vuarnet glasses. "Never! He's the kindest man I know."

I'm distressed that Brandon remembers Paul's attack but relieved his memory sparked Jeanne's curiosity. I've been desperate to learn how much Paul was drinking and how he treats her, but was hesitant to start that conversation.

In mid-January, five months after our first date, Steve moves in. I *married* Paul after six months but don't foresee any problems, as the only apparent quality both share is their love for Brandon. Steve is even-tempered and practical, has a huge savings account, doesn't smoke, has never done drugs, and drinks only on special occasions. Though Paul's parents never accepted me, Steve's parents treat Brandon as if he were their grandson and encourage us to join them for Sunday dinners. Steve and his family seem perfect.

I want this relationship to work so I can give Brandon a stable and traditional home.

A few months later, as I prepare dinner, I suddenly feel a pair of strong arms wrap around me, and a bouquet of beautiful lilies dances in front of my face.

"Steve! Thank you for my favorite flowers. What's the occasion?"

He pecks me on the cheek. "Only that I'm happy we're living together! Don't you agree taking care of Brandon is easier?"

Before I can answer, he points toward the salad bowls and says, "We agreed you'd make salads fixings one way."

"They are one way."

"No, they're not."

"Yes, they are. Each bowl has lettuce topped with chopped, sliced, and diced vegetables."

His face reddens. "I meant for you to make them the way I like them."

"Brandon and I don't like *all* our vegetables diced, but I will dice yours."

"That's too much work. I want you to dice *all* the vegetables, *every* day."

"No."

"Fine. Be ridiculous. Make more work for yourself."

On the surface, my unwillingness to bend to his demands may seem silly, but his determination is about more than being fussy about food. From experience, I know this is how control starts, subtly and about something minor. His need for conformity—and control—jolts me with a lightning strike *aha* moment. My life is *easier* but not better. I care for him because he loves me, because he loves Brandon, because he wants to make our lives easier, and because I love the stability and commitment of marriage.

He's easy to be with, reliable, and a fabulous lover, but his placid consistency is dull.

Somewhere, there must be a man who's steadfast—and stimulating—but not a control freak.

In March, in spite of Dwaine's predation at the swimming pool, or perhaps because of his behavior, he agrees to host my government grant for a multi-engine course that trains me to fly aircraft with two or more engines, and an instrument course to allow me to fly through clouds. I almost forgive him until I realize he agreed, not because he wants to help, but because the grant represents easy income in a competitive business with minimal profit margins.

During my training, I ignore Dwaine's rebuffs of "Females aren't charter pilots . . . especially females who have children at home," and convince myself that his smile means he's teasing.

I pass the flight test in May 1981 and expect he'll promote me to copilot on charter flights. When a male instructor hired after me gets that coveted right-seat position that should be mine, I'm furious but let my anger simmer.

Before making changes to my personal and professional life, I must consider how those decisions will influence Brandon. I mull possible alternatives in my head and rehearse what I'm going to say to Dwaine—and Steve.

A week or so later, Steve and I watch *M*A*S*H* reruns on television. He holds my hand and giggles as Hot Lips Houlihan rolls around the tent floor with Major Burns, until I say, "There's no easy way to say this—our relationship isn't working for me."

He jerks his hand away as if immersed in boiling water.

"Tell everyone it's my fault. I was desperate to make a better life for Brandon."

"I thought you loved me!" His voice trembles and cracks.

I touch his arm. "I do love you, but not—"

He crumbles against the cushion.

"You're a wonderful man but not the right wonderful man for me."

He closes his eyes, refusing to look at me.

As kindly as possible, I say, "Before you came into the picture, I had to be Brandon's mom *and* dad. I was responsible for everything. I was exhausted, physically and emotionally. After you moved in, I realized I wanted this relationship to work because of Brandon."

He removes his glasses, leans forward, and hides his face with open palms. Heaving sobs of despair fill the room. I squeeze my eyes shut, unprepared for the honesty of his anguish, but aware I deserve to see and hear the pain I've caused. "I was wrong, and I'm sorry."

After a few tense minutes, I say, "I hope you'll forgive me, after you've found the perfect partner, after you've been happy with her for twenty years instead of unhappy with me for twenty years."

He looks at me with bloodshot eyes. "I'll move in with my friends tomorrow."

His finality scares me. I guess my face indicates I expected a gradual separation because he says sarcastically, "Don't look so surprised. If it's over, it's over. If you don't want me to go, say so."

The television blares end credits.

He says, "I want to see Brandon once a week."

I nod. In my desperation to give Brandon a traditional family life, I hadn't fully considered possible consequences if our relationship faltered. I'd introduced a father figure into my son's young life, and now I was ripping their bond apart.

I'm pleased Steve wants to continue his relationship with Brandon. I don't know how long their relationship will continue, but at least the rip might feel more like a gradual tear than a brutal slash. I vow never to jump into another relationship and risk hurting another person the way I've hurt Steve—and maybe Brandon.

I search for jobs at larger schools with an active charter business. I receive a few offers to instruct but none offering charter pilot opportunities. I stew in silence until one warm autumn morning in 1981 when a twin-engine Piper Navajo whirls onto our ramp. Willy, the owner of the flight school where I had my first flight lessons, steps out onto the wing.

He hails me with a goofy smile, loosens his tie as if it's a noose, and hitches up his pants. "My passengers are investors looking to expand their farming empires. They'll be gone at least an hour—let's get tea at the terminal."

We chat about aviation and old friends until he asks, "Do you have your multi-instrument rating yet?"

I contort my mouth. "Yeah, but Dwaine won't use me on charters."

His brow creases. "Ridiculous. I don't have enough business

to hire you full-time, but I can hire you part-time. In fact, I can use you one day a week starting immediately."

I can't believe my good luck and can hardly restrain my enthusiasm as we discuss the details. I don't bother consulting Dwaine because Willy offers to hire me on my day off.

After several weeks of flying as copilot, Willy offers, "I'd like you to be my copilot two to three days weekly."

Trepidation shakes my shoulders. "Not sure if Dwaine will agree."

"Don't see why he wouldn't. We share business—sometimes his planes are gone on a charter or in for repair so he calls me and vice versa—so we may as well share employees."

I hug him and he says, "Leave the negotiations to me."

My first big chance. I can't sleep that night I'm so excited.

Willy calls the next night, but as soon as I hear his voice, I know something is wrong. "Dwaine rejected my suggestion. He offered Kev, his charter pilot."

"Can I still work for you on my days off?"

He groans. "I suggested that. He said if I hired you, he'd stop referring clients to me."

My high spirits disintegrate like a fighter pilot shot from the sky. I hang up and flop onto the couch, my tears erupting like Mount St. Helens. *Why is Dwaine making my career—my life—so difficult? Why did he hire me if he won't give me a chance?*

Brandon stops playing with his Lego blocks and snuggles onto the couch beside me. "Don't cry, Mommy."

I can't let this little guy see me fall apart. I've made his life so confusing with a real dad and an ex-partner. I never wanted Brandon to experience the tension I felt as a child with parents who stayed together for my sister and me, but the upheaval I've caused might not be a better solution.

I squeeze my tears away and say, "Let's go to Dairy Queen!" His little face smiles.

The next morning, I request a meeting with Dwaine who suggests a meeting the following afternoon, at six. When I enter his office at the appointed time, he's lounging in his leather recliner, feet crossed on top of his single-bed-sized oak desk, hands behind his head.

"So you want to be a charter pilot, do you?" he asks, his cadence slow and lazy.

"You know I do."

He shifts his feet to the floor and slaps both palms on his leather blotter. "I hired you as an instructor, and you're gonna stay an instructor."

"Your business would profit with instructors able to fly charters."

He rests his chin on his right fist and taps his index finger against his lips, seeming to consider my suggestion. "If Willy needs a charter pilot, he can have Kev."

"What if Kev's away on a charter? I could be Willy's copilot."

He regards me with half-closed eyes, stands abruptly, then ambles to the door. I expect he's going to usher me out but instead he shuts and locks the door. Swaggering with assurance, he cruises toward me, a smug expression of conquest smeared across his face. He brushes papers from the desk onto his chair. A wide sneer curls his upper lip into a ghoulish grin. He pats the desktop with his hand and asks in a voice as soft as a kitten's purr, "We could do it right here."

I despise him but finally understand if he can't get anywhere with me, I won't get anywhere with this company. I leap to my feet, ignore my desire to slap the smarmy grin of expectation from his face, and shove past him toward the door. As my hand grasps the doorknob, his outstretched arm darts past my head. His palm thwacks against the door, holding it closed. His moist breath tickles my neck. My body stiffens. Blood pounds in my ears. I struggle to breathe, as if a rapid decompression has sucked air from the room. I press my body against the door.

He says, "Now you know how you can become a charter pilot."

"Yes, I do."

I feel his body relax and, when he shifts slightly, I twist the handle to release the lock, and push backward, full force into his body. He stumbles and I whip open the door.

He hisses, "I'll be waiting."

I dash out, trying to process the terrifying realization that I've encountered another man who thinks boorish behavior will change my mind. I want to believe I have bad luck because the alternative hypothesis is that many men think women are theirs for the taking, using anger, violence, or coercion.

I continue teaching at Dwaine's school because I need the money but keep searching for another job as an instructor because he won't let me get experience as a charter pilot. I can't just quit—I have a child to support.

Mostly Dwaine and I ignore each other, but a month later, when I ask if he'll pay for a flight test to upgrade my instructor status from Class III to Class II, he agrees. *Does he still hope to get laid?* After my successful test, I'm more marketable, and within two months, I accept a flight instructor job as manager of a flight school in British Columbia. I can't work for Dwaine a minute longer.

I dread discussing this long-distance move with Paul, but when I do, he seems relieved, not angry. He looks at Jeanne, slowly finishing his cigarette. "Actually, we were hoping . . . since we're home every night and weekends . . . we're hoping Brandon can live here during school and stay with you during summer."

I roll my lips inward and feel tears gathering in the corner of my eyes. "I hate to admit it, but I think staying with you two is best for him."

Paul squeezes Jeanne's hand.

I smile at her. "Jeanne, Brandon couldn't have a better step-mother than you."

I'm envious of their relationship but happy for them. In a perfect world, I'd have a happy marriage, a perfect home for our son, and a career, but so far, that hasn't worked out. This might be a long separation, but Brandon needs parents at home, at night and weekends, and he needs to attend one school, not bounce between different cities and different homes.

22

RECOVERY

My head flops against my chest, then jerks upright like a demented marionette, shuddering me awake as if from a deep sleep, though I can't recall going to bed. My eyelids flutter, then reflexively close to block a searing glare of sunlight bouncing off the plexiglass windscreen. I feel weightless, suspended in time and space, with no sense of movement. Yet, when I scrunch my eyelids into narrow slits, a dizzying pinwheel of emerald, gold, and brown twirls before my face.

Understanding bolts like an electric shock through my body as I remember what I'm doing—or rather, what I'm supposed to be doing—before the nebula of lost time sucked away a sliver of my life. I gasp and choke on a rush of humid summer air.

I'm inside an aircraft—a real aircraft, not a simulator—pirouetting toward green grass, yellow hay, and ploughed fields. The altimeter indicates three thousand feet between us, terra firma, and death. *What if I hadn't recovered from my blackout?* My heart gallops inside my rib cage; tension straitjackets my body.

But I'm not alone. I'm with Fred, a student pilot, evaluating him to see if he's ready for his private pilot flight test. I remember asking him to demonstrate a spin, but instead of requesting an immediate recovery (as all pilots would do if the plane entered an *accidental* spin), I'd instructed him to spin until my command to recover. To ensure he understood my expectations and to compensate for the roaring engine and the whooshing wind, I'd yelled into his ear, "Any questions?"

A wide grin had filled his face. "Sounds great. I love spins!"

The last thing I remembered, the 1,600-pound aircraft whipped left and flipped onto its back. After that, my memory is a black hole.

What if Fred had passed out, too?

I shoot a sideways glance at Fred, seated to my left. He's calm and focused, acting as if everything is normal. I banish all questions about why I blacked out. Why can wait. Recovery can't. I say, "Recover!"—a brief command to ensure my quivering insides don't betray me.

Fred stops the spin and transitions the aircraft into a dive, the most dangerous phase of spin recovery. As our Cessna plummets like a juggernaut, the airspeed indicator needle swoops out of the green zone, rips into the yellow zone of caution, and sprints toward the red line—the never-exceed speed, the limit of engine capabilities. Wind hisses between the worn gaskets of the doors and windows.

Fred pulls us out of the dive—slowly, slowly—to avoid ripping the wings from the aircraft, then shouts, "What a blast! I've never performed a multirotational spin."

How long did I black out?

He levels off, now one thousand feet closer to the patchwork quilt of farm fields, pounds his flat palms against the control column, and whoops, "*Woo-hoo!* I wondered how many rotations we'd do before you decided to recover."

Fred's excitement implies this would be a highlight of his flight training. He swivels toward me. "*Seriously*," he asks again, "how many times did we spin around?"

His question echoes my thoughts. Based on our altitude loss and the tightness of the spin when I woke up, I made an educated guestimate.

The movement of an aircraft in a spin is the opposite of a child's top. When a top begins to spin, the spin axis of the top is vertical and rotates around the central plunger. As the top loses momentum, the rotation becomes wider and slower until the top topples.

Conversely, when a spin begins in an aircraft, the rotation is wide. As the spin progresses, the spin axis becomes nearly vertical. Recognizable objects on the ground become kaleidoscopic blurs streaking past the windscreen. Exactly what I'd seen when I returned to reality.

I casually say, "Almost two full rotations."

"Fan-TAS-tic! Can't wait to tell the guys. Didn't expect a girl to enjoy spinning."

A girl. I despise being reduced to child status, but now isn't the time to discuss semantics. I'm lucky to be with an experienced student who, even without my command, would've recovered before we corkscrewed into the underworld.

Why did I, an active twenty-five-year-old without any health concerns, pass out, without warning? Something is wrong, and whatever that something is snuffed me out like flame without oxygen.

Should I continue this practice flight test or return to the airport? I weigh my obligations to students and employer. I only need to test Fred on two more exercises, and if his performance on these final exercises equals his performance of those completed, I can recommend him for his flight test with our examiner. If I terminate now, Fred will need to spend more money to rent a plane to maintain his skills at a top-notch level. Finishing his pretest today is important.

Besides, I feel fine now. I'm healthy and fit, and I never visit Doc Templeton except for the annual renewal of my aviation medical that, to his amusement, includes an annual Pap test (every year, he says, "Funny, you're the only pilot I've ever known to *need* a Pap test!"). And I've never been hospitalized, except to give birth. I've never called in sick because of my period and never want to provide my colleagues (all male), my supervisors (all male), and the school's students (all male but two) with any reason to support the pervasive idea that I, an unofficial representative for current and future female pilots, am physically, intellectually, or inherently unsuited for aviation.

On the other hand, I've never succumbed to "get-home-itis," an aviator's jeopardy, a compulsion to demonstrate derring-do by refusing to change plans when confronted with unpredicted bad weather, systems malfunctions, or illness. Airline passengers and flight students are not sacrificial pawns for a captain determined to see how many challenges the aircraft and crew can withstand before the flight falters and topples, an airborne Jenga block tower.

I say, "Turn left, toward the airport on a heading of one-eight-five. We'll finish this pretest as we head home."

Back at the flight school, I congratulate Fred, who bounds like a kangaroo to book his flight test. I retreat to the instructors' office, reschedule my afternoon students, call Doc Templeton, and beg for an appointment today.

During the fifteen-kilometer drive to town, my hyperactive imagination scrolls through images of aviation disasters. Each gruesome scene chases another as random thoughts dart through my convoluted brain. My stomach squirms like a can of worms as I envision cadavers and mutilated airplanes and shudder at what might have been the shattered remains of our blood-splattered aircraft.

Today's blackout probably relates to the abrupt change in the aircraft's attitude relative to airflow over the wings as we entered the spin, but *why?* I've been flying since 1979 and, in those two years and twelve hundred hours of flight time, never experienced anything medically unusual. My thoughts dart through tunnels and around corners, a fugitive from shrouded ghosts, dodging bullets of incurable illness.

What if I have diabetes like my great-uncle? Or a tumor churning my brain into mush?

By the time door chimes announce my arrival at the medical office, I'm convinced Death hovers on my shoulder, a cackling devil mocking mortality. Classical music flows from overhead speakers and soft lights caress tawny walls. Neither nudges dread from my knotted shoulders.

White-haired Doc Templeton ushers me into his private office, a windowless box dominated by two walls of floor-to-ceiling bookshelves. He sits behind his oak desk and gestures for me to sit in one of two leather chairs, one red, one green—chosen to determine color blindness.

I describe my blackout.

He frowns. "Never liked spins much." He plucks an otoscope from his collection of instruments, then sticks the cold steel instrument into my ears. "Your right ear is infected."

I sag with relief.

"No pain or dizziness?"

I say no.

He knits his woolly, white eyebrows together and scribbles on my chart. "The infection trapped liquid inside your ear canals and sent your brain a garbled message about balance. Surprised you can walk without toppling over!" He hands me a prescription for amoxicillin, and as I'm wishing all my difficulties could so easily be resolved, he says, "No flying for seven days."

"I have a child to support."

He sighs. "Make sure you finish the prescription, but since you drove here and you're walking just fine, you can start flying day five."

I decide grounding is an opportunity to spend more time with Brandon, who arrives in two days for his two-month summer vacation. He's used to spending time at flight schools while I work, but instead of being there all day, I'll only be teaching ground school theory for two or three hours daily.

23

EAVESDROPPING

Unlike most students who never leave the comfort of their first flight school, I've studied at two different flight schools and, as a commercial pilot and instructor, I've flown in southern Ontario's densely populated flatlands as well as British Columbia's rugged, snowcapped mountains and dangerous box canyons. Day and night, through good weather and bad, I've navigated cities and forests, tundra and mountains, maintaining course by flight instruments, by visual reference to towns, rivers, and roadways, and sometimes by intuition and pure dumb luck.

This diverse experience encourages me to keep applying to larger airlines with charter and scheduled air service. The odds are stacked against me—95 percent of commercial pilots are men. Despite this, as my twenty-seventh birthday approaches, I land a job in northern Ontario as a charter pilot. After seven months of flying the mountains, I'm back home, closer to Brandon, and can't believe a major regional airline has hired me.

Though Brandon will be with Paul and Jeanne during the school year, I find a basement apartment for two because he'll be with me for holidays and summer vacation.

On my first day at Northern Air, Chief Pilot Victor greets me at the employee entrance and takes me to his office in a corner of the vintage WWII hangar.

We complete paperwork, then I have to ask, "Why *did* you hire me?"

"You forced me." Victor's dark-chocolate eyes twinkle from deep recesses. "Your monthly letters and telephone calls wore me down. Anyone that persistent deserves a chance."

Life gets better every day.

When he ushers me into the hangar, I'm overwhelmed and amazed. Though the actual floor space probably equals a football field, the space seems bigger than Madison Square Garden. The curving, Quonset-style roof soars thirty feet above six or seven twin-engine airplanes, two of which are Twin Otters, each the width of five or six cars, lengthwise. I'll be flying smaller twins, the Piper Navajos, similar to the model I flew with Willy.

After two months flying charters and medevacs, I need an annual flight proficiency test, with me at the controls observed by a Transport Canada inspector to assess my ability to keep the plane right-side up during flight while combatting simulated fires and systems failures.

The upside of reliable equipment is that pilots rarely, if ever, deal with real emergencies. In contrast to this daily life of a professional pilot, described by most pilots as "hours of boredom punctuated with moments of sheer terror," the proficiency test resembles an hour on a medieval torture rack.

All commercial pilots must pass this test, and if I fail, I won't have a career—anywhere in Canada. The hovering threat of failure followed by probable job loss intensifies the experience. If that isn't torment enough, to simulate flight through cloud I'll wear an uncomfortable hood (similar to horse blinders) that restricts my field of vision within the cockpit.

Vic schedules my test and says, "We don't have a simulator, and it's too expensive for us to let you practice in the air and pay for one of our pilots to supervise you. The second-best option is to *get in bed* with the emergency procedures by simulating the drills inside the Navajo with the engines shut off."

At our hangar the next day, I meander through the space, weaving between two late-model cars, a dozen mechanics and their toolboxes, a six-seater Aztec, and a single-engine Cessna, before arriving at the Navajo. I climb inside and, as per company policy, leave the rear door of the aircraft open to ensure a quick exit in case a real emergency occurs.

I grab the laminated pages of the Emergency Procedures Checklist and begin one of the drills. I intend to practice these drills until they're as familiar to me as the skills I use to drive my car. I ignore the drone of engines and cacophonous maintenance tools until a strident male voice overpowers the grinders, drills, and rivet guns used by the maintenance men.

"Another female! Can you believe it?"

It's Mr. Cocky, my secret nickname for the handsome, but arrogant, son of a successful lawyer. I can hear him clearly, so he must be standing near the rear door. My stomach clutches, but I force myself to focus on the emergency drill procedure.

Another voice booms, "I wanna know what kinda fuckin' woman wants to fuckin' fly anyway!" This must be barrel-chested Kurt, another captain, identifiable by his trademark foul mouth.

Should I ignore these wisecracks or poke my head out the door to tell him what kind of *fucking female* wants to fly?

Then Kurt asks, "Why the fuck can't she get a goddamn job that normal women get?"

I'm probably three standard deviations from his definition of a normal female.

Kurt says, "Boobs don't belong in a fuckin' cockpit."

Mr. Cocky says, "Vic's been married a long time. Probably needs to get his 'oil changed.'"

An unidentified voice says, "I hear Vic's scheduled her flight test."

"Maybe she *won't* fuckin' work out," Kurt says.

Mr. Cocky says, "Guess *he* thinks she's good enough."

The unidentified voice sneers, "Good enough to fly—or to fuck?"

I can't take another minute of this verbal abuse. I need to stop cowering in my den like a rabbit surrounded by wolves. As I prepare my rebuttal, dwindling voices indicate they're leaving.

I wonder how entering the conversation would have influenced the outcome. If I'd displayed emotion, would they label me an emotional female? Or would emotion make me more normal in their estimation?

I don't know the answers to these questions, but chide myself for being afraid, for hesitating, for not wanting to draw attention to myself. I want to forget their conversation, but I can't. Whether by accident or intent, Mr. Cocky's opinion about female pilots encouraged cruel comments. Tears roll down my face as I sit, flattened against the aircraft seat, conflicted and confused about my new life.

I've escaped abuse by one man—and flown straight into a storm of abuse by several.

Not wanting anyone to see my weepy face and expose my pain, I sit for a few minutes, attempting to control my emotions, but my thoughts keep swirling back to my first encounter with Mr. Cocky, who tossed a lukewarm hello in my direction, and Kurt, who grunted a hello. I've only flown with the two youngest pilots at this company, both in their mid-twenties (compared to Kurt's probable forty), neither overtly hostile.

Nausea grips my stomach as I contemplate the inevitable prospect of working with men who don't want to fly with me.

Murray's advice about the silo filters into my brain. These men represent the obstacle of prejudice that I can overcome if I ignore their negative comments and focus on my objectives. Instead of packing it in, I'm determined to prove them wrong. Tomorrow.

Now, all I want to do is to devour a Caramilk bar.

I wipe the tears from my eyes, sneak out of the hangar unnoticed, then drive to the butcher shop to buy a fresh roast for dinner.

As the beef roasts, I savor each chocolate square oozing with caramel and flip through *The Right Stuff*, Tom Wolfe's 1979 chronicle about aviation and NASA's space race. Wolfe wrote, "The unspoken premise was you either had the right stuff, or you didn't," and based on NASA's selection of an all-white, all-male, all-Protestant crew for the Mercury program, only white males could ever have the right stuff.

My anger rises as I remember Bessie Coleman, a sharecropper's daughter from Texas. When flight schools in America refused to train anyone who was female *and* Black, she sailed to France to take flight lessons. Then I remember the unsurmountable challenges created for Helen Richey, America's first female scheduled service airline pilot. *What if my all-male colleagues band together to force me out of the company like the all-male pilot union did to her in the 1930s?* Five decades later, despite women's proven capabilities in science, technology, and aviation and their contributions during WWII as pilots and factory workers, the bias toward white male superiority persists.

The kitchen timer trills, and when I open the oven door, the pungent aroma of roasting beef transports me to Mom's Sunday dinners. I combine flour with cool water, add a thin stream of boiling beef juice, and whisk with increasing vigor as I contemplate my fight for more than dishes and diapers. My rage simmers as I stew about the assumption that gender defines women's roles and characteristics. Men are pilots, doctors, or engineers, but women are *female* pilots, female doctors, or female engineers. On days like these, I want to give up.

I splash an ounce of B&G Haut-Medoc into the thickening gravy to justify the generous pour in my glass. Moments later, Brandon throws open the door and races toward me, arms outstretched, tilting his slender torso left and right imitating an airplane. He flaps a sheet of paper in his hand and his impish grin reveals two missing upper incisors. "I got perfect on my arithmetic test today!"

I kneel and scoop him toward me. "Congratulations, sweetheart. I'm proud of you."

He sniffs the air. "Mommeeeee . . . do I smell roast beef?"

"I must've guessed this was a special day for you!"

"I love you, Mommy."

After supper, we cuddle in bed, taking turns reading *The Lion, the Witch and the Wardrobe* aloud. Fifteen minutes later, he falls asleep, and I return to the living room where the implications of Mr. Cocky's oil change comment demolish my attempts to study.

Victor doesn't seem the type to try to get me into bed, but that's what Steve and I thought about Dwaine. Victor has me scheduled to start Twin Otter training, and if I start flying as first officer on those planes, I'll be away overnight with male captains.

What will I do on an overnighter if Victor expects sex?

What if any of them expect sex?

$=$ 24 $=$

THE TRAINING
CAPTAIN

I buckle into the Twin Otter's five-point harness, ready to tackle the last hour of training for my flight test. Though Vic hired me as copilot, I'm training for a captaincy position and therefore seated in the left seat, the captain's seat. Kurt, the designated training instructor, sits in the first officer's seat on the right side of the flight deck.

During the previous four training hours, Kurt and I were alone, but now Kurt's father, a retired commercial pilot, occupies the jump seat. I'm about to ask why anyone other than a Northern Air employee is onboard when Kurt growls, "Whad'ya think? Is it true women have half the brains of men?"

Is he trying to provoke me—or get a laugh from his father?

Either way, Kurt's comment doesn't encourage friendship. Neither has his attitude toward me. Whenever I asked a question, he revealed his impatience with snarly responses such as, "Haven't you read the manual?" I hope he knows the answers to my questions but can't be bothered to tell me.

As a person and a parent, I've learned that encouragement and support produce better results than anger and criticism.

As an instructor, I've learned that a question from one student often means others might have a similar question. Maybe the subject is complex and needs more explanation, or perhaps an explanation using different words or examples, relating the known to the unknown, is required. Or maybe, I didn't explain it correctly.

Halfway through this final hour of the standard five training hours, Kurt announces, "You're done."

I'm astonished. "My training hour is only half over—"

Kurt snarls, "I've got it," as he grabs his control column and starts grandstanding with steep turns and side slips.

His show-off stunts annoy me. "I want to use the remaining time to practice—"

But he's insistent. "Change seats with my dad. He's gonna fly."

I start to protest until I see his father standing, ready to take over.

I change places but resent Kurt's reallocation of the remaining thirty minutes—10 percent—of my training time for joyriding. Moreover, the remaining thirty minutes of practice time would be especially beneficial, as I haven't yet been offered the De Havilland training course taken by the other pilots a few months ago, prior to my arrival.

However, my training has gone well, so I interpret Kurt's decision to mean I've completed the required syllabus in less than standard time. My confidence surges. He's the instructor and a ten-year veteran with this company, but I'm a novice with three years and two thousand total flight hours.

On the day of my flight test, the Transport Canada inspector details the exercises on the test. I nod and smile until he says, "The last test item will be an approach to the airport followed by a missed approach with a simulated engine failure."

My stomach jitterbugs. Kurt didn't include this critical combination in my training. In fact, he didn't even include a missed approach, also called an overshoot. The inspector continues talking about something to Jim, the pilot who'll fly with me, but I'm zoned out. *Should I cancel the flight test or give it my best shot?*

I've done missed approaches with a simulated engine failure in other multi-engine aircraft but never in this plane—and never in a crew situation. My gut feeling tells me to explain my dilemma, but if I pass, Vic won't need to reschedule the flight test and inconvenience the government inspector who's flown several hundred miles to meet us at the halfway point.

Forty-five minutes into the test, I've successfully performed all the maneuvers and am feeling confident when the inspector announces, "That's all good. Now let's return to the airport for the instrument approach. We won't be landing, but sometime as we approach the runway, I'll instruct you to start the missed approach. Then, sometime soon after, I'll tell Jim to reduce power on one of the engines."

My approach to the airport, using instruments only, is perfect. Half a mile west of the airport, the inspector says, "Uh-oh. Moose on the runway. Overshoot!"

I apply full power and start climbing. My hood prevents me from seeing outside but also prevents me from seeing the inspector or Jim. Because Twin Otter throttles are on the ceiling of the cockpit, I can't see which throttle Jim will slide to idle.

The simulated engine failure will come soon—but when?

Which engine will the inspector choose?

Wham! Suddenly, the right rudder punches against my right foot. The unequal rudder pressure means the right engine is still at full power, but the left engine has "failed." I press hard against the right rudder, turn slightly right to return to my assigned heading, and keep climbing.

After this acceptable start, I feel myself crumble. My knees vibrate and my feet chatter on the rudders. My brain seems frozen so, instead of the cue-and-response checklist conversation I'm supposed to initiate with Jim, my copilot, I can't speak. Invisible hands clamp my throat and squeeze tighter and tighter. Silently, I begin the emergency checklist, and although I follow the correct procedure, I should've estimated that the probability of anyone performing this exercise without training, coupled with the added pressure of an inspector judging the performance, would be subzero.

I realize I'm close to losing control.

So does the inspector, who says, "That's a fail. Take me home!"

We return to the airport in silence. They aren't talking, and I can't.

I whip myself for botching the exercise. My decision to wing it and not discuss my concerns before the test was the wrong decision. I should've trusted my gut feeling and realized that reading about the missed approach is as related to the performance of that maneuver as reading *The Joy of Sex* is to having sex.

My desire not to let others down has let everyone down, including myself. All my years of studying and training have been futile. My successes feel meaningless in the face of this failure. I feel worthless and shrink in disgust, embarrassed to be my humiliated self.

I'm sure my good performance on the other test items will be ignored and my poor performance on one exercise will provide fodder for the cynics delighted to spread the word that Victor's new girl is a loser like the previous girl. Worst of all, I'll probably be fired.

I marinate in misery in the jump seat as Jim and Dave fly to their next destination. Jim and Dave include me in conversation, but I'm so consumed with wondering what they're going to say behind my back and to the other male pilots, I rarely respond.

Maybe I should quit aviation and focus on graduating university and being with Brandon. However, because distance education enables me to study anywhere, maybe I should get an aviation job in another city or province. Moving to another province would make Brandon's travel between his parents' homes more expensive, but if I agree to pay that extra cost, Paul will support my decision.

After landing, Jim shuts down the engines and says, "Please, come join us in the terminal for a coffee."

A rush of blood tingles my cheeks. If I look at him, I'm sure I'll see my shame reflected as scorn on his face, so I focus on the floor and shake my head.

When they disappear into the terminal, I bang my forehead against the bulkhead and unravel. I'd contained my emotions during the flight, but alone with my self-loathing, tears seep onto my cheeks. I strive for perfection as a pilot, but obviously, I've proven I'm far from perfect. Doubt runs circles around deprecation. *Should I have been able to perform the missed approach without instruction?*

Jim returns in fifteen minutes, hops into the captain's seat, then turns toward me. I've regained my composure, but watery eyes betray me. He says, in a voice deliberately soothing, "Cheer up. Vic will give you another chance."

I bite my lower lip. "Thanks for your encouragement—but why?"

"You're not the first person to fail a flight test."

I laugh through tears. "I suppose not, but it feels that way."

He grins sympathetically. "Vic will give you more training. You won't need a retest for the other exercises. In fact, you were doing well until the final exercise. What happened? Seemed like you'd never done it."

"I haven't."

Jim's placid face tenses. "Did Kurt use a checklist?"

"I don't think so—but he did use the last half of my training to showboat for his father."

Jim's jaw drops.

"Then Kurt made me move to the jump seat so his dad could fly."

Jim's eyes blaze with anger. "You gotta be kidding. Vic needs to know."

I want to believe Kurt's omission was unintentional, but his comment, "Maybe she won't fuckin' work out," now rings as a promise. Jim and I meet with Vic that afternoon, and soon thereafter Vic deposes Kurt from his role as training captain, a decisive action that suggests previous problems. I'm thrilled to have a new instructor for the balance of my training but realize my future flights with Kurt as a senior captain may be very unpleasant.

Two days later, I'm in the pilots' lounge waiting for Doug, the new training captain, who strolls into the lounge dressed as if for a *GQ* photo shoot. He shakes my hand and greets me with prep-school manners. I blink to convince myself I'm not face-to-face with Steve McGarrett, the erudite and handsome undercover detective from the TV show *Hawaii Five-0*.

Before sitting down, he removes the ashtray from the table and dumps the two butts into the trash. He lights a Camel and speaks as crisply as his starched white shirt. "Vic's allocated two hours for additional training."

I shift with the jitters but manage a confident smile. "That's generous."

"Once we get airborne, I'll demonstrate, then you'll mimic me. Questions?"

"Why did Vic pick you as the training captain?"

"I'm a flight instructor. Any other questions?"

"No."

"I'll debrief you in the air after every missed approach, so you know where you need to improve." He tosses an impish grin. "I'm familiar with some difficulties female pilots face. My girlfriend, Megan, works as an instructor at one of the local flight schools."

He's nicer than Kurt, but can I trust him? I raise my eyebrows. "For instance?"

"Despite her credentials and professional attitude, students question her competency. The guys here give me grief about living with a female pilot."

I lean forward, cupping my chin between my palms. "What do they say?"

He twirls his Bic lighter like a mini baton. "'Who's in the captain's seat at home?'"

"How's that make you feel?"

He winks. "Their wives have more control than they let on."

I don't restrain a laugh. "I guess they haven't flown with Megan?"

He takes a drag on his cigarette, then stabs it into the clean, glass ashtray. "Of course not. Usually, their comments aren't specific to her. They make rude comments about all female pilots." He pauses. "Actually, all females."

This information makes me wonder if I'm really so lucky to be working here.

In the air, specters of my ignominious failure dance through my brain and ruin my first few attempts to correctly perform the missed approach/engine failure sequence.

Doug says, "Let's sightsee for five minutes and try again."

Thankfully, his relaxation technique works, and after two flights, he schedules my retest for the following week. On test day, I force the memory of flubbing the exercise from my mind and smile at Doug, seated to my right, acting as copilot.

I take a sidelong glance at the Transport Canada inspector peering over my shoulder and say, "Let's do this."

Twenty minutes later, we're back on the ground and I'm a Twin Otter captain.

I realize how successful I feel today compared to the woman

who flew back to the airport following my previous flight test. That one failure, which happened in an instant, devastated me and made all my previous aviation successes feel meaningless. With that one failure, I labeled myself a loser. I knew I wasn't a failure, but I couldn't help feeling that way, at least for the first few hours. When my rational mind took charge and the embarrassment filtered away, I knew my attitude would determine whether I ultimately succeeded. I could've stopped flying after that single disastrous demonstration, but I didn't.

With the support and encouragement of some of my colleagues and the chief pilot, I'm finally steering my life in the right direction, professionally and personally.

I'm working as a pilot, for a major regional carrier, and making the same amount of money as my male colleagues.

Brandon is doing well in school, an important indicator that he's adapted to two homes, in two different cities. Jeanne's had a big role, not just because she adores Brandon, but because she convinced Paul to quit drinking.

I learn this from Brandon who says, "Jeanne told him we'd have more money and he'd lose his beer belly."

I guess the timing was right, and he was ready to quit.

I've decided to start dating again—for fun, not keeps. Lynn was right when she urged me to take time to heal and let myself discover the root of my desperate craving for security.

Grampa provided love and security but paradoxically minimized that security every time he returned me to my parents. As with all other adults in my parents' lives, Grampa couldn't know that love was a stranger in our home.

To avoid creating a heartbreaking fiasco like the one I created with Steve, I'm not searching for a father figure for Brandon. To prevent me from focusing on one guy, I'm seeing three, casually as dinner or movie companions, on dates squeezed between my obligations to Northern Air, university classes and assignments, and being a mother. This arrangement allows companionship without commitment and works well—until I meet Matthew at the flying school where I teach advanced flight training part-time. I love working with people motivated to complete their commercial or instrument training, unlike 90 percent of student pilots who quit, due to financial or time constraints or because their partner disapproves. Plus, the extra money I earn from teaching helps me treat Brandon to more dinners and movies than I could using only my Northern Air salary.

As we proceed through the stages of Matthew's commercial pilot training, I learn he's a chemistry grad and tech geek working for a major pharmaceutical company. At the end of his flight training, he asks me out. He doesn't kiss me at the end of the first date or at the end of the second, third, or fourth. This aloofness counterbalances my tendency to leap into a relationship, but just as I'm beginning to think he prefers men, he kisses me on date five. Soon, we're sleeping together, though I continue seeing the other three socially.

Vic schedules my first few flights with Doug or himself to familiarize me with our routes to northern Ontario's subarctic tundra communities before I confront captains less than enthusiastic about a female pilot. However, a June snowstorm alters his good intentions, so on my second day, I'm jousting with Captain Kurt, the ex-training captain.

Six towering feet of nastiness, the broad-shouldered, beer-bellied, angry bear glares at me. "If you *fuckin'* think you *fuckin'* deserve to *fuckin'* work here, *fuckin'* open the *fuckin'* hangar doors."

No platitudes. No good mornings. No clichéd queries about my health.

Just go fuck yourself.

But first, open the hangar doors.

I have enough work experience to realize that any new job,

in any profession, can be intimidating. No matter who you are or where you work, acceptance requires time. But I've also heard via the Moccasin Telegraph (northern lingo for gossip) that aviation is littered with arrogant captains who treat copilots as imbecilic scum, regardless of gender.

Instead of helping me learn the ropes, Kurt might use them to lynch me.

I glare into his eyes, hoping my stalwart posture portrays a brave Jeanne d'Arc ready for battle against his pepper-sprayed-with-profanity orders, not an immobile coward with leaden feet. Ugly memories of Paul's ornery snarls and clenched fists crash inside my skull, but just as I weathered his rages, I'll overcome this new bully. I won't let his don't-fuck-with-me persona stomp me, a "snotty-nosed newbie first officer," into the ground.

I turn toward the doors and Kurt hurls at my back, "Gaaahd-dammmmmmmit, check the fuckin' weather, too."

To get the plane outside, I must open six of the twelve doors, each fifteen feet high by seven feet wide. My prima donna days are over.

My previous employers had new hangars with electronic door systems to slide massive doors along unsullied tracks. But even then, the maintenance crew was responsible for opening hangar doors, pulling planes onto the ramp by hand or with a motorized tug, and aligning them wing tip to wing tip for the pilots. Here, no system and no one other than me is available to move these hangar doors along tracks encrusted with four decades of dirt.

Getting these doors to budge will be a challenge, but I hold my head high and select one of two doors positioned slightly ajar to circulate airflow. At the base of the first door, I stand firm, a female David dwarfed by Goliath, then grip the four-inch end of the door with both hands, lean my one hundred and thirty-seven pounds against the five-hundred-pound door, and shove.

The *rat-a-tat-tatting* din of the maintenance crew stops.

From the corner of my eye, I see their heads rivet toward me. If I fail, I'll be the laughingstock of this company—and maybe the entire airport.

The bearings creak. I push. The massive door shifts, crawling as fast as an ancient Galapagos tortoise. I keep pushing. The door moves slower than a sloth, but after two feet, momentum becomes my friend, and the door becomes a jackrabbit sprinting for her life. I slam the first of six doors so hard against its stops that the door bounces back about six inches. I jump in surprise. The thud reverberates through the hangar.

The maintenance crew rushes to help, and though I wave them away, one of them says, "We help the guys, so we'll help you."

Kurt stands firm, watching.

Somehow, Kurt and I survive each other for ten flights, two days, and one night. Though he speaks to me only when safety and professional courtesy require crew coordination, he isn't the ogre he pretends to be. I've heard of captains at other airlines who believe FO means fuck off, not first officer, an opinion revealed by attitude or the directive, "Shut up, and let me fly my plane." To my surprise, he lets me fly every other leg, the only way any pilot gets experience.

Nevertheless, I'm looking forward to spending the night with Matthew, my only sex partner for the past three months. Tonight's plans coincide with Brandon's school break visit with his father and are perfect because Matthew doesn't have to make excuses for excluding Brandon in our dinner plans. I can stay overnight at Matthew's without the guilt of shirking parental responsibility clouding my evening.

At the terminal, I shut down the engines, glad to see Matthew on the ramp, ready for our prearranged photo shoot. He hops into the plane, and as he snaps photographs of me at the controls, I grin into his Canon T50, pretending life is perfect. We share a love of scotch, aviation, and Trivial Pursuit. After photographs, he bends his slender six-foot-four frame over me, brushes a lock of straight hair from his high forehead, and kisses me.

He says, "We should hurry to my place."

Imaginary butterflies tickle my groin until he says, "The chicken breasts have marinated long enough in Burgundy."

During supper, I say, "I want to tell you about the radiation biophysics course I'm taking." I'm also studying genetics and abnormal psychology, but he'll be more impressed with the science course. "I didn't take many science courses in high school, so this course is difficult."

He delicately places his silverware on his Royal Doulton plate, then with chin supported by elegant fingers Beethoven would envy, he says, "Impressive. Tell me more."

He slices a slender strip of chicken, chewing slowly and precisely.

I say, "Last night I muddled through a chapter about cations and anions."

He laughs, chokes, and grabs his throat, gasping for breath. I leap up and thump my fist against his back. As vague memories about how to perform the new Heimlich maneuver whiz through my mind, he catches his breath and gulps half his glass of Burgundy.

To my surprise, his hooting laughter begins anew. "I apologize, but those ions are pronounced *cat*-ions and *an*-ions." His laughter continues, "Not kayshuns and anyuns."

Scarlet with fury and embarrassment, I rally, "Maybe you'll choke on your pearl on-ions so we can end our communicat-ion."

Matthew's derisive laughter stops. "Logical. Clever. But wrong."

After sex, I leave. Being with him makes me feel lonelier than when I'm alone. We sleep together twice more before drifting apart without drama.

= = =

The following week, during our first flight together and the first time we've chatted since my flight test, Vic initiates conversation. "I talked with Kurt about your training."

"I suppose he blames me for losing his position as training captain?"

"He admitted he 'might have missed a thing or two' but insists his training wasn't to blame."

"Thanks for making Doug the new training captain."

He says, "Kurt said you didn't meet flight test standards because"—he hesitates—"aviation isn't a woman's job."

"I hear that way too often."

"He wondered why you didn't want to stay home with your son."

"You omitted at least four f-bombs." We laugh, then I ask, "Did you ask him why he doesn't want to stay home with *his* children?"

Vic turns away.

I can't blame him for Kurt's actions, but as chief pilot he's responsible for ensuring that flight training follows the guidelines. Calmly, but with a deliberate edge to my voice, I say, "The bottom line is that the person preparing me for my flight test assessed me as incompetent before I got in the plane."

Vic adjusts his yellow Ray-Ban sunglasses. "You could look at it that way."

This is a grudging response, but my optimism persuades me to look on the bright side. He hired me and supported me after I failed one test item by giving me two more hours of training. And he recognized the benefit of having a former flight instructor, Doug, become the new training captain. This man is an ally I can count on.

$$= = =$$

Sometime in the next few weeks during a scheduled flight with Sam, one of our many senior captains, he asks, "Do you know Vic hired you instead of Pat?"

"I'm guessing Pat isn't short for Patricia?"

Sam ignores my jibe. "The guys told Vic that Pat would be a better choice. He's a local boy. He used to work here, so he knows our routes and our planes. Plus, he's stronger."

"Many women aren't as strong as some men but I'm strong enough."

He doesn't respond.

"Why *did* Vic hire me instead of Pat?"

Sam brushes a lock of black hair away from his eyes. "When you two are on an overnight layover, what do you do at night?"

My defenses bubble but I keep my tone casual. "Doing what you and I do. Eat, have a drink, go to bed early for the zero-dark-thirty departure."

Sam smirks. "Yeah, but we're all curious. Do you go to bed *alone?*"

I look outside for a few moments until I feel sure some of the rage has disappeared from my face. "Do you *really* think Vic hired me for sex?"

"Have you noticed you're sched with Vic on overnighters more often than the rest of us?"

"I only check to see who I *won't* be flying with." We laugh together, then I say, "You guys have more experience, but we wrote the same exams and took the same flight tests."

A slash of scarlet races across his high cheekbones, then he hunkers deeper into his stoop shoulders.

"Your loyalty to Pat is impressive but I'm offended you think I was hired to fuck, not fly."

= = =

Two days later, after Sam and I returned to our home airport, I visit Vic in his office. He's hunched over his desk, shuffling papers and drinking coffee, but waves me in. "Have a good flight with Sam?"

"He was friendly and helpful. At first, I thought he supported equality and opportunity for women, but then he told me about Pat."

Vic slouches against his high-backed executive chair. "I wondered if he might. Sam asked me to rehire Pat."

"Why'd you hire me instead?"

"Pat's a great guy but I'll wager Sam didn't mention Pat is an alcoholic?"

"He forgot that detail."

"Pat's their friend. He needed a job, but he had his chance. Ignore their whining. They'll get over it."

"Will they?"

"Give 'm time."

I'm grateful for support from three of my colleagues—Victor, Doug, and Jim—so rather than tackle my detractors head-on, I bury the war-whoop warnings and hope time will dissolve resentment. But the brutal truth curdles in my stomach. Why should I expect support and encouragement from strangers, men who'd rather work with men, when I don't get support and encouragement from my parents?

25

LIFE IN
THE BOX OFFICE

"Hell-o, young lady. I recognize that uniform you're wearing! Guess you'll be joining us on the flight?" asks the fifty-something man clutching a Vuitton briefcase. His London Fog overcoat ripples in the breeze, exposing a steel-gray suit with coordinating shirt and tie. He exudes a power-broker-financier aura from Toronto's Bay Street area, a pleasant change from the typical northerner's jeans, toque, and plaid lumberjack jacket.

I wear my company uniform with the pride of accomplishment. Three gold stripes on the coat sleeves indicate my status as first officer, so his perspective that I'll be joining him seems skewed. I wish he'd shrivel up and die—I've chosen a far corner of the prefab aluminum terminal building for a few precious moments of silence and spring sun before the next flight—but reply courteously, "Yes. Did you enjoy your flight from Toronto?"

He waves his hand dismissively. "Just another day. I fly a lot. Great to see your airline has hired a stewardess. What're you serving for lunch?"

I turn my head so he can't see the grimace flashing across my face. Licks of evaporating snow tickle the Twin Otter's tires, parked for our thirty-minute turnaround. I say evenly, "Stewardesses prefer to be called flight attendants."

"What's the difference?"

I clench my fists. "Flight attendant removes gender from the job. And speaking of job and gender—I'm one of the two pilots on your flight today."

"I've never seen a female pilot." Doubt riddles his voice.

My fingernails dig into my palms through lightweight gloves, but I try to be upbeat. "There aren't many. In fact, though the uniforms worn by my male colleagues are ready-made, my uniform had to be tailor-made. These three stripes mean—"

He scowls and deliberately adopts an irritated tone, as if he's offended. "I *know* what they mean. Didn't you hear me say I fly a lot?"

I clamp my lips together as Mom's voice resonates, *Don't say something you'll regret.*

He gawks. "Didn't you borrow that jacket?"

Breakfast performs somersaults in my stomach. I force my mouth into a rigid smile and ask through clenched teeth, "If you saw a man wearing this uniform, would you ask if he borrowed the jacket?"

He blushes.

I don't have time to discover if he's ingenuous or chauvinistic. "I'll see you on the plane," I say, and then spin toward the trolleys of cargo and luggage parked beside the Twin Otter.

During the flight, as I relish the pleasure of soaring through the sky, proud (and still somewhat amazed) to be operating a magnificent hunk of heavy metal, Gavin, the captain, says, "There's a saying that if women belonged in a cockpit, it'd be called a box office."

I want to believe his remark is a crude attempt to be friendly, but coupled with the passenger's remarks prior to the flight, I feel like an unwelcome novelty.

Though flight schools welcomed me (my money), my experiences in commercial aviation suggest that many people consider a female pilot on the flight deck less capable than a monkey. A patri-archal society with inequality of opportunity harms everyone, yet every day, at work or play, I encounter men and women unaware or disinterested in feminist struggles for equality of opportunity and equal pay for equal work. The frequent barrage of bias, rejection, and absurd assumptions based on gender is galling—and psychologically debilitating. I'm thrilled when some nod with understanding but crushed when they follow with, "But you'll quit when you get married and have children."

I imagine the few other women employed as commercial pilots endure challenges similar to mine, but there's no easy way to connect with any of them. The nearest female pilot flying for an air carrier lives seven hundred kilometers away. As a solitary female unable to share frustrations—and accomplishments—with female colleagues, my enthusiasm for this job is withering from lack of workplace support and friendships. *I can only hope that the loneliness of my struggle makes it easier for future female pilots.*

A few weeks later, Liam, one of my colleagues, helps me under-stand both sides of the dilemma. He's fair-haired, muscular, and broad-shouldered like my ex-husband. However, Liam's gentle nature overrides any real connection between their physiques. Swaddled by a few more pounds than svelte Paul, Liam seems less Greek god and more cuddly Teddy.

Liam and I crisscross the expansive hangar floor, a cement sea of mottled oil stains, toward our aircraft parked outside. We dodge islets of cat litter absorbing oil spills, duck under aircraft, and navigate around aircraft parts, overall-clad mechanics, and their dresser-sized, candy-apple-red toolboxes.

He arrives at the pilots' access door before me and grasps the door handle, but instead of opening the door and walking through, he hesitates. He twists to face me and says, "I need to ask you something."

My heart flip-flops like the syncopated synthesizer in Queen's "Radio Ga Ga." I suffer through an unendurable pause until he says, "The problem with you—"

What does he mean—the problem with me?

"You confuse us. We don't know how to treat a female pilot. Should we open the door for you, like on a date, or should we go through first?"

My shoulders relax. "Opening a door is sometimes appropriate"—I pause—"but we're employees with the same status, in the same age group."

He opens the door, smiles a lopsided grin, and walks through first.

Liam's curiosity has made me happier than if he'd asked for a date. Well, maybe not, but I value his candid question. I doubt his ultimate goal is to get me into bed (though at this point in my career, this tactic wouldn't surprise me), but if it is, his unique approach impresses me.

I'm thrilled he respects me enough to ask about the commonplace logistics of opening a door, a question that highlights the complexity of interactions between men and women and helps explain why a female pilot generates tension. Though the necessities of WWII prodded against the doors of resistance barricading women from most professions, not much has changed in aviation, at least not in this nether northland between the 49th parallel and the North Pole.

My presence injects confusion into the established equilibrium. The company roster reinforces the status quo of accepted gender-appropriate roles. The secretaries and check-in clerks are women, but a man owns the company, the aircraft mechanics are men, and the pilots are men—except me. Maybe some don't resent my intrusion but are afraid of public censure from those who do. Or maybe they want to accept a female but, like Liam, are awkward and unsure about establishing friendship. The male pilots and I share a passion for aviation but not much else. I don't like to watch or participate in organized sports. A couple of times I've gone with them to local watering holes but don't typically frequent bars. When I'm not at work in the air, I'm at home as a single mother and a full-time university student, who studies and writes papers.

Other than being a mother, I don't conform to their norms. I have little in common with my colleagues' wives or our female employees. The wives of my colleagues have dedicated their lives to their husbands and children, and with one exception, the girlfriends of my unmarried colleagues are not career professionals. I love my son but don't enjoy chatting about children and prefer cuddling kittens and puppies to somebody else's baby. I'm a decent cook and sewed my clothes during high school, but I dislike both.

Though I grew up in Ontario, the province is larger than the countries of France and Germany combined. In contrast to the southern, populated region where I spent my first seventeen years, the northern part of Ontario feels like a different planet, a spatially and experientially different world, light-years from the opportunities and opinions of cosmopolitan southern Ontario. The behavior of real-life characters like the mayor of northern Ontario's largest city, Thunder Bay, emphasizes the difference between populated southern Canada and the sparsely settled north. When Queen Elizabeth II and her husband, Prince Philip, visited soon after Jolly Wally's mayoral term began in 1973, he instructed the audience to "please welcome His Royal Highness and his lovely wife," then patted the royal bottom as she ascended the podium. Despite these breaches of royal protocol, citizens elected Jolly Wally for a second term beginning in 1981.

In northern Canada, I encounter men (and more than one woman) who remind me of Bob and Doug McKenzie, fictional TV show hosts created in 1980 for *Second City Television*. Beer-swilling, good ole boys Bob and Doug live in the "Great

White North," wear plaid shirts, toques, earmuffs, and winter coats year-round, and guzzle a lot of beer.

The cavernous misunderstandings between men and women aren't limited to pilots. Though a few passengers recognize the value of a role model and introduce their daughters, when I perform my role as baggage handler at our remote bases, passengers often refuse to relinquish their bags. Women protest but men push me aside, politely, but vigorously. "Ma'am, you'll hurt yourself."

My standard response is always, "All copilots load baggage at remote locations."

Some respond, "Women can't lift a fifty-pound suitcase into a four-foot-high baggage compartment."

When my polite words aren't effective, I seize the handle with my right hand, haul the luggage to chest level, and move my left hand to the bottom to support the bag. Then, balancing the heavy load near my neck and shoulder, I slide my right hand to the rear vertical section and, emulating an Olympic shot-putter, hurl the case into the compartment. The crash of the suitcase into the metal baggage compartment always changes their opinion, and instead of seeing me as a female unsuited to the task, they see me as a person doing my job.

Other passengers write letters of complaint to our Head Office in Toronto. This classic, presumably twigged by legendary sexcapades between "stews" and pilots, is a favorite.

"The stewardess spent the flight flirting with the captain. She sat up front with him in the copilot's seat for the duration. Not once did she attend to the needs of her passengers. They even held hands together on takeoff."

In fact, we were complying with standard operating procedure for takeoff specifying that the pilot not flying (PNF) must shadow the hand of the pilot flying (PF). I'm annoyed that passengers don't question two men holding hands in the cockpit until I remember that my education, my parents, the media, and society have informed all of us that men deserve positions of power and control.

Men are pilots. Women are stewardesses.

Pilots are gods. Women serve the gods and have their children.

Weeks after my conversation with Liam, an older, bolder blonde named Brenda destroys my schoolgirl crush on him. He tells a colleague, who tells a colleague, that she's an enthusiastic gymnast in the sack. Soon, we all know and are envious of different people for different reasons. During flights and layovers, Vic comments about Liam's sexual activities. Though statements such as, "I'd like to try that position, wouldn't you?" don't directly suggest *we* have sex, his inappropriate remarks are laden with implications. I ignore him, but instead of getting the hint, he becomes bolder, and I begin to think Sam and the boys knew exactly what Vic had in mind when he hired me. Anticipation of flights with Vic whips my insides to a frenzy. Overnight layovers are my greatest challenge. During otherwise boring airborne moments, he mentions Liam's latest riotous romp with Brenda in explicit candor. I never comment, terrified he might interpret any spoken response as interest.

At all our overnight locations, our company pays for two separate bedrooms or two hotel rooms, one for each pilot. I want to be sociable and make friends, not enemies, but I want to sleep in my bedroom (alone). The hotel room offers privacy, but when our accommodation is suite-style with a common living area, escape is difficult.

Vic isn't the only captain who takes advantage of the opportunity layovers provide, but he's the only captain to persist. He starts at the opposite end of the couch and sidles closer or sits a couple of feet away, facing me with his arm resting along the top of the couch. On one occasion, when he strokes my hair, instead of shifting position, I go to my bedroom and shut the door. When

I hear footsteps in the hallway, I brace myself against the door, relieved when they continue to his room.

After that, I adopt several strategies. I switch flights to avoid him, occasionally bring Brandon as a passenger, or sit on the La-Z-Boy. This works well . . . for a while. One night when Brandon isn't with me, Vic straddles the ottoman in front of the La-Z-Boy, leans forward, and tries to force his tongue into my mouth. I push him away. Vomit scalds my throat as I race to the bathroom. I slam the door and flip open the toilet lid just in time.

I wash my face and hands, then slowly turn the door handle, opening the door a sliver. I hear the TV. *Is Vic watching TV—or waiting for me in my bedroom?* I don't want to lose my job, but I don't want to sleep with him. The agony Mom suffered from my father's infidelity serves as a reminder to never get emotionally involved with a married man—especially my boss.

I peek into the empty hallway, then dart to my bedroom, a tiny room with nowhere to hide. I silently shut the door and prop the chair against the door. Wearing all my clothes except my suit jacket, I try to sleep. My brain whirs with rage and fear. *What if he barges in? What will we say to each other tomorrow?*

I don't blame him or any man *directly*, but I do blame an institutionalized inequality, which perpetuates the notion that women are commodities with value equal to their beauty, not their intelligence and skill.

The following day, during our three-hour flight home, neither of us mentions the incident, but the shadow skulks nearby, like a malevolent stranger with a knife. I can't imagine how we'll get past this incident. Even if rumors abound about our alleged affair, even if he fires me, even if he overlooks me for promotion, I know I haven't slept with him.

I'm certain this is all that matters.

26

WHERE DO WOMEN "BELONG"?

"D o ya see that?" Gavin points into the sun-saturated sky. Convinced he's spotted an aircraft about to crash into us, I scour the clear, blue sky.

He points again. "Take a goooood, looooong look."

I see nothing but clouds and sky and wonder why he's jeopardizing our safety by not telling me about a conflicting aircraft. I'm about to say something snarky when he harrumphs with annoyance at my obvious stupidity. "Just tell me. What color's the sky?"

"Blue."

"Son of a gun! Don't you know that if girls were meant to fly, the sky would be pink?"

My stomach bubbles like fermented broth. Only fifteen more minutes with this asshole and a couple of hours before dinner with Matthew. Occasional encounters with Gavin at the hangar are unpleasant, but flights with him are like being caged with a rapacious tiger. I have no proof, but my inner self telegraphs he's sabotaging my job by sharing his contempt of me with the more tolerant captains, hoping to turn them against me.

Today's light wind makes landing the Twin Otter easy and uneventful. The oversize Michelin Aviator tires tweet onto the seven-thousand-foot-long asphalt. No matter how hard he tries,

Gavin wouldn't be able to find fault with this landing. I taxi the aircraft to the terminal, basking in the soothing rays of spring sunshine. The illusory greenhouse effect inside the aircraft poses a teasing contrast to the subzero temperatures that will flood the cabin when the doors open.

This landing ends our scheduled jaunt to seven far-flung northern Ontario airfields at isolated cities and towns north of the Trans-Canada Highway, a meandering link snaking coast to coast. I'm glad to be home after two days and twenty-four bush takeoffs and landings in remote communities where I, as the first officer, am required to load massive duffel bags, hunting and fishing gear, and freight into and out of the plane. I accept that first officers double as ground crew and treat this as bonus exercise in a job that provides minimal physical activity, but I'm tired. Though I never expect assistance, most captains help unload a few bags, but Gavin prefers to watch.

Initially, I believed Kurt disliked me as much as Gavin, but as Kurt's crust flaked away, I recognized him as a caring father and dedicated husband. His initial attitude and behaviors to me were inexcusable, but I think he's a good man coping with unresolved confidence issues concerning his pilot father.

Gavin will never be my friend.

When I'm pilot flying and he's pilot monitoring (with the responsibilities of talking with air traffic control and assisting me during takeoff and landings), he slouches against his door and twists his torso to watch for any mistake, however small. Instead of encouraging me to build my skills and gain confidence while supervised by a senior pilot, Gavin's determination to find fault and criticize makes me second-guess my performance. Instead of relying upon my knowledge and experience, I overthink my actions and develop performance anxiety. Instead of flying with the fluid, second-nature actions of the accomplished professional that I am, my flight performance under Gavin's scrutiny often becomes a series of mechanical actions like a student's step-by-step progression.

I soon learn Gavin's a master at throwing me off guard with questions such as, "How come you can't keep a husband?"

I'm shocked into silence.

"Well, *how come?*"

"That's none of your business."

"I'll bet you're frigid."

"That's not your business either."

He tips his head. "Are you a dyke?"

"Are you serious?" I expect a snarky retort, but his widened eyes fixate on me like a puppy awaiting a treat. "You met my boyfriend."

He scratches his beard. "Maybe he's a cover."

"Why do you think my husband left *me?*"

"Why would a woman leave a man?"

"My ex has anger issues."

He raises an eyebrow. "Maybe because you don't like sex."

I shake my head in disbelief. "And he's an alcoholic."

With genuine interest, he asks, "Isn't a bad husband better than no husband?"

"Are you afraid your wife will leave you?"

He focuses on his instrument panel, suddenly lost in thought.

Our overnight accommodation at one airport is an apartment rented by our company for our exclusive use. Pilots keep personal items including clothing, food, books, and a variety of men's magazines ranging from hunting and fishing to *Penthouse* and *Ilustler.* I ignore these magazines and study for my anthropology and genetics classes at university until one of the crewmembers who'd stayed the previous night positioned one of the raunchier publications on the first officer's single bed.

In the centerfold, spread out in Technicolor, is a splayed-leg model named Lola.

On a positive note, and to my immense relief, Vic has abandoned his sexual pursuit of me and stopped all sexual references. Flying and overnighters with him are now an intellectual pleasure. Life and work are challenging enough without the added pressure of worrying about losing my job because I refuse sex.

Although the Canadian government has recently formed a task force to evaluate the impact of workplace harassment of women in nontraditional occupations, harassment isn't a crime in 1983. Our company doesn't have a human resources department, and the legal requirement for voice recorders doesn't apply to the DHC-6 (or any plane carrying fewer than thirty passengers). If I report a captain, my testimony will be the word of a junior pilot against a senior captain, the voice of a woman against a man.

Even the word "testimony" derives from "testes," an affirmation that women are not qualified to provide evidence in court or that a woman's opinion is worth less than a man's.

Without legal recourse or a support network, I have no alternative but to muddle on with my own coping skills, doing my job and silently dodging harassment.

During a summer morning flight, while I'm flying and enjoying the sunny weather and Sam is the pilot monitoring radios, he says, "Did you hear about the time Karen let the plane drift off a two-hundred-foot-wide runway?"

I laugh. "That's hard to believe."

He snorts. "She didn't even notice!"

I say, "That's ridiculous. A five-year-old on a tricycle knows if a wheel drops off the sidewalk on to the grass."

He doesn't respond, so I ask, "Were you flying with her?"

He fiddles with one of the radio dials that doesn't need

adjusting. "Well, no." He drags out 'no' as if it has two syllables.

I ask, "What's she doing now?"

"Flying for another company."

Though my own errors (and Karen's alleged errors) might not differ in kind from those made by male pilots, our male colleagues gossip, magnify, and report our mistakes to supervisors rather than accept we all make errors. I strive for perfection but I'm not perfect. I'm an average pilot. As a first officer, I make mistakes, but I'm not the only first officer (or captain) who has bounced the aircraft in a crosswind landing or had trouble staying on course during an approach in turbulence, rain, and impossibly bad visibility. Others have failed tests, nicked propellers, and mangled an aircraft tail while trying to taxi under the wing of a taller plane.

I can't know if other women endure the same scrutiny and sexist attitudes, but for me, the metal tube that is my office feels as transparent as a glass globe. These years of continued resistance to my presence have distorted my inherent optimism. Although I ignore individual snips of gossip, the cumulative effect is overwhelming. Some seem determined to barricade the road map of my career with boulders and make my life miserable so that I'll quit flying, at least with their company.

They're succeeding. I am miserable. I love flying but hate going to work. When doing my job means I have to enter the dispatch office populated by even one of my detractors, I feel as if I'm parading naked in front of a jeering audience. However, I'm determined to disprove the idea that women have no place as pilots in commercial aviation, a task that seems insurmountable thanks to the zeitgeist of the time.

Despite these adversities, nothing will destroy the thrill I get from the freedom of flight and the opportunity to see the world from a different perspective—above the clouds, watching the sunset from the sky.

— — —

On the rare occasion I hear a female voice on the airwaves, I try to pair the voice with a face. I'm keen, almost desperate, to befriend a female pilot, someone who understands the special challenges faced by female pilots, a special someone with whom I can share the everyday problems of life and love, hopes and dreams.

Rebecca's the first female pilot I befriend.

I'm surprised when she tells me, "I was a flight attendant for a decade, but when the airline announced a surplus of flight attendants, I volunteered for an eighteen-month unpaid leave of absence so I could get my airline transport rating."

"I hope the airline is grateful. Thanks to you and others on leave, they're saving money."

"Exactly. Plus, my colleagues who can't afford to take unpaid leave don't have to deal with reduced shifts or forced early retirement. Plus, the opportunity was perfect for me. Many senior captains will retire within five years, and when the male copilots become captains, I want their empty seats!"

During her leave, her charter-flying job originates from a different province, so we rarely see each other. Whenever possible, we chat over the airwaves. During one conversation, her voice bursts with delight as she announces with pride, "I just sent in my application for my airline transport rating!"

Several months later, our flight paths intersect, albeit briefly, when her half-hour layover meets my flight, which is late. Arms spread wide, with great grins, we race to each other on the ramp facing the passenger terminal. We catch up on our personal lives, something we don't broadcast over the airwaves for our male audience to hear, repeat . . . and judge.

Airport employees maneuver baggage carts and fuel trucks between parked aircraft, and though no one can hear us, I lean conspiratorially close to her face. "Since I last saw you, Matthew and I broke up and . . . I have a new beau!"

"Ooooooh! Do tell!"

"Devon. He's super-smart, good-looking, fun, thoughtful, and has a great job."

"Doing what?"

"Runs the IT department of a major agribusiness company."

"*Another* tech-geek?"

"Yeah, but this one is *definitely* heterosexual."

She giggles.

"He doesn't have Roman hands or Russian fingers, but he did kiss me on our first date."

She nods her approval as I continue. "For our third date—I can't believe that was four months ago!—he took me to a steak house for dinner, then *Flashdance.*"

Her eyebrows arch over wide, hazel eyes. "Bet *that* movie energized you!"

I giggle. "Halfway through the movie, I wanted to take him home and rip off his clothes, but I'm trying to be cautious about leaping into love."

"He sounds great."

I remember the pain I caused Steve. "Most of the guys I've dated would make fabulous husbands—for someone else!"

She glances at her watch.

I ask, "Any news about keeping your seniority at the airline and transitioning from flight attendant to pilot?"

She scuffs her loafer against a few pebbles of winter grit. "Human Resources said I could apply, but I'd have to quit my job as flight attendant."

"But they'd hire you as a pilot?"

"No guarantees. And if I quit, I lose seniority and travel benefits."

"That's crazy. You're bilingual and a university grad."

Rebecca sighs. "A monkey would have a better chance."

I wag my finger. "You mean a *male* monkey! Do they even have female pilots?"

"Two."

"Have you talked with them?"

"I've never met them."

"With your qualifications and work history, I thought you'd be an obvious pilot candidate. What *are* your plans?"

She tosses her curls and raises her chin. "In two weeks, I start first officer training—with the competition."

I shout, "Congratulations!" and give her a big hug.

As I watch her walk to her plane, my insides jumble with mixed emotions.

I'm happy for her and proud she's paving the way for future generations of female pilots. During her unpaid leave, she accumulated fifteen hundred hours, acquired a multi-engine rating and an instrument rating, qualified for an airline transport pilot license (the highest license possible), and clocked more than one hundred hours of jet time.

She's worked hard and deserves this big break, but I can't help being a little jealous. No matter how hard I work, my less-than-perfect eyesight eliminates me from flying with *any* major air carrier.

And I'm *a lot* outraged. The airline that she worked for as a stewardess is the same airline that hired my first instructor when he had only three hundred hours and a commercial license, but they've rejected her. Despite national legislation, systemic assumptions based on arbitrary and irrelevant qualifications persist—and limit the career opportunities and upward mobility of women, half the world's population. A reluctance to hire women in nontraditional roles and occupations is a deliberate decision to avoid using all available resources, much like deciding to use one arm instead of two, when both are available and functioning.

27

THE APPROACH

Jennifer replaces Rebecca for the courier service, and her new flight schedule meshes with my schedule. I'm delighted to have found another female who understands the emotional impact of being a lone female pilot surrounded by male pilots, antagonistic or accepting.

One afternoon, Jennifer invites me for supper at her house, a small two-bedroom home, eclectically decorated with artifacts of her life. I point toward an oil painting of the African savanna on the wall. "Since I read *Out of Africa*, going on safari has been on my wish list."

She pours tea and selects one of the Voortman Dutch Windmill cookies from the plate of fresh cherries and assorted sweets she's arranged. She snaps it in half, then says with cultivated detachment, "I've been on safari *many* times."

"Many times!" I exclaim, my voice expressing wonder and admiration.

"I was born in South Africa."

I peer closely at the artist's signature. "Wava. That's an uncommon name—is the artist Black?"

Her back stiffens. "Wava's my mother."

I say, "She's talented. Living in South Africa must have been difficult."

Her pale blue eyes pierce like hail against glass. "Why?"

"Apartheid."

Her words flame like a blowtorch. "Apartheid does not exist!"

"Many people disagree."

Her back arches. "Blacks are attacking other Blacks. Blacks *want* to live with *their* kind."

I'm astonished by her anger, but she speaks with such conviction. I say, "Perhaps I've misinterpreted the turmoil in South Africa. I've never been there and maybe the constant barrage of media reports are false."

During dinner, we struggle with conversation, so instead of staying overnight as originally planned, I return home. I dread our next encounter but that never happens, as she's soon transferred to another base.

To compound my problems finding a female pilot with whom I can relate, Devon and I are having trouble. At least, I'm having trouble. I should be happy to have found an educated, dependable nonsmoker who loves his parents. Though we see each other almost daily, I'm reluctant to move in with him. One night after supper, I try to explain. I've dropped hints before but now I'm determined. I turn toward him, lean my elbow on the couch, and look into his eyes. "Your favorite meal is roast beef, right?"

His black eyes flash an avid *yes*.

I run my fingers through his black curls. "Let's say you eat roast beef for supper"—he licks his deep-red Cupid's bow—"then dessert, then a midnight snack, then breakfast, then lunch, then a late-afternoon snack."

He stares blankly.

I sip my Pinot Gris. "The point is . . . you'd get tired of roast beef."

"What are you trying to say?" He laughs.

I'm bungling this. "Sex six times a day is too much for me."

"Other women thought I was a good lover," he says with a pout.

"You *are* fabulous, but—"

He recoils as if slapped. "You've found someone else."

This reminds me of Paul who insisted I was leaving for another man, rather than accept any blame. "There's no one else."

"Flying takes you away at least two nights weekly. That makes our daily average four."

I roll my eyes.

He squeezes my breast and fondles my nipple through my blouse. I brush his hand away and he says, "What if we skip love-making at noon? I'll work through lunch and come over early."

"If you get here before Brandon's home from school, you'll want sex."

He pulls my hand onto the bulge in his pants. "I can't keep my hands off you."

I pull my hand away. "You're not listening. Or maybe I'm saying this wrong. I've been concerned about our relationship for a while. I'm not sleeping well. Being tired hasn't affected my flying *yet*, but I'm exhausted."

"I thought you loved sex."

"I do—but I have to break up with you because of sex. Ironic but true."

His fingers trace my lips. "Sweetheart, let's make it work."

"My parents spent years trying to make it work. When Mom tried to explain her concerns, Father wouldn't listen. When he had an affair, she still tried to make it work." My hands clench involuntarily, and my voice rises with anger. "She stayed with him for ten years—ten *wasted* years—only to have him leave."

He looks at me with puppy-dog eyes. "Let's try."

"I tried to make it work with Brandon's father, but our problems didn't go away—we just buried them. If we try to make it work, it *will* work—for a while—but soon the same old problems surface. Life is too short to rehash problems."

He says, "You're worth waiting for. I'll give you time."

For several weeks, Devon calls every few days. His determined pursuit flatters me, and just as I'm about to let him back in my life, I realize that something far deeper than too much sex keeps me from putting my future into his hands. We could work through that problem, but we can't work out his inability to understand me. If he doesn't understand me, I can't trust him to be my life partner.

All thoughts of reconciliation screech to a halt when I remember my mother's grief when Father, a man she thought she could trust, abandoned her. If she'd left instead of trying to make it work for thirty years, she might have found happiness with another man.

Devon stops pursuing me soon after I say, "I want to be friends, but I'm not going to change my mind about dating you. In fact, I've decided to stop dating anyone. My life is busy with work, school, and Brandon."

Though this is true, the truth is that I need to be on my own, until I find a man my heart trusts.

Professionally, I've established a tenuous harmony with my colleagues. Four are supportive, the others are ambivalent, and Vic has accepted my insistence that our relationship be platonic. Occasionally, I experience a burst of acceptance when I'm included for drinks at the pub, but mostly, I watch their private party through impermeable glass.

The one obvious exception is Gavin, who, if he wanted to share the knowledge acquired during ten years and ten thousand hours in the air, could be a mentor equal to Vic or Doug. Most flights with him are worse than any flight test because examiners are impartial and follow specific and quantifiable guidelines, but his hawk eyes search for mistakes and his cutthroat tongue slashes my confidence like a raptor's talon.

However, on flights without passengers, Gavin almost always

transforms from surly to mischievous. One winter day, when he's flying as captain, he winks. "Let's surf the treetops and see what we find." And with those few words, he fills the flight deck with the magic of curiosity.

We descend to two thousand feet. Sunlight twinkles on pure white snow, unblemished by civilization. He spots a pack of wolves loping like a skein through a forest clearing and reduces power to idle. We float silently to one thousand feet and admire their agile bodies running across a counterpane of unbroken snow.

I say, "This reminds me of landing on an inland lake in the BC interior when I saw a pair of bald eagles on their nest, maybe fifteen feet away."

He nods. "I miss the freedom of flying charters into the backcountry."

For the first time, I can relate to him. "Taking time to enjoy the solitude."

"Sticking around to shoot the shit with the guys."

The wolves snake around sparse evergreens, then vanish like mythical creatures into the forest. I ask, "Have you seen *Never Cry Wolf* yet?"

He shakes his head. "Read Mowat's book in school."

"The movie's different but has the same message—wolves are essential to the ecosystem, not ruthless predators."

I consider the impact of education and understanding on ignorance and fear. Mowat's story reached thousands of people in many countries, but the few female pilots in North America are like wolves in the wilderness, fighting to change public perception of women as less capable and less intelligent than men.

When we land, I show him a cartoon strip pasted into my logbook. The left half shows an unshaven pilot flying a floatplane thinking, *There has to be more to life than hauling fish. Airline pilots have it made. Clean planes, clean clothes, big bucks to sit in that office in the sky.*

The right half shows a first officer in the jet, saying, "Bored! Bored! Bored!"

The captain responds, "I know what you mean . . . sometimes I wish I was hauling fish again."

We laugh together, and I'm glad for these rare moments of camaraderie with him.

"Gavin, you should use a couple weeks of summer holidays to fly floats."

His sulkiness returns. "Yeah, right. That'd make the wife happy."

In autumn 1984, during my third year with the company, Jim (my copilot on the flight test when I botched the missed approach) and I have spent the last two days fighting turbulence, fog, and heavy rain inside a wicked low-pressure system covering central Canada. Despite the best high-tech navigational aids in the plane, we've had to abort landing at two of our scheduled stops because fog and rain reduced visibility to zero.

Now, after an overnighter, we're on our way home. Sheets of drizzle smother the landscape, and we can't see farther than ten feet. Though the visibility at our home airport is terrible, home is a major airport with the best instrument approach aids. We're glad to be finishing our two-day shift, tired from the extra vigilance demanded by relentless bad weather.

About twenty miles from the airport, all Jim's instruments suddenly wobble, sway like drunkards, then keel over. Jim says, with his usual calm, "Holy crap. I've never seen anything like this before."

He leans toward me to get a better look at my instruments.

I say, "Mine are still working. Thank goodness."

While he tries to determine the cause of the bizarre failure, I say, "I'm glad this is our last leg because if it wasn't, I'd be flying all the legs."

He can't find any obvious solution. I fly on, mostly because there isn't another alternative. The problem relates only to Jim's side of the plane but, *What if my instruments fail?* I don't dwell on that and repeat to myself, *The engines are fine. We have lots of gas. We'll be home soon.*

Then Jim tells me the latest weather report. "Cloud two hundred feet with one-quarter-mile visibility."

Now, the possibility of weather extending our duty day flashes across my personal radar. We can legally and safely descend to two hundred feet, the same level as the cloud, so we *should* be able to see the ground, but the weather office is two miles east of the runway, and the runway is one mile long.

What if the weather at our end of the runway is worse than at the weather office?

I shudder when Jim says glumly, "I hope we find the runway."

I begin the instrument-guided approach toward the runway, and though I reassure myself, my stomach starts to rumble. We're on target to find the runway—if Jim is able to see it. He calls out our altitude each hundred feet of descent and says, "You're doing a great job. I'm looking outside, but everything is solid white."

At two hundred feet, I level off, eyes glued to the instruments. The plane hurtles forward, flying parallel to pavement. I hope to hear Jim say, "Visual contact. I have control," but my confidence in this outcome is decreasing rapidly. He has seconds to spot the runway and decide to land—or abort.

He says, "Can't see a damn thing. Fuck. Missed approach."

This is a command. He's the pilot monitoring, responsible for spotting the runway, and the captain. I climb to a safe altitude while he gets updated weather for the airport we left an hour before.

After a few minutes, he says, "The weather's worse. Clouds are lower, the precip is heavier, and the vis is worse, but it's good enough."

We stare at each other. His frown suggests his thoughts mirror mine.

What if the weather gets so bad, we can't find that airport—even with instruments?

An hour later, Jim broadcasts on the radio, advising our intention to begin the instrument approach and land. Gray pellets of rain stream over the windows, restricting our vision to inside the flight deck. With our connection to the real world blocked, I experience the surreal sensation of suspension inside a floating bubble. To avoid disorientation, I devote all my attention to the instruments that confirm I'm flying the correct heading with the wings level and descending about three hundred feet per minute.

I hope Jim will see the runway. If his instruments were working, he'd be flying this leg, but his instruments are still lifeless. If he, or any pilot, attempted to fly in cloud without instruments, control of the plane would be lost within a few minutes. I clench my teeth, focus on the instruments, level off at two hundred feet, and mentally start preparing for another missed approach.

Jim says, "Runway in sight! I have control!" He grabs the captain's set of dual controls on his side of our Y-shaped dual control column.

I let go and start breathing again. I hadn't dared hope he'd see the ground but there's the runway, in front of us.

Jim touches down, and our massive tires plow through puddles of standing rainwater, creating mini tidal bores. Inside the terminal, we take turns pacing and checking dismal no-fly weather reports. He flips through a motley collection of donated magazines while I study genetics, occasionally distracted by *People* magazine covers: "The Kennedys: 20 Years Later" (difficult to believe someone assassinated JFK twenty years ago) and hunky Richard Chamberlain in *The Thorn Birds*.

After two hours, a special weather report indicates slight

improvement. The increasing wind has rustled the low clouds grazing the earth and driven them to higher pastures. We corral the passengers from the two-waiting-room terminal and take off for home. Again.

Jim gets another weather report, indicating the weather has decayed during our flight. "Jesus Murphy, this sucks," he says with a sigh. "By the way, you're doing a great job." I've never heard him swear before this flight. I'm pleased to hear his praise, and hope his words aren't some of the last words I'll ever hear.

What if I have to do another missed approach?

If we were flying in southern Canada or in mainland America, there'd be ten airports within a twenty-mile radius. Even if some of them were unpaved, a Twin Otter is a versatile airplane able to land on pavement or grass. But we're in northern Canada, where there are few airports. And we don't just need an airport, we need an airport with good weather.

Where's the nearest airport with acceptable weather?

Again, I start the approach, then descend to the minimum safe altitude. We race along at two hundred feet. Seconds pass like hours as I wait for him to find the runway.

What if we don't have enough fuel to get to that airport, wherever it may be?

Suddenly, I feel pressure on the controls. Jim seizes his control column and shouts, "We're visual! I've got it." I let go, suddenly aware my fingers are stiff, not realizing until then I've been gripping my control column.

The wheels connect with the ground.

Jim exhales a blast of air, ruffling his lips. "That felt like my last night on death row."

"Yeah"—I nod—"hoping for a stay of exccution."

I breathe deeply and allow myself to contemplate my future, now that I have one.

———

Months later, Gavin is my captain on a series of scheduled flights into a weather system forecasted to be sensational. On the drive to the airport, raindrops thump against my windshield and sluice in gullies along the sidewalks. Dead leaves spiral into the air, and discarded plastic grocery bags become Arizona tumbleweeds.

When I enter the pilots' lounge, Gavin snaps, "You're late."

I shove my watch into his face. "You're early."

He brushes my arm away. "Did ya get the weather?"

"Of course, it's my job." I flutter the weather reports in his face. "The met office resembled a barroom brawl with a dozen pilots versus one weatherman. Everyone needed advice plus hardcopy printouts of the weather. Almost as soon as he printed a report, a newer and much worse report came through."

Gavin stands with his left leg folded onto one of the two steel desks, pretending to look busy examining paperwork. Economical but unflattering fluorescent tubes on the fifteen-foot-high ceiling highlight the pitted grooves of his weather-wounded face.

Pony-tailing my long hair, disheveled by the tempest brewing across much of central Canada, I say, "We're in for a treat today. Surface winds are already thirty knots gusting to forty-five. Gale-force upper winds sixty to ninety. Forecast much stronger, up to one hundred knots."

He focuses on the papers clutched in his hand.

I say, "Those crazy strong headwinds will almost move us backward."

A smirk spreads across his face. "Little wind got the little girl scared?"

His tone rankles but I say, "Even if *you* don't mind, it'll be a rough ride for passengers." I point to the reports for current and predicted weather. "The storm spans three provinces. We can expect extreme thunderstorms, turbulence, torrential rain, and fog."

His eyes bounce from the reports to my face.

I say, "We don't have a legal alternate airport if our destination craps out. Winnipeg's forecast is okay, but it's too far away." Sneaking onto parchment-thin ice, I venture, "Some of the pilots at the weather office decided to delay their departure while others are canceling."

Sarcasm spills across his lips. "Do yeeeoooouuuu think we should cancel the flight?"

"Yes."

"Too bad. All the passengers have checked in, plus there's important freight."

"I'll bet the passengers would rather arrive alive tomorrow than dead today."

He stands up, walks toward me until his nose is six inches from mine, and glowers. "We're going."

A shiver shakes my spine, but I hold his mocking gaze.

I hadn't expected him to agree, but I needed to voice my opinion, even though captains could quash suggestions from lowly first officers without explanation or censure. A confident captain will listen and explain, but an arrogant tyrant lacks the confidence to weigh the opinions of junior pilots.

Gavin might not like me as a pilot or as a person, but his determination to make this flight stuns me. He's a senior captain with this company, with a decade of experience flying in the wilds of northern Canada, and he's not known to make foolish decisions. I'm surprised he's not following the lead of other captains who delayed or canceled flights. I want to bail but figure the weather will hold, at least to our second stop.

I board the passengers, then Gavin does the takeoff. He'll fly the first leg and I'll be the pilot monitoring, a nonflying, auxiliary role. Today, my rotation as pilot monitoring will mean scrambling for updated weather and requesting altitude changes, route changes, or radar vectors around weather.

As instrument-rated pilots navigating with instruments only, we aren't required to use any maps other than those designed for instrument flight. However, whenever I don't have hands-on control of the aircraft, I use topographical aviation maps to determine a precise location—and keep myself occupied. Today, identifying landmarks will be a major challenge rather than a casual pastime.

Rain skates along the curved windscreen and transforms the transparent shield into opaque pewter-gray. Turbulence tosses us up, down, and sideways. Anxiety tosses my stomach up, down, and sideways. We tighten our seat belts, a five-point harness that secures our shoulders and hips, with a belt between our legs to prevent us from slipping forward. The rhythmic drumming of relentless rain changes my simmering headache, caused by our confrontation in dispatch, to a full-tilt boogie. Blood pumps against my temples with the steady thumping beat of a bass guitar.

One hour out, I notice our ground speed has reduced to an absurdly slow value on our distance measuring equipment (DME). The Twin Otter is renowned for stability and reliability, traits desired in a friend or partner, but their bulky bodies, thick wings, and permanently extended landing gear aren't pinnacles of aerodynamic efficiency. Both engines produce the correct power for our standard cruising speed of one hundred and forty knots, but the wind must have shifted to head-on because now we are going seventy knots.

I point. "Look at our ground speed."

I'm surprised when he responds. "Yeah, I saw it. Probably wrong."

"Superstrong headwinds were predicted."

This time, he can't be bothered to respond.

I say, "For fun, I'll use the instruments to triangulate our position."

He drawls, "Don't bother."

I ignore him, and like the pioneer aviators, use my manual

flight computer (a circular slide rule) and the topographical map to plot distance flown against time in the air. "My calculations agree with the instrument calculation of seventy knots."

He grunts and settles deeper into his seat. Lured by the siren song of familiarity, inside a dependable aircraft with reliable instruments, it seems he's entered la-la land.

Cars on two-lane highways are moving faster, but he doesn't seem worried.

I should've refused this flight, even if that meant canceling the flight and inconveniencing passengers. More likely another first officer, lurking in the shadows, would have jumped to replace me. The flight would have proceeded, and the passengers and the company would be happy—unless an accident occurred. I visualize the Transport Canada poster, "Complacency Kills," depicting an airplane, smashed into the ground by a pilot who pushed the limits of weather.

What if we crash?

Our company doesn't pressure pilots to take foolish risks and my no-go decision might have the support of the chief pilot and the sympathies of my peers.

Or perhaps not. Pilots are supposed to be gutsy—not gutless.

My refusal wouldn't mean termination but might mean I'd be scheduled less frequently next month and perhaps not at all in six.

Radio chatter increases as pilots request updated weather for their destination or radar vectors around embedded thunderstorms revealed on the radar. Others turn around, but not us. Gavin drives us westward, deeper into the vortex of silver clouds bubbling toward the stratosphere. My terror increases when the unruffled voice of a Boeing 737 pilot requests revised routing to avoid the weather. Our Twin Otter sports cutting-edge technological navigation-communication radios, often better equipped than major air carriers, but if a one-hundred-and-thirteen-thousand-pound Boeing 737, carrying one hundred and twenty passengers, diverts to avoid weather—*What fate will befall our twenty-passenger, twelve-thousand-pound turboprop?*

I say, calmly but with a deliberate sense of urgency, "Let's turn back," but all I get is a scathing, sidelong glance as if I were a buzzing fly that won't stop pestering him.

What's he trying to prove?

My luck to fly with a captain deluded by "get-home-itis," a syndrome akin to the "show must go on." This might be great for show business, but afflicted pilots equate termination or cancellation of a flight with defeat. Each successful push beyond the limits of aircraft or pilot capability, each evasion of the Grim Reaper, increases the temptation to push further the next time.

Abruptly, the LED numbers on one of our three navigation-communication radios change to a dashed line, indicating that the radio has power—but isn't picking up a signal.

I'm already reaching for the dial when Gavin says, "Change the station. See if you can get a signal from another navigational aid." His unnecessary directive pisses me off, but I ignore him, select several different stations, and wiggle the dials.

I can't pull in any stations. "No joy."

He says, "Strange. Guess the radio went tits up."

This is a hassle but not a catastrophe because our other two navigation-communication radios continue to function normally. I'm not worried until a minute or so later, when the remaining two radios keel over. Now, bundled inside clouds without sight of the ground and without navigational equipment, we can't confirm our position or plot a course to our destination. Without communication radios, we can't contact a controller for radar-assisted routing direction, get weather updates, or contact our station agent.

My chest constricts as if swathed in a straitjacket.

The problem might be similar to signal interruption to television or AM/FM reception during an electrical storm, but I have no way of confirming this or knowing how long the interruption might continue. Two minutes? Four hours? Invisible hands strangle my breath.

Gavin's body jolts as if electrified by a massive blast of current from an electric chair. He blurts, "Ho-*lee*-fuuuuck! We don't have a damn thing left!"

"No shit. Any idea why?"

He inhales sharply, holds his breath, then sighs deeply.

I force a deep breath of air, then deliberately synchronize my breathing with the steady throb of the engines. *Be calm.* I fiddle with the radios, change frequencies, and attempt contact with anyone. Nothing works, so I say, "Maybe the electrical storm disrupted signals from the ground stations."

He says, "We still have our basic flight instruments. And strangely, the distance measuring equipment."

"That's a plus."

But we both know that flight in cloud using basic flight instruments plus one navigation radio, the DME, is impossible and dangerous, not to mention illegal, especially carrying passengers.

Gavin says, "Based on our elapsed time, we should be directly overhead."

"You're right. We shou—"

"D'ya see anything on the ground?"

"Gavin, 'should' is the key word." I realize he hasn't considered the implications of our reduced ground speed. "You've flown these routes hundreds of times more than me but . . . we haven't covered the amount of ground we normally cover." With increased emphasis, I say, "My calculations indicate the wind reduced our speed over the ground by seventy knots."

He's the captain, so I wait for him to suggest a plan, but he says nothing. I'm hesitant to make suggestions but remember reading about crashes that might've been averted if the junior pilot had spoken up. I say, "I don't want to argue but our incredibly slow ground speed means we're farther east than we should be. Can you see anything?"

He seems hypnotized by the instrument panel. *I might as well chat with the altimeter.* I don't expect small talk, but we need to communicate. The initial shock of our systems failure thunderbolted through him, but now his body slumps characteristically. Forward visibility is impossible, so I squash my face against my side window and peer straight down, hoping to identify anything.

He says, "I see trees!"

"If we were on track, we'd see water."

He says, "So, smarty-pants, where *are* we?"

"I'm . . . not exactly sure. What should we do?"

I hope his continued silence means he's considering a solution and not detached from the reality of our predicament. With each passing second, as he impersonates a zombie instead of a captain, my dread quadruples. I have no idea how to get out of this mess, and apparently, he doesn't either. We continue—because we have no other choice.

Why's this arrogant smart aleck suddenly spineless? My frustration increases exponentially. If he weren't always so quick to criticize and find fault with me, his current apathy might be easier to accept.

Horrific images battle for my attention. I see our mangled bodies, bloodied and alive—or broken and dead. Inside a crumpled aircraft, on fire and about to explode. A flash of black humor whizzes through my mind—if I die, Devon will have to move on. I force these counterproductive thoughts out of my head and say, "We need old-fashioned dead reckoning—and a break in these fucking clouds."

I'm annoyed he insisted on this flight and furious with myself for not standing up to him. I don't want to die. I don't want to leave Brandon without a mother. I want to help him become an adult. *What if I pay for Gavin's mistakes with my life?*

On the topographic map, I draw a circle around our last confirmed geographic location. Then, using our seventy-knot, half-normal ground speed, I approximate our current position and determine a rough heading to our destination. One of us needs to make a decision. I say, "I guesstimate we're forty miles southeast of the airport. Steer heading three-two-zero."

To my amazement, he complies. Time stops as we drift in an ocean of burbling clouds, floundering without an island of safety in sight. *What if the cloud layers thicken and obscure the airport?* I push this out of my mind because I know the result—we'll sail above the airport, unaware we've missed our only chance to land before another systems failure—or our fuel is exhausted.

My heart jackhammers against my ribs. I blot out the gruesome images dancing through my mind and replace them with my eight-year-old son, waiting at home with his babysitter. I'm not sure I'll see him again.

Suddenly, unbelievably, the cloud layers shift to reveal a skinny splinter of land. I pump my arm like an excited schoolgirl desperate to answer a tough question and point at an airport's rotating beacon, a hair's width north of our present course.

Gavin says, "Thank fucking god."

This isn't our destination, but we recognize this small airport, ten miles southeast of it. We're in the right place, at the precise moment, to reestablish our bearings. We're ten agonizing minutes to safety, but the approaching twilight in the relentless rain makes visual flight increasingly difficult. I scan the instruments, hoping one might spin to life.

What if something else goes wrong?

Seconds later, cotton-batten clouds engulf our plane. My pulse races as I check the map to confirm we're not going to mash into life-terminating towers. Gavin descends cautiously, two hundred feet per minute, through a layered hell of cloud levels. Fractured glimpses of Shangri-la taunt us until a good fairy creates a V-shaped valley between the clouds. To my amazement, directly in front of us, about four miles away, I see a grassy field surrounding a strip of asphalt. I shout, "There's the runway!"

Gavin descends, faster now that we can see the ground.

When we're about one half-mile from the runway, a diabolic meteorological treachery reduces our cloud crevasse to a narrow V. A surge of bile stings my throat, but I don't dare lose sight of the runway. Sheeting rain streaks the windscreen. My vision blurs, and I realize I'm crying. Crepuscular gloom sinks onto the misty runway. Gavin squeaks onto the runway seconds before the cloud drops to the grass, burying us under a coverlet of steel-gray fog. Lumps of lunch pool in my mouth. I choke them down my throat.

Flickering lights on our instrument panels catch my attention. Now, safely on the ground, the red LED lights on our radios spring to life and dance. The devil has released his choke hold grasp on our lives.

We stare with astonishment at each other.

Gavin steers us to the ramp, creeping foot by foot, shepherded by the edges of the tarmac, darker than the grassy border edges, and by an occasional sighting of lights along both sides of the taxiway. At the terminal, he shuts down both engines, then without a word, hops out and darts inside the terminal.

A gaggle of black umbrellas flaps open as fifteen passengers mill around while I unload luggage. Our flight took longer than normal, but because we are at our intended destination, none of the passengers ask questions. The last passenger and I dodge inch-deep puddles as we dash to the terminal. I pause under the eave to let water seep from my clothes. My shoes slobber and squish as I walk inside the terminal and into our company's dispatch office.

Gavin interrupts his conversation with Angela, our station agent, and orders, "Get the weather for our next leg."

"I'll get the weather, but you'll be going alone."

His ruddy cheeks darken to mulberry, but he smiles at me as if we were good buddies. "Aww, c'mon, be a good girl."

"Just because our radios and navigational aids are working now, we have no way of knowing if the same electromagnetic forces will affect them once we're in the air again."

His body tenses, ready to explode. I can almost feel the malevolence shooting toward me from his slit eyes. I'm terrified of him but more terrified of another flight through the wicked storm.

"Angela, get us a taxi and two hotel rooms. We'll leave tomorrow morning."

Her jaw drops. *Is she shocked a woman would defy a man? Surprised he agreed? Or does she merely disapprove of a first officer giving an order to a captain?*

The taxi ride is quieter than Tutankhamun's sarcophagus. I want to discuss this experience with Vic, who'll document my concerns, speak with Gavin to determine why he wanted to fly into bad weather not once but twice, and discuss his reactions to the systems failure.

But my word will be the word of a junior first officer against a senior captain, and making a big stink is more likely to get me fired than resolve my concerns. So, I say nothing and hope Gavin will evaluate the experience without intervention.

The weeks pass but my memories of that horrific flight and Gavin's attitude linger. Some of the guys tell me Gavin can't wait to tell them about my mistakes, even though those blunders might be similar to the ones made by male pilots. I remember reading that when Marvel Crosson crashed her plane in the 1929 American National Air Derby, male reporters touted her error as proof that women—*all* women, not just Crosson—have no place in aviation. It seems women must perform all facets of the job perfectly, every time. And that just isn't possible—for me, for anyone.

In contrast, all but the most atrocious errors by a male pilot are justified, perhaps because men understand and empathize with other men. In a notable instance, one of our pilots was heading east when the heading indicator control flipped one hundred and eighty degrees. He didn't notice until air traffic control asked why he was flying in the wrong direction. His negligence might have caused a midair, but colleagues only laughed and said, "Those instruments aren't for decoration!"

I approach Vic, not to rat on Gavin, but to discuss the implementation of a training program so pilots can learn from the experiences of other pilots, and hopefully, avoid making the same mistakes. One idea is to establish a no-names-mentioned reporting system that doesn't point fingers but encourages discussion about systems failures; another is to promote the idea that terminating a flight exemplifies expertise, not cowardice.

But, before I fully formulate my proposition, Vic accepts an offer with another company, Gavin becomes chief pilot, and the University of Waterloo in southern Ontario approves my application to transfer from correspondence studies to on-campus studies in the fall. I don't want to abandon flying, so I accept a supervisory position at Waterloo Flying Club, a major aviation school with five instructors, ten aircraft, two hangars, an executive boardroom, and a ground-school classroom for twenty-five students.

I say goodbye to a few of the guys and want to hug Dave, one of our best pilots and a graduate of a college aviation program, when he says, "I'll fly anywhere, anytime with you."

Yet, despite my many confrontations with Gavin, I transform one of his observations into a bittersweet memory. Whenever I see a blue sky metamorphose into a firestorm cognate of J. M. W. Turner's canvases of carmine flames, rosy drizzles, and clouds trimmed with coral pink, I tell everyone, "*Look!* Girls *are* meant to fly."

28

CHOCOLATE AND ROSES

My drive south toward a new life in Waterloo, seventy miles west of Toronto, retraces pathways of my youth, camping adventures led by my parents or my grandparents. I stop at Wawa's giant Canada goose then meander through Lake Superior Provincial Park, stopping at Old Woman Bay and Agawa Bay to remember the good times, then press on to the Sault, the halfway point of this journey.

The next morning, my journey continues east in an almost straight line along Lake Huron's north shore, past Bruce Mines, Iron Bridge, Spanish, and Espanola—towns with names that reflect the settlers and their reasons for settling—past pleasure boats bobbing in the waves. Somewhere south of Sudbury, ABBA's "Waterloo" comes on the radio. Seven years ago, I did my flight instructor training at Waterloo and loved every minute. I feel like I'm coming home and I can't stop singing the bouncy lyrics, reassured about my decision to return to southern Ontario.

My duty hours at the flight school will change every four months to accommodate a new semester at university. I have a full academic load and, each week, spend forty hours in the air as an instructor and teach a three-hour-long evening class to commercial or instrument students. In addition, I wrench personal time into this and maintain joint custody of Brandon. I'm outrageously happy with my staggering schedule until Richard Chamberlain swaggers into the flight school and takes up an incredible amount of space at the flight dispatch desk. My brain hums. A hurricane of desire swirls in my groin and shoots through every nerve in my body.

This isn't the clean-shaven priest in *The Thorn Birds*, the 1983 TV miniseries. This is the bearded adventurer in *Shōgun*, the 1980 miniseries. Of course, this isn't the real Richard Chamberlain at all, but this ruggedly handsome man could be his stunt double.

My knees buckle. I grip our receptionist's chair and pretend to examine the aircraft logbooks on her desk while she answers Shōgun's questions about airplanes or aircraft parts or something. I glance up, and he flashes the most assured grin, then strides out the door, trench coat sailing behind.

I look calm but inside I'm trembling. I ask, "Cookie, who *was* that?"

She looks at me, shakes her head slowly from side to side, and scowls. "You *don't* want to know."

I persist. "Is he a pilot?"

She shrugs. "Scott has a private license, but he's a maintenance engineer at Wardair."

"Why haven't I seen him here before?"

"He's usually at his hangar building an aircraft. Never seen him with a woman."

I throw up my hands. "Are you saying he's gay?"

She sniggers. "Definitely not gay. Definitely gorgeous. Smart but uncouth."

"He seems polite."

"He wanted to meet you. He's a philistine. Forget him."

So, I do.

Until the next week when he arrives at the flying club three days in a row, late in the afternoon. Each time, he invites me to join him for coffee, just the two of us, at a table in the club's Compass Rose Café, a laid-back lounge where pilots and passengers share coffee, meals, and bullshit. As Cookie suggests, he's not a debonair raconteur, but our conversation flows and he's pleasant and polite. The location of his aviation work experience—up north, in the bush—parallels mine.

On day two, he asks, "Did Cookie tell you I'm building an airplane?"

Though I'm fantasizing about his beard and moustache tickling my flesh, I shrug. "She mentioned it."

"A Formula One air racer. Cruises at two hundred knots."

"Fast! Do you have enough experience to fly it?"

"Probably not." He leans toward me. His hot breath sears my face. My skin tingles. He speaks softly into my ear. "But you do."

On the third day, he gulps his coffee, then stands abruptly. "Maybe you should see my airplane."

Is this an invitation to accompany him? A vague promise? A question? Or the aviation version of Mae West's coy offer of sexual dalliance, "Come up and see me sometime"?

I check my watch. "I'd like that."

He hesitates, then asks, "Maybe you'll be around tomorrow?"

I pause, trying to be cool, though my insides smolder. "Maybe."

He smiles. "Maybe I'll see you."

The next day, we have our first date. Sort of. He doesn't woo me with dinner, wine, or flowers, and I can't imagine many women who'd want a second. Our voices fill his hangar with nonstop chatter for three hours, without food or drink, admiring an immaculately crafted, wood-and-fabric aircraft he's been building for five years, one vintage 1970 Lotus painted original racing green, which he rarely drives, and in an upper corner of the hangar, a loft bed we don't use.

Date two ends like the first, inside his hangar, but begins with *Highlander* at the cinema. I'm not sure who's teasing whom, but as we share popcorn, every brush of fingers to fingers sends a tingle up my spine.

For date three, we dine at the Blue Moon, a pub-style restaurant in an eighteenth-century brick building. Once a thriving hotel for stagecoach travelers, now buried in a small town deep in Mennonite farmland, the proprietors serve German-inspired dishes. He suggests ribs cooked in sauerkraut and, between mouthfuls, says, "This is my favorite. Mom can show you how to make it—if you're interested?"

"I'd love to." I'm not quite ready to take cooking lessons from his mother but my spider sense of danger from another bad choice is at an all-time low. Instead, I feel Scott will ground me, yet let me soar. He still hasn't kissed me or held my hand. Though this reminds me of Matthew who didn't touch me until our fifth date, the sexual tension is unbearable.

Back at the hangar, we examine his airplane, standing side by side, soon sidling toward each other until our shoulders and thighs touch, body language that informs me he's interested but patient. We're testing the water, waiting for the right time to plunge.

For our fourth date, two weeks after our first, I invite him to my townhouse for dinner. He arrives on time, brandishing a six-pack of Foster's Lager. Though I rarely have time for TV, I recognize the Australian beer from the barrage of billboards featuring charismatic Crocodile Dundee.

He shrugs. "Victim of advertising."

He devours my spaghetti and meatballs. "Delicious. You are multitalented."

Dinner is fun. Petting on the couch is more fun until he says, "There's this woman I've been dating a couple years."

Instant pain pierces my temples.

I manage a flat, "Oh."

My back reflexively arches away.

He snugs me closer. "She lives near Orillia. I see her about once a month."

I feel duped.

"Before I met you, I planned to see her this weekend."

Another short, flat, "Oh."

"We get on okay"—*Does he mean me?*—"but my relationship with her is nothing like ours."

"Oooohhh."

"I want to break up with Maggie in person. And, um, I didn't plan to go this far tonight." We're lying on the couch, facing each other, his hand stroking my breast. "I want to make love with you, but I won't cheat on her."

My breath returns to normal until his tongue explores my mouth with a kiss so sensuous and deep, it mimics intercourse. I gasp. "I want to make love with you."

Half an hour later, as we approach the point of no return, my amygdala is screaming, *Yesyesyes*, while my rational brain counters with, *Slow down, slow down.*

Suddenly he says, "It's nearly midnight. After work tomorrow, I'm driving north to see her. I should go home to pack."

At the door, his tongue makes love to me again, then he gazes at me. "I'm working nights next week. Maybe I'll see you at the club. Maybe Friday?"

That nebulous "maybe" has returned. I say, "Maybe."

Then, he's gone.

My gut tells me he'll keep his word and break up with Maggie, but life offers few guarantees. Until I spend more time with Scott, I can't know if he'll be Mr. Forever—or just Mr. Right Now. I make myself forget about him—at least for the weekend. Brandon's coming tomorrow, and if Scott were around, my enthusiastic optimism would tempt me to introduce them.

Late the next afternoon, Brandon and Jeanne meet me after work halfway between our homes for our weekend exchange. Rather than wait in a parking lot, we arrange to meet inside Kelsey's Roadhouse Restaurant and wait comfortably if one of us is delayed by work or traffic.

Brandon and I cuddle on the bench across from Jeanne who says, "Let's share a big plate of the barbeque chicken wings."

Brandon stabs his stubby finger on an image on the menu. "Hawaiian pizza, too, please!"

Jeanne says, "Brandon, show Mommy your painting."

He digs into his schoolbag and brings out a painting of me in an airplane. Despite my maternal bias, I'm impressed. "Sweetie, that's really good. Maybe you'll become a famous artist." He whips out his report card and I say, "Well done. Guess you like this new school?"

He nods excitedly.

Now that Brandon is ten, he often spends the day with me at the airport if I have to work that weekend. He reads in my office, watches television in the Compass Rose Café, or rides his bicycle. But this Saturday, after her lesson, my student Nancy says, "Why don't I take him into town and keep him occupied for an hour or so?"

When they return two hours later, he rushes into my arms. "Mommy, we went to McDonald's *and* Dairy Queen." Throughout supper at the steak house, Brandon jumps with excitement as he says, "She drives a Corvette. Why don't you have one?"

I'm delighted she offered to amuse him but a little jealous, too. I'm driving an old Pontiac Acadian, not a flashy red Corvette, but I can't have everything. "Sweetheart, Nancy and her lawyer husband are DINKs—double income, no kids. I spend my money on you!"

When he finishes his Caesar salad, I suggest, "Want to see

Back to the Future?" and he's all smiles. On Sunday night, we meet Jeanne at Tim Hortons, and he returns with her.

Our weekend was great, but now at home, alone, at night, concentration on anything but Scott is difficult. He's adventurous like Paul and gentle like Steve. Monday comes and goes. I hope he might call my home phone or my private line at the flight school, but he doesn't.

Or if he did, he didn't leave a message.

On Tuesday, I force myself to finish an anthropology assignment for university and fall asleep reading my statistics text. During the day, I focus on flying, but during silent moments inside the plane, unbidden thoughts cycle through my mind.

What if he tried to break up but Maggie persuaded him to change his mind?

What if he never really intended to break up with her?

Rather than allow these negative thoughts to overcome my natural optimism, I focus on the positives of this situation. The imposed hiatus gives me time to consider how a romantic liaison will affect my professional trajectory and my limited personal time.

Late Wednesday afternoon, as I review my notes for that evening's classroom lesson to commercial pilot students, Scott appears at the door of my office. His six-foot-two frame, covered by a massive work coat, dominates the doorway. He had suggested we might get together on Friday, but this is Wednesday. *Is his unexpected arrival good news—or bad?*

I grasp the edge of my chair to keep from leaping into his arms. "Did you see . . . *her?*"

He strokes his beard with his hand. "I stayed overnight."

I gather enough breath to ask, "With . . . her?"

"Orillia is a long drive. She insisted I stay rather than go to a hotel or drive home."

I hiss, "I'll *bet* she did."

His eyes twinkle. "I slept on the couch."

"Are you going to see her again?"

His smile penetrates every inch of my body. "I couldn't wait to see you. I have a couple hours before I leave for work." He sweeps into my office, lifts me out of my chair, and kisses my lips. Then he says, "Want to check out my airplane?"

Do I ever. He leaves, and a few minutes later, I casually say, "Cookie, I'll be gone a couple hours." Her smile suggests she's guessed where I'm going.

Scott whisks me inside his hangar, then shuts the door. Our bodies fly toward one another, unable to resist a moment longer, caressing each other with hands and mouth as he leads me to the ladder of his loft bed. The precise construction of his airplane suggests he's a master carpenter, but I ask, "Is this bed strong enough? I don't want to crash onto the cement floor."

He caresses my cheek with his fingertips. "We'll be like test pilots."

We ascend the ladder, then he explores my body with his magnificent tongue, a prelude to the best lovemaking ever.

After a few months of sleepovers at my townhouse or his hangar, where we sleep once or twice weekly while he works late on his aircraft, he moves in.

Cookie still maintains Scott is a philistine, and Joy, my petite student whose landings resembled controlled crashes until I realized she needed booster pillows to see the runway, insists he doesn't treat me well. I understand their rationale but disagree. He doesn't buy flowers or jewelry, gifts expected by most of my female friends, and some of his gifts are anything but romantic: a cast iron mallard duck doorstop, after I mention, "This reminds me of my duck-hunting grandfather"; a gleaming set of stain-less-steel cookware, after he complains about my mismatched pots; and an oak toilet seat—no idea why, but it's beautiful.

When I buy a new Honda Sport Coupe without air-conditioning, Scott arranges for me to purchase a unit at cost from his friend, a Honda executive. Scott says, "Installation will be a breeze. I have all the tools at my hangar."

That weekend, after a hangar sleepover and coffee at the Compass Rose Café, I organize the air-conditioning components. Scott tinkers with his airplane for thirty minutes until I explode with frustration. "When're you going to start the install?"

He laughs with genuine surprise. "I'm not. You are."

I say, "I can't!" and immediately regret the whining tone of my voice.

He ignores my moment of weakness and hands me the instructions. "Yes, you can. If you need help, I'll be here."

He doesn't help or offer tips to make installation easier, and I've no idea what position experienced mechanics use, but I spend most of the day upside down with my legs draped on the passenger seat and my torso under the dash. Somehow, I manage, using his tools and demanding his occasional assistance when the task requires more than two hands. At the end of the day, I have an air-conditioned car and an amplified appreciation of his love that's already lasted three hundred days longer than empty boxes of devoured chocolates and withered roses.

We celebrate our second year together with a diving trip to Flowerpot Island near the northern tip of the Bruce Peninsula on Lake Huron's Georgian Bay. The rugged isolation and no campers on the other five tent platforms make me imagine how my life might have been as an explorer, a *coureur de bois*, navigating these waters. Dozens of northern water snakes basking on the shoreline of jumbled boulders in the record-breaking 80°F temperatures of early autumn are the only evidence of life on the island.

For five days, we zoom around Fathom Five Underwater Marine Park in his inflatable Zodiac, then slip into the chill waters for a few final dives of the season. Each day is a sun-drenched panorama of clear sky reflected in ultramarine water, rippled only by our boat.

As we return home in his Jeep Cherokee, the golden sunshine of late afternoon strobes through the barren branches of some deciduous trees. I take one hand from the wheel and squeeze his burly hand. "Thanks for agreeing to dive the *Arabia* twice."

Scott chortles in his conspiratorial manner. "Never thought I'd find a woman like you."

I blow him a kiss.

Scott would be perfect if he spent more time with Brandon and me, as a family, but he isn't perfect and neither am I. Brandon has a father who loves him, so I appreciate what I have—a wonderful son, a good career, and a man who loves me. *What more do I need?*

Before returning to our townhouse, we stop at his hangar so he can glue another layer of fabric to the aircraft wing. After an hour, we then pop into the Flying Club to pick up my messages and paperwork. I unlock the front door, and we stroll inside, past the normally packed Compass Rose Café, today so empty a WWII De Havilland Mosquito could have screamed without impact through the emptiness.

I'm blinded by a blood-orange sunset piercing the western windows. As we approach my office, I jump, still with spots in my eyes, startled to see a human silhouette behind the dispatch desk. I make a visor with my hand. "Cookie, why are you working so late?"

She peeks at us between twin columns of paperwork.

I say, "I'm sure the school had a busy day, but can't the paperwork wait 'til tomorrow?"

She hesitates. When she finally speaks, her voice quivers. "I've been waiting for you."

I usually check in after a busy weekend, but she seems upset. "Why?"

"Did you hear the news?"

My eyes adjust to the chiaroscuro twilight. "What news?"

Her mouth opens and closes and opens again, like the wary fish who'd shared their peaceful waters with us. I want to say, "Out with it," but when she finally murmurs, "Will crashed his plane," I wish she hadn't.

I pucker my lips. "Oh my gosh, is he okay?"

Her tawny Mediterranean skin wanes to ashen, something I didn't consider possible. I notice her almond eyes are red-rimmed and lack their usual glimmer.

She blurts, "Will is dead."

My brain refuses to process this horror. "Are you sure?"

"They believe he died instantly."

My thoughts race to Joy, his wife and my former student. "I hope he was alone."

"Joy is . . . in critical condition."

I hear myself ask, "Wh-what-how-what happened?" but the words seem to stammer from someone else's mouth.

Tears tumble onto her cheeks. "Search-and-rescue found her on the ground, sprawled against a tree trunk."

Scott and I exchange glances. He shifts from one foot to the other, then transforms into Michelangelo's *David*, sublime, rigid, and mute.

Cookie says, "Apparently the engine started to vibrate and cracked the fuel tank. Gas leaked into the cockpit onto their legs."

Neither Scott nor I speak.

She snuffles. "Will shut down the engine. He picked a good field, but as he got close to the ground, he saw telephone wires in the way."

I groan. "*Uhhh-mmmm.*" I feel woozy.

Cookie says, "Apparently Will yanked back on the control column and tried to fly above the wires."

Internal screams puncture my eardrums. Cymbals clang in

my brain. My knees buckle and I clutch the counter. "Noooo. *Noooo.* They would've been gliding . . . at a low airspeed . . . trying to climb without power . . . the aircraft would have stalled, spun, and . . ."

I lean into Scott, who wraps his arm around my shoulders. I gasp for breath, then exhale. "Tell me I'm wrong."

"Joy was tossed out of the plane. She has some broken bones but no apparent internal injuries. They're keeping her for observation."

I gulp for breath. An invisible full-body vise squeezes tighter and tighter until I'm barely breathing. A primeval force propels my legs out the door, into the parking lot, and toward my car. I don't recall if I say, "Scott, let's get out of here," or if I say anything at all, but he follows.

My legs stop moving ten feet from my car. I sink toward the pavement, stopped from slumping onto tarmac by Scott's hands pulling me up into his arms. I dissolve into his chest, and we cry together. We admire Will and Joy for their determination, intelligence, skill, and courage. I'm sure his thoughts echo mine: *How could this tragedy happen to our infallible heroes?*

29

INTO THE BLUE

On a midwinter Saturday in 1988, during a relentless snow-storm that threatens to take us prisoner inside the hangar, Chief Instructor Martin and I plow through the endless but necessary paperwork. I'm half through the stack of student progress reports when Martin starts clicking the plunger of his pen in/out, in/out.

He knows repetitive pen clicking irritates me, so I glare at him across our identical 1950s-style teachers' desks pushed back-to-back. "Whatever you want better be good."

He clears his throat. "Wanna fly to the Caribbean?"

My stomach tightens, but I keep the sparkle of enthusiasm from my eyes. "Maybe."

Martin picks at a piece of laminate wood peeling from the edge of his desktop. "Mike, a former student of mine—you don't know him—wants an instructor to accompany him and his assistant on a business trip to the Bahamas and Jamaica."

"What's he do?"

"Owns a manufacturing company."

I lean back in my swivel chair. Something about this proposal agitates my amygdala. "He's *your* ex-student. Why don't *you* go?"

Martin flips both hands into the air, seeming to dismiss the charter as a routine flight. "I went last year."

"Two consecutive Caribbean jaunts will jazz up your resume for that corporate job you've been eyeing."

Martin runs the slender fingers of his hands through his carrot-orange curls. "I have previous commitments."

I scrunch my lips together. "It *sounds* fabulous."

He reaches for the telephone. "Excellent."

"I'll give you a few days to change your mind."

He dials. "I'm calling Mike now."

Though Mike will be financing all expenses and flying the plane, this unexpected charter will increase my flight time and provide experience flying to new destinations in new countries.

Three days later, Martin introduces me to Mike, who smooths his windblown hair and says, "Let me treat you to coffee and a sweet."

At the Compass Rose Café, he points at crispy swirls of glazed pastry dotted with raisins. "These are my favorites!"

After pastry and pleasantries, he thrusts his license and logbook toward me. I scan a few pages, then wrinkle my nose. "Impressive. You own your own business, but just for fun, have a commercial license, an instrument rating, and you've flown internationally."

He splays his fingers on the table. Massive gold rings inset with diamonds flash from both ring fingers. He balances the chair on its back legs and rocks. "My assistant, Cathy, and I fly south for business *every* year."

"That's a big annual expense."

"The corporate tax savings I get from having components made in the Caribbean more than compensates."

He stops rocking and pats my hand. "Don't worry. I'll do the flight planning, radio work, and, of course, *all* the flying."

"Why bother taking a senior instructor?"

He holds his palms skyward. "You're like insurance. Who knows what might happen."

Over continental North America, a pale sun hovers amidst acid-washed, blue-denim skies. The winds are light and the single engine of the four-seater Cessna purrs. Mike keeps the plane straight and level and on course, but the intrusion of his splayed legs into my half of our aircraft makes me feel more cramped than usual in these confined quarters. From a safety perspective, his stance blocks my view of some gauges on the instrument panel. When I gyrate to confirm the functioning of gauges, he shifts momentarily but resumes monopolizing my space. He doesn't seem to notice anything but his comfort.

Cathy, his slender assistant, reclines on the bench seat behind us, reading a paperback.

As we approach Lake Erie's northern shore, Mike whips his head over his right shoulder toward Cathy and tosses ad hoc phrases into her face, shouting the important words. "In the pocket—behind my seat—emergency procedures card—engine failure—ditching in open water—life jackets behind you—questions?"

Her wide-eyed Betty Boop expression indicates she's translated his terse staccato to "Emergency—crash—death" and "Ditching—open water—shark attack!—dismemberment—death."

His timing suggests he'd forgotten to give the passenger briefing on the ground, when the engine's roar won't drown the standard, well-rehearsed terminology learned by all pilots. Before departure, I attributed his omission to their frequent flights together. Now, I wonder what else he's forgotten, but since his pilot skills are technically good, I push this thought from my mind.

Until we approach Charlotte, North Carolina, when haze obscures our vision outside the aircraft and forces him to rely on instruments more than geographic features. He becomes slightly disoriented, unable to maintain heading or altitude with precision.

When the plane enters a descending turn and he doesn't correct these deviations and return to his assigned heading and altitude, this indicates he's responding to the sensory input from his body telling him the plane is straight-and-level—when, in reality, its turning and descending.

Finally, the combination of piloting, map reading, communicating with controllers, and weather overwhelms him. He's flying as if he's a novice private pilot with fifty flight hours, not a commercial pilot with three hundred hours and an instrument rating. But he's a good pilot in good weather, I have bags of experience, and we anticipate no major storms until Jamaica.

When he requests my help with communicating and navigating, I realize he's made the right decision, unlike me when I let Martin's praise for Mike lull me into bogus complacency. I should've trusted my intuition and spent a couple hours before departure to ensure his skills were adequate.

From Florida, we fly east into the Bermuda Triangle, where more than fifty planes and ships have mysteriously disappeared. Only fools believe this imaginary triangle harbors diabolic spirits, but an unexpected wave of foreboding washes over me. A flash of heat tingles my skin. I force myself to be rational. Though we'll be inside the triangle (in the air and on the ground in Freeport) for the next few days and won't emerge until an hour south of the Bahamian Archipelago, the sky is a cloudless blue, the engine purrs, and Mike's about to deliver us into paradise.

For the next three sun-drenched mornings, I wander Freeport while Mike and Cathy meet prospective manufacturers. Tension leaches from my body as I relax in sun-speckled floral gardens, drool over sleek sailboats moored at Bell Channel Bay, and the aroma of fried fish and succulent stews lure me into Port Lucaya's open-air market. Informed by a colorfully turbaned chef that the rich broth of one stew derives from pig's feet and another from sheep's tongue, I settle on fried conch.

After lunch, I laze in a woven hammock on the beach under coconut palms, wiggle my toes in warm sand, and read a few chapters of Margaret Atwood's *The Handmaid's Tale*, a Christmas gift from Mom. Late afternoon, I join my hosts in the palapa-roofed beach bar to slurp expensive cocktails and sing along with "Margaritaville" and other Caribbean classics.

Cathy wears a different color of the same sleeveless shift every day, looking glamorous without apparent effort. Mike's clothing is never wrinkled or soiled, and I conclude his wardrobe must consist of identical pairs of taupe Dockers and black, button-down shirts.

He emphasizes his pre-departure promise—"This is my trip. I'm paying. Enjoy yourselves"—and treats us to cocktails and decadent dinners of anything we desire, surf and turf for them and sweet, buttery scallops for me.

On day five, we depart the Bahamian Archipelago for Jamaica. Captain Mike does his best takeoff of the trip, and Freeport fades to a memory. My brain buzzes with the excitement of today's flight and exciting adventures in another new country. I marvel at the sublime southern shores of Xanadu and the shimmering beryl-blue sea that filter, but don't block, the intense sunlight. Manta rays glide in V formation like black brooches across the creamy seafloor. Their undulating wings wave farewell.

Fare well.

For the next three hours, we'll be airborne above open seas, my first flight over any body of water larger than the Great Lakes, farther south than I've traveled before. If the engine malfunctions, an improbable (but real) risk of flight beyond gliding distance from shore, we'll be floating on the shark-filled seas of the Bermuda Triangle. I tell myself these thoughts are ridiculous. The most recent disappearance occurred nearly ten years ago, in 1978, when St. Thomas Tower Controllers sighted Eastern Caribbean Airways Piper Navajo, then they didn't.

Over the years, many ships and planes have disappeared inside the Bermuda Triangle, but none have ever been found.

An invisible rubber band tightens around my forehead.

Mike fights to keep the plane on course as the haze increases and blurs the already indistinct horizon created by the merging of the sun-glazed sea with an incandescent sky.

Twenty minutes later, clouds encase the plane. Forced to rely on flight instruments and unable to see anything outside the aircraft, Mike struggles. I watch with concern as he allows the plane to stray from our assigned heading and altitude. He corrects all deviations, but seconds later the plane begins another slow descent and an almost imperceptible turn.

Manic butterflies scurry inside my stomach.

When I ask if he wants a break, he sits up straight, focuses intently, and maintains good control. I slump against the bucket seat and close my eyes, enjoying the calm for a few minutes until the unnatural silence of the radios shivers my spine.

I contact air traffic control to request a higher altitude. No response. Despite the cool outside air flowing into the airplane, a flush of heat surges over my skin. I try another radio frequency. No response. I try the second radio and check the maps to confirm I've selected the correct stations.

The butterflies inside of me transform into a flock of thrashing birds, pecking chunks from my stomach. I switch radio dials, returning to the first, still-silent frequency. The plane doesn't need radios to fly, but we need radios to communicate with the outside world.

I say, "These radios are too quiet."

Mike says with snarky confidence, "Probably 'cuz no one else is flying."

"Have you noticed anything unusual with the instruments or the radios?"

He shakes his head.

I ask him to cycle the battery/alternator switch on, then off. I hear nothing. No static. No voices. Nothing but dread screaming in my head. I say, "I'll try all our previously assigned radio frequencies."

The high-pitched shriek resonating inside my head drowns the murmuring engine noise—*Electrical failure . . . electrical failure . . . electrical failure.* At first, I refuse to listen, but the inescapable silence convinces me. Leaning toward Mike, I speak directly into his ear so Cathy can't overhear. "Our electrical system has gone south."

With his right hand, he pats the dash. Fractured sunlight bounces off his diamond ring. He flashes his salesman's smile. "I don't believe this beautiful lady has let us down."

He sounds confident, but his left hand chokes the control column, and his voice goes up an octave when he says, "I *need* to get to *Jamaica.*"

I say, sotto voce, "If we were over land, and if we were certain our destination had good weather, I'd continue with our flight planned route. But we aren't."

He rubs both palms on crisp, pleated Dockers. "What's the difference?"

"Communist Cuban airspace is the difference."

Cool, fresh air flows in from the vents, but droplets of sweat pool near his receding hairline. I touch his forearm with my fingertips and look at him. "We've flown a fifth of our route. We'd be foolish to continue in cloud, without radio contact, over open water, near embargoed Cuban soil."

He turns toward Cathy in the back seat, bracing his right arm against my bucket seat. Despite the cool air at eight thousand feet, an armpit crescent darkens his Hawaiian shirt. The scent of his fear penetrates my sinuses like an ice pick. He says, "Lola thinks we have an electrical failure. She wants to return to Freeport, but I want to continue to Jamaica. What do *you* want to do?"

Cathy responds with the unmistakable sound of retching. The tart smell wafts forward, and I adjust the outside air vent to force fresh air onto my face and open a window for additional ventilation. She retches again.

I ask, trying to keep the anger from my voice, "Why did you ask an experienced pilot to accompany you if you won't listen to advice?"

"I wanted Cathy's opinion."

"She doesn't know anything about flying. All you did was waste time and upset her."

Mike grips the control with his left hand and fiddles with the radios while I scrounge a paper serviette from my purse. I hand it to Cathy, who brushes moist, blonde bangs off her forehead, then wipes her mouth with the serviette.

Using my best "I know what I'm doing voice," I say, "Don't worry. The electrical system has failed but that does *not* affect the engine." I smile with confidence, glad my Ray-Ban aviator sunglasses mask the angst in my eyes. "The engine's fine. We have lots of fuel."

She clutches her folded Sic-Sac, speechless and terrified, but settles against the seat, somewhat reassured.

I squeeze her hand and repeat, "Don't worry," then turn to tackle our dilemma. I try to pull in signals from stations on both radios but hear nothing and have no way to confirm whether the signals or my voice transmit beyond our aluminum tomb. Flashbacks of previous systems failures fill my brain. Options to save our lives shoot through my mind. Mike's words of assurance during our preflight discussions in Canada mock me now. *"I'll do all the flight planning, talking on the radios, and, of course, the flying."*

"Mike, you're having trouble flying in cloud."

"No, I'm not."

"You're not maintaining altitude or heading."

"I'm okay."

"You're all over the sky. I can't monitor you *and* find a solution. I'm taking control."

He doesn't acknowledge my command or release his side of the control column. I jiggle my controls, but Mike's dual-hand death grip on his control column makes it difficult to move. I jiggle it again, abruptly, with vigor.

"Mike, let go! I'm taking control."

He throws his hands in the air. "Fine."

I exhale with relief, thinking he's accepted my decision, until his next directive. "Descend now. Break out of cloud. Just do it."

"I won't do that without a controller's approval. We might hit another airplane."

He says, "Don't be ridiculous. We haven't seen any planes, anywhere—even at Freeport."

"We only need to hit one other plane to have a midair."

His hands hover near the control column. "What are *your* plans?"

So far, Mike is fighting the urge to resume control, but I can't let that happen. Flying with reference to instruments had been difficult for him and now, to complicate matters, he isn't thinking logically. "Mike, unless you can suggest a reasonable solution, please—be quiet!"

He pounds the dash with his fist. "I rented this plane. I need to get to Jamaica." Cathy's sobs fill the airplane. I turn to console her, but Mike leans into my face. "Did you hear me? I rented this plane! I need—"

"We're ninety miles south of Freeport and have about four hours of fuel but—"

"With all that gas, let's continue!"

Instead of assessing the situation and determining alternatives, Mike's slapdash demands suggest he's perilously close to panic, a dangerous state of mind that escalates, spreads like an influenza virus, and forces a terrifying situation into uncontrollable chaos.

Mike's panic is dangerous to me because I need to determine the best strategy, not waste precious moments reassuring our passenger and Mike, whose preflight confidence had suggested savoir faire was his middle name.

My head aches as if squeeze clamps press against my temples. "Mike! Fear is normal. Panic is not."

Cathy retches between sobs. I understand why they're scared. I'm scared, too, but I'm also exasperated with men who exude confidence then buckle under pressure. I ask, "Do you remember Montego Bay is expected to have heavy rain?"

He shrugs.

I can't contain my contempt. "*If* I return control to you and *if* you manage to fly without getting into a spiral dive and plowing into the ocean, *how* do you plan to find the Montego Bay airport without radios?"

"We could . . . um . . . I guess . . ."

I lean toward him, my mouth almost grazing his ear. "Even if the weather in Jamaica is perfect, if we approach Cuba without talking to Cuban controllers, MiG fighter jets will escort us to our final destination—Havana!"

He whirls toward me, eyebrows raised, eyes wide. "MiGs?"

I poke my index finger into the soft flesh of his upper arm. "That's right. *If* we're lucky. *If* they ask questions first. *If* they speak English. Otherwise, we'll be target practice."

He deflates into his seat and crosses his arms. I'm not really certain MiGs will shoot down a small, civilian aircraft, but I'm glad my potential worst-case scenario convinces him to obey. He's sulking, but at least in silence. I scan the instruments, the radios, and consider our options for survival.

I'm about to admit, at least to myself, I haven't got a clue how to save our lives when a flare of white light floods the flight deck. The shifting cloud layers have moved to reveal a gash. Far below, I see whitecaps churning.

Should I squeeze through this narrow slash?

I have seconds to decide. Should I maintain my heading and altitude? Or dive toward the ocean? Fruit and granola tumble in my stomach, agitating like laundry in Grandma's wringer washer.

Should I wait for a larger opening?

If I wait, will the clouds shift again and obliterate our view of the waves below?

Will I get another chance?

Over water, we aren't in danger of colliding with communication towers, skyscrapers, or mountain-stuffed clouds. But what *if* another plane is on our route at a lower altitude? The narrow gash doesn't provide a wide field of vision for me to see other planes— or for them to see me. I half-expect other aircraft, but other pilots aren't expecting me.

We might fly an hour before another opening appears in the clouds or we may never get a second chance. Eventually we'll run out of gas. Eventually we'll be ditching into the ocean.

My mouth sours as if I've swallowed Cathy's vomit, but I force myself to speak. "Mike—you look left; and, Cathy, you look right. Do *not* stop looking. Tell me if you see *anything.*"

Tension settles in my shoulders as I gamble for what might be my only chance to get out of cloud—and out of this mess alive. Those imaginary squeeze clamps drill through my temples into my brain. If other planes are nearby, I hope they aren't in my flight path and that the cloud patterns don't change as we descend. I tighten my grip on the control column, tip the wings to check for traffic, then barrel into the crevasse.

Seconds later, we break out below clouds and enter a world of unlimited visibility. A spark of hope pulses through my body. Our situation has improved, but we remain stuck in an aircraft with a broken electrical system, surrounded by miles and miles of watery desert.

I turn the aircraft toward the north and retrace our path from

Freeport. I check on Cathy, whose ashen cheeks show a hint of rose. She hasn't abandoned her Sic-Sac, but instead of clenching it, she has placed it on the bench seat beside her. I give her the thumbs-up sign, then turn my focus on flying and Mike.

His hand hovers near the control column. "Now that we have good vis, let's continue on to Jamaica."

I grip the control column tightly, fearful he might overpower me, seize control, and turn us toward Jamaica.

High clouds dissolve as we near Grand Bahama Island. Two miles south of the Freeport airport, I begin the approach and landing procedures. Without electrical power, the three green lights (one for each wheel) on the panel won't illuminate and confirm that the gear is down and locked. I must rely on hearing the gear thump into place.

I say, "Unless you see another aircraft near us, please keep quiet."

Thump-thump. The main wheels are down, but I can't relax until the third thump indicates the nosewheel is down. The only traffic is a jet five or six miles west of the airport. I cross overhead the airport so the controllers can see our aircraft, join the traffic pattern, land, and exit onto the first taxiway. A ramp agent guides me into a parking position, and after I kill the engine, he flips his head toward the control tower. "Controllers wanta see ya."

Mike says, "You go. Cathy and I'll check out flights to Jamaica."

They collect their matching American Tourister luggage and race toward the terminal. A meeting requested by controllers was usually a bad sign except for the time that the gruff Canadian controller invited me up to ask for a date. I close my eyes for a few moments of serenity, then walk on quivering legs to the tower and buzz the intercom.

A crotchety voice asks, "Who is it?"

I identify myself, drag open the heavy steel door, and spin up the three-story spiral staircase, my Timberland hiking boots clanging against the steel steps. A blast of air-conditioning smacks me in the face as I enter the controllers' hexagonal aerie. The two occupants whirl their executive chairs toward me, then politely say hello with grim faces and eyes barricaded behind mirrored Ray-Bans. I ram my hands into my jacket pockets to avoid chewing my cuticles. The one wearing a ball cap taps his fingernails on the metal armrests of his chair.

"Why'd you deviate from your flight plan?"

Before I can respond, the older man, Darth Vader's double with black curls salted white, says, "Why did you come back?"

His baritone resonates like the iconic villain's and, despite arctic air-conditioning, sweat trickles down my spine. "We had a total electrical failure in cloud! Mike, the pilot who rented the plane, had a meltdown."

The men shoot sideways glances at each other.

"Mike wanted a more experienced pilot to come along in case he needed help. But when he needed me, he wouldn't listen. I was afraid he'd do something stupid. We needed to land. Yesterday."

Darth removes a pen nestled above his ear and writes on a yellow notepad.

I want to vaporize. "My biggest mistake was to believe he was pilot in command, but he thought we shared the responsibility, at least when my assistance was convenient for him. In Canada, we say too many cooks spoil the broth."

Darth stops writing and grins. "My grandmum says that, too!"

I pull my hands from my pockets and raise both palms to face Darth. "I *do* need to get the plane fixed."

"We recommend Island Aviation. Best aircraft repair company on the island. I'll call 'em and explain the pickle you're in."

We shake hands, then I skip down the hundred or so steps of the control tower and walk to the terminal building. Mike waves at me above the throng of passengers in the waiting room.

He announces with pride, "We're booked on a commercial flight to Jamaica. Leaves in an hour."

I sense he expected approval, but I'm puzzled. "What about the airplane?"

He shrugs. "You're the pilot. Get it fixed."

I snap my jaw shut like Iceman in *Top Gun*.

Mike spins toward Cathy, then, as an afterthought, says to me, "Call me when it's ready, and I'll fly her home."

I flick my wrist goodbye and head outside, into nature's sauna, relieved to be rid of Mike, if only for a few days—days I'll spend wondering what I could've done differently during our aborted flight to Jamaica.

30

PROMISED LAND

S purred by rage, I stride faster and faster along a potholed strip of dirt that promises to take me to Island Aviation at the airport's eastern edge. My anger rises as I reflect on the morning's debacle. I remember male colleagues, relatives, friends, and lovers similar to Mike. Men who have knowledge and skills, successful men who exude confidence, yet, when faced with unexpected challenges, act aggressively—or crumple with fear.

I'm not angry about their reaction. I understand why they're fearful.

I'm angry that men perpetuate the stereotype of women as weak and fearful.

The sun flames my cheeks; sweat tickles my spine. A hedge of hibiscus bushes dotted with wind-ripped shards of colored plastic and bleached paper guides me along the airport periphery. I stop to catch my breath and admire a fifteen-foot-tall poinsettia tree, amazed they grow larger than the two-foot-tall potted plants Mom has at Christmas.

From a distance, I can't identify any of the businesses in the row of six pointed roofs that appear to lean against each other for support. None of the wooden structures suggest prosperity and none advertise with neon or electric signs, just battered wooden, plank signs with remnant, indecipherable scribbles. About twenty feet away, I search the stretch of buildings, only to discover Island Aviation isn't the *best* repair facility; it's the *only* repair facility.

I turn the door handle, layered with a rainbow of chipped paint and grime. Inside, my eyes struggle to adjust from tropical sunbath to catacomb gloom. A bare light bulb droops from an electrical cord and drives daggers into my eyeballs. Somewhere behind the glare, I hear a singsong voice. "How-DEE-doo, miss. Controllers say you got a sick baby."

These premises don't reassure me, but I say, "I sure do!"

"Tell Bobby Jay all 'bout your troubles."

I squint toward the voice and my eyes lock on Bobby Jay. If his skills as a mechanic are half as impressive as his muscular torso, chiseled face, dark chocolate eyes, and mellifluous voice, I'll soon be home. "The alternator quit. Can you fix it?"

"Don'tcha fret. I'll have dis 'ere baby operating good as new. C'mon back tomorrow."

He arranges accommodation and transportation. The swank Pelican Bay Lucaya where we stayed is full, but the comfortable Holiday Inn can accommodate me for one night.

I dump my bags on my room floor, then contact the hotel's long-distance telephone operator and provide three numbers in order of priority. Once connected, I discuss the malfunction with Martin at the flight school. He gives his approval for the pending repair bill, then says, "Are you comfortable getting the plane fixed there? Maybe one of our mechanics who has a private license could fly down commercially, fix the plane, and accompany you back home?" That option hadn't occurred to me, but something about it sounds wimpy. "I'll be fine."

Next, I call Brandon. "Hi, sweetheart! How's my little angel?" I tell him about swimming in warm ocean water but nothing about the scary flight. "I promise to bring you a conch shell. When you hold it against your ear, you'll hear the roar of ocean waves."

Finally, I contact Scott to discuss the situation.

He says, "Now that you're on the ground, it's a simple problem for the maintenance engineers to fix or put in a new alternator."

He's right, so I force myself to be optimistic—even though the terrifying possibility of almost being lost at sea, with little chance of rescue, somewhere in an ocean of sharks, is still very, very real.

Logistics complete, I slip into my bathing suit and dash to a beach lounger at the poolside bar. Five minutes later, I'm swirling the last dribble of my frozen margarita from a tulip glass. I beckon the handsome waiter for a second, and as he ambles away, I contemplate my predicament.

A stench should've permeated the air when Martin offered this great opportunity last month in our instructor's office. *Why hadn't I listened to my gut?* Something too good to be true is too good to be true.

As the afternoon sun and the margarita soothe me, inside and out, I realize Mike's emergency briefing after takeoff should've jolted me into high alert. Pilots give effective briefings prior to departure, not after kissing land hasta la vista. Mike had flown well in good weather but needed practice flying in clouds, without visual reference to earth and sky. Today, after the systems failure in cloud, Mike hadn't been able to control the aircraft— or himself. Because modern planes are reliable, I conclude this has been Mike's first systems failure *and* his first experience with actual instrument flight in cloud.

The following morning, after a buffet breakfast of tropical fruits, imported cheeses, crusty rolls, and strong coffee that could have been tailor-made for me, I check out, then hop into a taxi bound for the airport. Island Aviation hasn't contacted me, but the mechanics should soon finish the repairs.

Bobby Jay saunters out of the office; a cigarette droops on his full lower lip. Another mechanic, identified as Chas by an oval name tag on grease-stained coveralls, joins him for a smoke.

Grins fill their faces as they gesture to my aircraft parked on the ramp, indicating it's ready to go, rather than inside the hangar as an in-patient. We high-five, then I drop my luggage in their office, do my preflight walk-around, and prepare for a quick test flight.

Things look good until midway through the pre-takeoff checklist, when the alternator quits. With wide eyes, I stare in disbelief at the discharging gauge and shriek with frustration. I return to the ramp, shut down the engine, and leap out, preparing to throttle Bobby Jay and Chas. I stomp toward them but slow my angry pace when I see their expectant faces.

Chas asks with surprise, "What's wrong, honey-chile?"

I shrug. "Still broken. Can you *get* a new alternator on this island?"

Chas wraps a reassuring arm around my shoulders. "She'll be fixed for tomorra."

I check back into the Holiday Inn, mostly because I don't have many alternatives, and I want to believe Chas can fix the plane.

Back at the airport the following morning, Chas greets me. "My best boy done fixed your plane. She's good to go!"

Once again, we high-five, I drop my luggage in their office, do my preflight check, and prepare for a quick test flight. When the alternator fails on the pre-takeoff check, I flop against the seat-back, close my eyes, and count to one hundred. The confidence of Island Aviation's employees, and their desire to please, had buoyed my hopes.

I want to kick holes in their particleboard walls. Instead, knowing this will make enemies, I smile and say, "You've done the best job with the tools you have. I'd love to stay on your beautiful island, but I need to get home. Any ideas?"

Bobby Jay slaps his hip and says, "Why, you jes' fly to Palm Beach."

My mouth gapes wide like an alligator waiting for an unwary egret. This man is a lunatic. "You want me to fly more than two hundred miles, over open water, in a plane that has *no radio*?"

He throws his head back and howls with laughter. "NORDO! Thas right."

"I've never flown an aircraft that didn't have a working radio!"

He says, "You flew *here* without a radio."

I shudder, remembering my unplanned return to Freeport when we had to fly NORDO because all the radios failed as a result of the alternator malfunction. "I've never *intentionally* flown an aircraft without a working radio!"

He asks, "What's the difference?"

I blink, astounded. "The *difference* is I'll be flying into one of the busiest airspaces in American airspace, using landmarks as reference points like Lindbergh used Maya pyramids."

Bobby Jay says, "Yes, ma'am. NORDO, like the pioneers." He tips his head toward the phone. "Arrange the flight with your friends in the tower, then call Atlantic Aviation in Palm Beach."

To my surprise, neither Darth nor the Atlantic Aviation employee who slots my plane into his schedule are surprised. Bobby Jay laughs with good humor at my expression and accepts my apology for doubting him.

Back at the Holiday Inn, I try to lose myself in the dystopia of *The Handmaid's Tale*.

On the third morning of my extended nonvacation, Freeport's meteorologist reports a massive area of high pressure bringing at least three days of what pilots call *no* weather. No clouds, no rain, and no winds. No weather is perfect weather.

I can't stop smiling. If all goes well, I'll soon be home, cuddling Brandon, and soon thereafter, in bed with Scott. I advise the Palm Beach repair facility of my imminent arrival, file my flight plan, and receive my departure clearance from the air traffic controller I've nicknamed Ball Cap. To make certain I understand, I repeat his clearance exactly, needing to confirm I've been given the very unusual preapproved landing clearance in America.

To Ball Cap, I say, "Thanks for all your help."

As much as possible, I've enjoyed my second visit to Freeport, but it's past time to leave.

All systems (other than the dead alternator) check out. I do an effortless takeoff in calm air, but instead of retracting the wheels after takeoff as the manual directs, I keep the wheels down. Wheels increase drag (resistance against the air) and fuel consumption. I have four-and-one-half hours of fuel, three more than needed, but I need landing gear to land and it's safer to keep them down than worrying about getting them back down.

Today, my biggest obstacle is the knowledge that I'll be flying an aircraft with a broken system into overstuffed airspace where jets transport about thirteen thousand passengers per day, and where dozens of private and charter aircraft take off, land, and transit each hour.

I climb to eight thousand five hundred feet, and every few seconds, scan the instruments, anticipating another mechanical malfunction. I twist my torso and wiggle my shoulders. I feel a release of some of the tension stabbing my back. The aircraft doesn't know the alternator isn't working. The aircraft doesn't know the electrical system malfunctioned (or that an electrical system existed in the first place) or that it's over water, well beyond gliding distance from shore, still inside the Bermuda Triangle.

Only I (and the controllers) know these things.

The silence of the radios calms me and provides an opportunity for reflection, but today I'd welcome radio chatter. I chew the cuticle of my right forefinger until it bleeds, all the while yearning for annoying belches of static.

On the water, frothy whitecaps indicate that the calm winds at takeoff have increased to fifteen knots or more. If the upper-level winds have correspondingly increased, my flight will be longer. However, these waves provide unexpected guidance because, if I keep them angled thirty degrees to my right, I'm on course.

Halfway through my estimated flight time of ninety minutes, I strain to see land in the distance. If the aircraft has flown half the distance, I should see Florida's coastline. But I don't. I'm certain the plane is bucking headwinds stronger than predicted.

I record the time, but so far, I'm not worried.

The engine hums and the plane cruises through an electric-blue sky. Lulled into meditation, I muse about the flights of aviation's female pathfinders, my childhood heroes. Though my flight across a short stretch of ocean meagerly echoes trailblazing flights across the expansive Atlantic, I feel a distant kinship with my hero Beryl Markham, the first person—male or female—to fly alone across the ocean from east to west, from England to Canada. Lost in reverie and finally comfortable in my skin, the hot sun makes me want to curl up with my cat.

Suddenly, a strip of aquamarine blue bisects the sea and sky. Snapped into the present, I bolt upright. This distant horizontal slash is land somewhere along America's coastline—but where? I can't see far enough to identify landmarks, and without radios, I can't determine my exact location.

I've flown sixty minutes of a flight originally calculated to take ninety minutes, based on predicted winds. The first hour has been perfect, and I hope the rest will be as easy. However, without geographic reference points to confirm my specific location, I don't know where I am, other than inside the Bermuda Triangle, somewhere above a vast ocean.

Does the aircraft battery have enough juice to power one radio? I don't know, but if I don't try, I'll never know. The battery may work for a while but conk out quickly. The worst-case scenario is that it won't work at all. I hold my breath and flick the battery switch on. Gauges whir to life. Needles spin into position. I try one navigation radio, plot my position, and turn off the battery.

I'll be landing in forty-five minutes.

Unless the engine quits. Then I'll be swimming with sharks.

Minutes later, the misty horizon transforms into a mystical oasis of mansions shimmering in hundred-degree heat. Uniquely shaped capes and coves ripple the shoreline and cradle distinctly patterned cities. Twenty nautical miles out, I tentatively identify Palm Beach International Airport. Fifteen miles out, I make a positive identification by comparing the schematic drawing in my airport handbook to the distinctive crisscross runway pattern I see in the distance.

I'm close. So close.

Should I risk using the battery again? On the day the alternator failed, multiple systems had killed the battery, but today I've used the battery less than five minutes. Maybe, just maybe, it'll work.

The Palm Beach controllers expect me to fly into their airspace as a NORDO aircraft, unable to talk to them on the radio. They don't need to hear from me, but I want to be reassured by a human voice. If something goes wrong now and I must ditch into the ocean, somebody should know my last known position.

What if the plane doesn't float?

I shift in my seat and flick the battery on for a second time during this flight.

How long will my life vest keep me afloat before the sharks arrive?

I turn on one of the two communication radios and hear emptiness. I turn up the volume. My belly fills with Mexican jumping beans. Dead air is not reassuring. If the battery is working and supplying power to the radio, I should hear constant chatter in this congested skyway corridor linking busy airports. Has another weird system failure occurred? If yes, Murphy is a permanent stowaway. Everything that could go wrong, has gone wrong.

I inhale deeply, hold my breath, and exhale slowly, repeating several times to force composure, then try the second communication radio, reminding myself that today's flight is a planned flight in beautiful weather, not a traumatic systems failure in cloud. Perhaps the controllers and other aircraft can hear me, though for some unexplained reason I can't hear them. I broadcast my aircraft call sign, my position, and my intention to land.

I jump with surprise when an unexpected voice answers, his voice filled with relief. "This is Palm Beach Approach. *Greeaat* to hear you! Cleared to land runway 28 Left."

Normally, an aircraft would be cleared to land by a tower controller, not an approach controller. However, I've been given priority because of the aircraft's NORDO status. Neither the controllers, nor any pilots flying near me, want a disabled aircraft flailing around the skies or bailing into the ocean. Getting my plane on the ground and off the runway is imperative for everyone. Consistent with emergency or unusual situations, the controllers will keep runway 28L clear of all arrival or departure traffic until I land and clear the runway.

The flight is over. Almost.

About one mile east of the eastern end of the runway, I know that even if the engine quits now, the plane can glide to the runway. The muscles in my back twitch, then relax. Slightly.

Twenty feet above the runway, I reduce power to idle and float through blankets of heat percolating from the black tarmac. I cross the threshold, then whoop with delight as the rubber tires squeal against scorching hot tarmac. My spine sags with relief. Just being in America isn't being home yet, but it's close enough.

I park the aircraft on the ramp and stroll into Atlantic Aviation, where two employees greet me. The female receptionist smiles like Vanna White. "Our maintenance crew informs me that unless you've misdiagnosed or they discover another glitch, your plane will be ready tomorrow."

I've heard that before, but I force excitement into my response. "Excellent. Can you call a taxi and reserve a hotel somewhere near here for me, please?"

"We recommend the Airport Hilton."

The second employee, a twenty-something male wearing coveralls, says, "I'm taking my commercial flight test soon. If you promise to give me some pointers, I'll take you to the Hilton."

He listens to all the details about flying over open water in a single engine without a radio, then says, "Weren't you scared?"

"Scared shitless. But less than during the total electrical failure in cloud over the ocean between the Bahamas and Cuba."

He shudders involuntarily. "I never want to find out how scary that must have been!"

Inside my hotel room, I flop face-first onto the queen-size bed and dissolve into the fluffy white duvet, inhaling its lemony fresh scent.

Today's flight had been *almost* routine, but worry had riddled my sleep for the previous nights.

I'm thankful to be here, a step closer to home, but the plane isn't fixed yet. I need some stress-free hours and a scotch from the bar fridge. I pour two ounces, sink against all four king-size down-filled pillows, and within minutes, feel my taut muscles soften from the combination of pillows and booze. I still can't believe I flew NORDO into one of America's busiest airports, and it was easy—and fun. I begin to savor my grand adventure and remember the engine's pulsing melody and the artistic beauty of the lathered surf. I've flown over open water in a plane with undiagnosed problems, continually concerned about another absurd malfunction. I remember the willing assistance from determined mechanics and helpful controllers in the Bahamas and America.

And I remember how far I've traveled from the bullied wife, trapped in a monotonous routine as a bank employee.

Just as I begin to imagine Scott's naked body, the telephone warbles. I'm tempted to ignore the intrusion. I've been waiting to see what's wrong with the plane before contacting the school, Brandon, or Scott, so only Atlantic Aviation employees know I'm here. *Will they have good news—or bad?*

I pick up the receiver and a man with a lilting Irish cadence says, "Good news, lassie—you diagnosed the alternator problem correctly. Bad news—you need a new alternator. And"—he clears his throat—"a new battery."

"That's why we lost electrics so quickly!"

"And . . ."

The scotch tumbles in my stomach. *What else has malfunctioned?*

"You'll be on your way tomorra'."

I finish *The Handmaid's Tale*, then surf TV, expecting nothing interesting on any of the twenty cable channels. A commercial for *Cry Freedom*, Attenborough's new docudrama about Steve Biko's fight against apartheid, forces me to remember my pilot friend Jennifer's denial. I shudder, imagining her reaction to this mainstream movie. I add the movie to my must-see list, then whip through the channels again, landing on the curiously synchronistic *World without Walls—Beryl Markham's African Memoir*. Filmed two years earlier, in 1986, during the final months of her life, Beryl comes to life amid the panoramic scenes of the infinite savanna, bursting with wildlife and the colorful Maasai.

My flight over a fraction of the ocean paled in comparison to Beryl's achievement of flying west with the night across the entire Atlantic in 1936, but my short hop bonds me emotionally, in some small way, to my teenage hero.

The show ends and I turn off the television, wanting to think more about this tribute to Beryl and other pioneer female aviators. *What flashed through their minds as they plowed against fierce winds sandwiched between ebony skies and surging ocean swells, or navigated continents bombarded by rain and tossed by turbulence, or were forced to land by swirling sandstorms?*

When fate forced me to deal with aircraft systems failures, images of my imminent death pranced before my eyes, taunting me. I foresaw flailing in the ocean, surrounded by ravenous sharks, waiting for the pain of jagged teeth ripping my flesh or being stranded in the air by bad weather, unable to land, running out of fuel, crashing in the tundra, or disappearing into the Bermuda Triangle.

Despite these terrors, soon after my feet touch the ground, the freedom of flight always lures me back into the sky and grants me another opportunity to view the far horizons of our world from a different perspective.

Just as the joy of motherhood dulls the pain of labor and childbirth, the joy of flying overrides those terrifying flights when I thought I wouldn't live to see my son again.

Just as Beryl overcame adversity, changed careers, and reinvented her life each time to create the life she wanted, so have I fought the shackles of traditional female roles and male dominance. Despite setbacks and a circuitous route, I've maintained my feminist stance throughout marriage, motherhood, and a rebel career. While searching for authenticity, I made many mistakes and hurt many people, but finally, I know who I am and who I want to be. Life is a privilege I've chosen to fill with challenges, but without these opportunities to learn and grow and find my true self, my life would be a different kind of death.

GLOSSARY

AGL. Above ground level.

ATC. Air traffic control.

CFB. Canadian Forces Base.

C-FDMZ. Using the phonetic alphabet, I refer to my plane as Charlie (or Canadian if abroad); Foxtrot; Delta Mike Zulu—designed to prevent confusion between single letters. For example, the letters D and Z sound similar but Delta and Zulu are unmistakably different.

CFI. Chief flying instructor (Canada) vs. certified flight instructor (US).

Cumulonimbus. A cloud of vertical development up to sixty thousand feet above Earth, having an anvil-shaped top; produces thunder, lightning, and severe turbulence.

Cumulus. Small, puffy, white clouds.

CYYZ. Identifier for Toronto International Airport (Canadian airport identifiers begin with "C").

DME. Distance measuring equipment.

FPM. Feet per minute (rate of climb/descent).

Heading indicator. Provides directional guidance.

Malton Airport. Toronto Airport; renamed Lester B. Pearson International Airport in 1984.

Medevac/medivac. Medical evacuation.

NAV/COM. Radio with navigation *and* communication capability.

NAVAIDS. Navigational aids, e.g., various instruments on the pilot's dashboard.

NORDO. No radio.

PF. Pilot flying.

PM. Pilot monitoring.

PNF. Pilot not flying, an auxiliary role in which a qualified pilot is responsible for changing radio frequencies, preparing maps and airport approach charts, and talking with controllers on the radios. Now called pilot monitoring.

Run-up. With reference to a checklist, the satisfactory operation of the engine, gauges, and flight controls is checked before departure.

Transponder. A *trans*mitting and res*pond*ing system.

Twin Otter DHC/6. entered aviation in 1964 designed for rugged fields requiring short takeoff and landing (STOL) capabilities. More than nine hundred have ventured around the globe carrying short-hop commuters and performing specialty operations in the subzero polar climes of the Arctic and Antarctica, sweltering deserts of Africa, and mountainous regions of Asia.

ACKNOWLEDGMENTS

This book spans three decades of my life, from the little girl discouraged from following her dreams to the adult woman who achieved those dreams. Though I cannot express my gratitude to everyone, I am indebted to my teachers and the many readers for guiding me along the pathway.

I wish to express specific appreciation to Shahnaz Habib for her encouragement at the beginning of my writing journey; Lee Gowan for his spontaneous support of my vision; Ayelet Tsabari for leading by example personally and professionally; Cheryl Rodo for her friendship and generosity of time; Sarah Chauncey for making me realize I wasn't writing about aviation, but rather using aviation as a vehicle for women's struggles in the ongoing battle for equality in the home and in the workplace; and Erin Spaeth, Prue Mason, and Pat Valdata of the Aviatrix Writers Group.

I also wish to express my gratitude to Jodi Fodor, Lorraine Fico-White, Krissa Lagos, Lauren Wise, and Brooke Warner at She Writes Press.

Finally, I wish to thank Jeff, my husband of twenty-six years, whose unconditional love and support have helped make me a better person.

AUTHOR BIOGRAPHY

Lola Reid Allin is a commercial airline transport pilot, flight instructor, scuba divemaster, and an award-winning author and photographer.

Lola's adventurous spirit spurred her to move to Mexico, to live with the Maya, and to explore more than sixty-five countries. She's trekked in Canada, Guatemala, Morocco, Nepal, Peru, Scotland, Tanzania, and Viet Nam; summited Africa's Kilimanjaro and Toubkal; earned her dog-mushing certificate; crossed deserts on camel; and been on safari in eight African countries.

To encourage others to travel and to promote the role of women in aviation, she creates personally narrated PowerPoint presentations for schools, service groups, and libraries.

Her professional aviation affiliations include Women in Aviation International, The 99s International Organization of Women Pilots, and the Northern Lights Aero Foundation. With Robin Hadfield, she created the New Track Scholarship for Female Aviators in 2022. She lives with her husband and Kalurra, their beloved Aussie Shepherd-Siberian Husky, a few miles east of Toronto, Canada.

Contact her at lola@lolareidallin.com.
Visit her at lolareidallin.com.

Looking for your next great read?

We can help!

Visit www.shewritespress.com/next-read
or scan the QR code below for a list
of our recommended titles.

She Writes Press is an award-winning
independent publishing company founded to
serve women writers everywhere.